PHILOSOPHICAL READINGS
IN
CARDINAL NEWMAN

PHILOSOPHICAL READINGS IN CARDINAL NEWMAN

edited by

JAMES COLLINS
Professor of Philosophy
Saint Louis University

HENRY REGNERY COMPANY
CHICAGO 1961

*To the devoted priests and students
working with the Newman Foundation
in many American colleges*

ACKNOWLEDGMENTS

THE PUBLISHED works of Cardinal Newman are used here with the kind permission of Longmans, Green, and Company, in the editions specified in the Bibliographical Note. The use of all manuscript materials, including papers and letters, rests upon the generously given permission of Rev. Charles Stephen Dessain, C. O., present superior of the Oratory at Edgbaston, Birmingham, England. In addition, I am grateful to the following publishers and authors for permission to use Newman materials found in their publications: E. J. Brill Company, for Dr. Zeno, *John Henry Newman, Our Way to Certitude;* Burns, Oates, and Washbourne, for M. H. Allies, *Thomas William Allies;* Johns Hopkins Press for G. H. Harper, *Cardinal Newman and William Froude, F.R.S.: A Correspondence;* Longmans Green, for Wilfrid Ward, *The Life of John Henry Cardinal Newman;* Publications Universitaires de Louvain (E. Nauwelaerts) and the author, for J. Seynaeve, W. F., *Cardinal Newman's Doctrine on Holy Scripture;* and the Clarendon Press and the editor of *Gregorianum* for an unpublished Newman paper printed jointly in *The Journal of Theological Studies* and *Gregorianum* in 1958.

CONTENTS

PHILOSOPHICAL READINGS
IN
CARDINAL NEWMAN

NEWMAN AND PHILOSOPHY

THE PERSONALITY and mind of John Henry Cardinal Newman (1801-1890) have been thoroughly scrutinized from
a good many perspectives. Special attention is always paid
to his leading role in the Oxford Movement and the details
of his conversion to Catholicism. He is acknowledged to be
a master in describing the interior world of religion and in
doing the work of a modern apologist for his faith. Some
readers also turn to him for an account of how deeply the
Christian way is involved in the cultural problems of the
modern world. In the area of theology, indeed, Newman's
position was obscured for some years because of the misuse
of his writings by the Modernists and the excessive rigidity
of his orthodox defenders. Today, however, we can take the
true measure of his theological contributions, especially in
the areas of the act of faith, the developmental nature of the
Church and its doctrines, and the modes of Scriptural interpretation. The growth of Patristic theology and the new
views on Biblical inspiration and miracles have quickened
the interest in Newman's religious teachings.

A fresh assessment of Newman's significance for philosophy is also being made by many scholars, who are now suffi-

1

ciently removed from the controversy over Modernism to permit them to take a calmer and more accurate look. His philosophical views can now be examined in their own setting, without always being nervously defended against the misleading charge that they foster nominalism, historicism, and an anti-intellectual disdain for doctrinal truth and certitude. In the past, the posing of these issues only served to distract attention from Newman's positive achievements in the philosophical field and his distinctive way of philosophizing. By consulting his writings directly, we are in a better position to understand his peculiar problems, his own way of resolving them, and the reason why it is worthwhile to consult him on many questions facing us today. The present collection of readings is intended to encourage people interested in philosophy to turn to Newman himself as a helpful guide in exploring some important regions of inquiry.

In this general introduction, a threefold foundation is laid for making an intelligent appraisal of Newman's contribution to philosophy. First, we must become acquainted with those aspects of his own education and reading which influenced his approach to philosophy. A second task is to determine more precisely those specific areas in philosophy where he has done some valuable work. And finally, we can notice those themes in his thought which are particularly relevant to our present-day concerns in the philosophical order.

It will be wise to avoid claiming that what emerges from this threefold approach is the whole Newman. First and last, he was a religious thinker, apologist, and theologian in the concrete mode. Yet in the course of a lifelong wrestling with religious issues, he found it necessary to reflect on a restricted but highly important cluster of philosophical questions. In his blunt and downright way, Newman tells us that he was always haunted by the following problem.

The great mass of Catholics know nothing of argument, how then is their faith rational? . . . How can [the Catholic's] belief be called rational? How can his treatment of his intellect be called honest or dutiful to its great Maker and Giver? . . . If a religion is consequent upon *reason,* and at the same time for *all* men, there must be reasons producible sufficient for the rational conviction of every individual. . . . I would affirm that faith must rest on reason, nay, even in the case of children, and of the most ignorant and dull peasant, wherever faith is living and loving; and of course in a great many other cases besides. I start then with a deep conviction that that is the case on which the objection I am to answer bases itself; viz. that faith not only ought to rest upon reason as its human basis, but does rest and cannot but so rest, if it deserves the name of faith. And my task is to elicit and show to the satisfaction of others what those grounds of reason are.[1]

Out of his grappling with this fundamental matter, he launched into a number of questions requiring a philosophical treatment. Our purpose is to concentrate upon this latter phase of Newman's work, without forgetting that the root and goal of the entire investigation lie in his abiding concern for the religious existence of men and the soundness of their faith.

1. *Newman's Philosophical Formation*

Newman's import would be missed, were we to attempt to read him mainly in the light of some Scholastic system or some variety of Bergsonian philosophy. Neither set of categories can be imposed upon his thought or made the primary frame of reference for understanding his mind. It is true that he conscientiously consulted the Scholastic authors and was sensitive toward the crisis in religious belief out of which grew the philosophies of immanence. But the mind which he brought to bear upon these matters was already formed and matured, already shaped by other influences into a personal instrument for analysis and reconstruction. And we in turn must take Newman's mind where we find it, rather than remove it to an alien setting.

From the philosophical standpoint, six sources are specially pertinent to the philosophical formation of his position. They are: the logic of the Noetic school, the natural philosophy of Newton and later French advances in mathematics, British empiricism, Joseph Butler's religious argument, the cosmic outlook of the Alexandrine Fathers, and the philosophy of Aristotle. It is in terms of his critical and creative use of materials drawn from these sources that we must try to understand Newman's own line of philosophical vision. The attempt to do so is made difficult by the fact that the cultural situation which originally made such a synthesis possible has now disappeared. In a retrospective mood, the mature Newman himself realized that the Oxford of his early years was irrevocably gone. He did not mourn over its loss, since he felt that he had brought forward into a new age all that was worth retrieving from that past condition. But we find it difficult to return historically to the Oxford which existed prior to the time when Mill and Darwin and Jowett became the intellectual leaders in Victorian England.

When the young Mr. Newman was elected a fellow of Oriel College in 1822, he joined the most brilliant intellectual company of the day, the Noetic or Evidential School gathered around Richard Whately, afterwards archbishop of Dublin. Whereas the Enlightenment had driven many continental Christian intellectuals into fideism and romanticism, it served only to stiffen the trend in the Church of England toward a rationalization of Christianity into those doctrines which survive the strictest logical tests. Indeed, the Noetics claimed that no one has the right to believe until he has given a formal demonstration of the doctrines patterned after the proof required in mathematics and natural science. The honest believer must apply to the religious sphere the same canons used by the mathemetician and physicist, on pain of losing his integrity and failing to show the rational character of his religious conviction. Conversely, the Noetics held that when the support of formal logical argument is obtained, it compels the assent of any rightminded person to the articles of Christian belief. In thus establishing a proportion between the reasonableness of one's belief and the rigor of objective proof, this school tended to reserve a well-founded Christian faith for the scholarly few who can master the technical proofs from rational evidences.

Newman's initial comment on his association with Whately was typically laconic and pointed: "He, emphatically, opened my mind, and taught me to think and to use my reason."[2] Whately gave him an intellectual discipline and critical turn of mind, even inviting Newman to collaborate on portions of his influential textbook, *Elements of Logic.* Anyone who has felt dismay in confronting the mass of definitions and divisions heaped up in the opening pages of Newman's *Grammar of Assent,* and who has then noticed how rigorously Newman adheres thereafter to them, can gauge the deep impact made upon him by Whately and the

Noetics. They quickened Newman's search for intellectual content as well as evangelical fervor, and made him suspicious of a purely emotional hold on religion. They also encouraged his tendency to make a cool, bluntly honest evaluation of the evidence available in particular religious topics, a tendency which sometimes made Newman a disturbing force for believers and unbelievers alike.

From his own observation of the religious mind at work, however, Newman judged that the Noetics' criterion for reasonable belief is artificially narrow. Many believers do have a reason for their act of faith and do distinguish it from an ungrounded commitment, without being able to put their evidence into a formula. Their minds operate through an implicit kind of reasoning, even when they do not put it into syllogistic mood and figure. Granted that a formal logical analysis can clarify and defend the religious position, still the human mind does not have to await such analysis before accepting in a reasonable way many natural truths and the revealed truths of faith. Indeed, Newman maintained that, even in the case of highly reflective religious minds, much of their inference from evidential grounds cannot be properly stated and weighed in the modes of the syllogism.

This ran contrary to Whately's assertion that "*all* Reasoning, on whatever subject, is one and the same process, which may be clearly exhibited in the form of Syllogisms."[3] From his experience with men of faith, Newman suggested that the Noetics' purported relation between the degree of evidence and the degree of formalization does not in fact exist. He added that the syllogistically stated argument does not even cover the entire field of logical analysis, since there is a distinctive pattern for the concrete logic used in implicit and nonformal types of reasoning. Not only the ordinary man but also the practicing natural scientist avails himself of the resources of this latter kind of inference. Furthermore, Newman's work with souls convinced him that there is no mechanical way of coercing the assent of faith, simply by presenting apologetical arguments in a demonstrative form. All these points of disagreement inclined him to reconsider the whole topic of how the mind actually works in dealing with concrete and historical matters, such as those involved in faith.

Although the mathematical and natural sciences were not emphasized at Oxford until after Newman's departure, he did benefit by expert tutoring and readings in these fields. He did not excel at mathematics as a Trinity undergraduate, but he took a keen personal delight in what he called in his autobiographical memoir "the laborious and nerve-bracing and fancy-repressing study of Mathematics, which has been my principal subject."[4] Using "mathematics" in the current Oxford sense inclusive of the natural sciences, Newman was here indicating the intensive work he did not only in the infant science of geology but most particularly in Newtonian mechanics and mathematics, supplemented by the advances made by Lagrange, Laplace, and Cauchy. He continued these studies as an Oriel fellow, until in 1830 he had to make a professional decision about specializing there or in the scientific history of the German scholar, B. G. Niebuhr, or in the theology of the Church Fathers. Although he chose the latter path, his scientific readings made an indelible impress upon his thought.

The scientific impact is readily seen in the prominent position which he assigned later on to the teaching of science in the university, as well as his confidence about its ultimate relationship with religion. Less noticeable but perhaps more significant is the recurrent comparison made by Newman between scientific and religious reasoning. In one respect, he regarded the two as quite similar. Both of them are paramountly concerned at some phase with matters of fact, and hence they must move beyond pure mathematics and its abstract type of demonstration. They deliberately use several methods of investigation, instead of confining themselves to one rigid pattern, such as Francis Bacon had imagined. Just as religious inquirers must take a personal approach to the problems of faith, using all the virtualities of informal reasoning, so "it is remarkable that not even in [Newtonian] physics can real genius submit to the trammels of that *Novum Organum* of investigation, which, as Bacon truly says, is so important, so necessary, in the case of the many."[5] Both the natural scientist and the religious mind must employ methods of discovery which are not fully formalizable, must attend to the import of probabilities (in the sense of concrete factual findings not previously given in mathematical constructions), and must recognize unsounded depths in our universe calling for a personal sense of the mystery of being.

As Newman moved into his mature speculation, he was obliged to emphasize also some of the differences between the scientific and religious outlooks. Particularly in the course of sketching his notion of a university and in his lifelong correspondence with his scientific friend, William Froude, he came to realize the points of conflict which can arise, not precisely between religion and science but between religion and a philosophical naturalism attempting to restrict all knowledge within the range of a scientific method and its revisable conclusions. Yet Newman always upheld the theme of one of his Oxford sermons, namely, that Christianity has nurtured the temper of mind required for modern science and modern empirical philosophy. He anticipated Whitehead by observing that, on the objective side, "Science and Revelation agree in supposing that nature is governed by uniform and settled laws."[6] And the Christian faith has fostered the modern empirical habit of investigation by criticizing an excessive attachment to grandiose systems at the expense of observational data, by supporting a cooperative approach to problems, and thus by being "the first to describe and inculcate that single-minded, modest, cautious, and generous spirit, which was, after a long time, found so necessary for success in the prosecution of philosophical researches." Concerning the religious influence upon the modern empirical temper of mind, Newman agreed with Robert Boyle and the founders of the Royal Society. Whatever his opposition to a philosophical naturalism which appeals to the scientific and empirical way of thinking, then, Newman remained confident about synthesizing that way of thinking in science and philosophy with the Christian faith itself as an alternative to a closed naturalism.

He is well read in the philosophical tradition of his own country, and he has his countrymen chiefly in mind whenever he speaks about the modern currents in philosophy. In Newman's eyes, the leading British philosophers are Bacon and Locke, the former in respect to the method of studying the external world and the latter in respect to man's inner universe. Both his own early Calvinism and his study of Macaulay's influential essay on Bacon incline him to accept the distinction of the two words uttered by God: in the book of nature and in Sacred Scripture. Newman agrees with Bacon on the distinction of methods and the ultimate harmony of doctrines in science and religion, but he stresses

more than does the Lord Chancellor the analogous relations obtaining between these two accounts of the universe.
God's presence in nature and history is much more effective
and capable of being discerned by our natural intelligence
than Bacon is ready to admit.

It is safe to say that we cannot really grasp the philosophical aspects of Newman's mind without considering his
close acquaintance with Locke's *Essay Concerning Human
Understanding*. This book, rather than the masterpieces of
Descartes, Kant, or Hegel, constitutes for him the central
achievement in modern philosophy. Its terminology and
problems permeate his own thinking and become visible in
the structure of the *Grammar of Assent*. Newman's intimacy
with Locke and the empirical approach in philosophy dif-
ferentiates him sharply from most other Catholic thinkers
of his time who are more closely related to the continental
rationalists. He does reflect upon the method and starting
point of Descartes, as well as Kant's view of perception. But
he feels that Locke stands more firmly on common human
soil than do the systematic rationalists, whose notions he
regards as too vaulting and artificial for the human mind.
Indeed, Newman's major criticism of Locke is that he is not
sufficiently empirical, not thoroughly enough committed to
the historical plain method of studying the human mind in
its concrete operations and limitations. In treating man not
as a pure reasoning machine but as a sensing-reasoning-
feeling-believing-acting animal, the English cardinal regards his own standpoint as being not only opposed to the
rationalistic analysis of man but also as adhering closer to
our experience of man than Locke himself does. Similarly,
he makes a critical use of what Shaftesbury teaches on the
moral sense and the sense of beauty.

Newman's relationship with Berkeley is much more tenuous, and with Hume much more avidly critical, than it is with Locke. He regarded the Irish bishop as a minor and somewhat eccentric thinker and denied having any close dependence upon him, even when friends pointed out a similarity between Berkeley's immaterialism and Newman's boyhood persuasion about the unreality of matter. Actually, Newman resembled Locke more on the score of accepting both the existential reality and the essential unknowability of matter, and resembled Berkeley in regarding sensible things as the message of God to man. It was on this latter point that he came into conflict with Hume, with whose writings he was familiar from his youth and whose naturalization of religious belief constituted one of his lifelong problems. The Hume whom Newman read and criticized was not the pure epistemologist and theoretical skeptic, but rather a Hume much closer to our present conception of him as a philosophical naturalist and moralist. Newman did not regard Humean naturalism as being the inevitable outcome of using the empirical approach in philosophy. But as with the case of Locke, he maintained that Hume deviated from the experiential method and became infected with some rationalistic presuppositions. Newman specified his criticism of Hume around three issues: whether we can know that God transcends nature, whether the scientific notion of laws of nature makes miracles impossible, and whether conscience is fully explainable in psychological terms of association and utility. John Stuart Mill's position came into the ascendancy during Newman's maturity. This philosophy constantly provoked Newman's astonishment at the number of unexamined assumptions which had to be introduced in support of phenomenalism. He did agree with Mill and

11

Bacon, however, about the serious limitations which the logic of science places upon the mind when it tries to base a theistic conviction on the argument from design in nature. His manuscript notes on the Scottish School and on the *Logic* of Mill testify to his continuing study of empiricist sources as a means of clarifying his own position.

The one British thinker whom we must range alongside of Locke as exerting a major positive influence upon Newman's mind is Joseph Butler, the eighteenth-century Anglican bishop of Durham. Currently, he is enjoying a minor renaissance among analytic philosophers interested in his moral theory. During the early nineteenth century, however, the staple fare of university students such as Newman and Darwin was his *The Analogy of Religion Natural and Revealed to the Constitution and Course of Nature*. The introduction to that book contains two golden sentences which worked seminally upon Newman, and which he summed up as the principles of probability and analogy. Butler writes:

Nothing which is the possible object of knowledge, whether past, present, or future, can be probable to an infinite Intelligence; since it cannot but be discerned absolutely as it is in itself, certainly true, or certainly false. But to us, probability is the very guide of life. . . . It must be allowed just, to join abstract reasonings with the observation of facts, and argue from such facts as are known, to others that are like them; from that part of the divine government over intelligent creatures which comes under our view, to that larger and more general government over them which is beyond it; and from what is present, to collect what is likely, credible, or not incredible, will be hereafter.[7]

Newman agrees with Butler about the broad role of probability in the human mode of inquiry, which is not governed by the rationalist alternative of having either mathematically demonstrated propositions or nothing at all worthy of being deemed knowledge. Newman contrasts probability with formalized reasoning, not with certitude and demonstration, since informal inference can yield certitude of an appropriate demonstrated sort in concrete matters of fact. Moreover, there is an analogy rather than a reductive identity between the scientific description and the moral-religious conception of the world.

Yet, in order to notice the analogical relations between the physical, biological, and spiritual orders, we must remain open to the religious interpretation and not close our minds in the face of initial difficulties. In this connection, Butler makes a striking translation from Origen: "He who believes the scripture to have proceeded from him who is the Author of nature, may well expect to find the same sort of difficulties in it, as are found in the constitution of nature."[8] It is part of Newman's program to translate this remark by Origen into the modern context of the noetic methods behind the scientific and religious ways of interpreting natural reality. In a realistic appraisal, Newman finds that human intelligence operates both in scientific and religious matters through the use of probable indications and analogical suggestions, without being confined to Euclidean demonstration and the formal syllogism.

The statement quoted from Origen also reminds us of Newman's considerable debt to the Church Fathers even for his philosophical position. They enlivened his historical awareness, drew his attention to the general plan of historical development in ideas, and encouraged him to examine the nonformal modes of reasoning. Philosophically, he was aided more by the Alexandrine Greek Fathers than by St. Augustine. What attracted him most to Origen and St. Clement of Alexandria was not their specifically theological teaching but their philosophy or general view of the cosmos.

13

They regarded nature as being both a sacrament or visible sign of God's perfection and a veil concealing his full beauty and providential intent from us. Moreover, Newman found something congenial in the Alexandrine conception of philosophizing as a personal activity, carried on within the context of humanistic learning and one's Christian faith, and directed toward discerning and incorporating the seeds of truth, no matter how widely scattered they may be. Along with his senior colleague at Oxford, John Keble, Newman looked for a synthesis between personal reflection and the mystery involved in God's powerful yet hidden presence in nature and history.

The Oxford stress upon the classics also sharpened his philosophical vision. In a moment of excess, one of his friends (the ill-fated Blanco White) hailed Newman as his Oxford Plato. Although Newman had done some reading in Plato, the "Platonic" strain in his thought came primarily from his study of the Alexandrine Fathers and the English Romantics. The classical philosophers in whose heritage he most intimately shared were Cicero and Aristotle. The 1824 essay which Newman wrote on Cicero for an encyclopedia contained a solid account of his philosophy. The section on skepticism displayed that capacity for a sympathetic penetration of an opposing viewpoint which was to set off Newman from so many of the churchmen of his century. Cicero grounded him in the various Hellenistic philosophies, a knowledge which Newman subsequently used to keep Hume's naturalism and skepticism in perspective.

If Bacon and Locke are Newman's main teachers in modern philosophy, Aristotle holds this place in regard to ancient philosophy. It is the Grecian Aristotle, rather than the Stagirite filtered and transmuted by the medieval commentators, whom Newman studies and admires. Whenever he thinks about philosophy precisely as a human discipline and without reference to the influence of revelation, he finds in Aristotle the prototype of philosophical wisdom.

While the world lasts, will Aristotle's doctrine on these matters [the kinds of knowledge and their ends] last, for he is the oracle of nature and of truth. While we are men, we cannot help, to a great extent, being Aristotelians, for the great Master does but analyze the thoughts, feelings, views, and opinions of human kind. He has told us the meaning of our own words before we were born. In many subject-matters, to think correctly, is to think like Aristotle; and we are his disciples whether we will or no, though we may not know it.[9]

Neither Newman nor Locke (who also displays a genuine admiration for Aristotle himself) intends to surrender his critical function simply because of the great debt we are all in to Aristotle. But especially Newman regards his Greek source as an anchor for his own intellectual continuity, remarking that in the midst of many religious changes he still kept Aristotle as his master in human philosophy.

At Oxford, Newman did source readings in both the speculative and the practical parts of Aristotle's philosophy but, unlike the Schoolmen, he did not focus mainly upon the Aristotelian logic, philosophy of nature, and metaphysics. Rather, he became engrossed with the practical philosophy—particularly the *Nicomachean Ethics, Poetics,* and *Rhetoric*—not only for its own sake but also for whatever hints it might furnish about the general structure of human knowledge. As a footnote carefully inserted into the *Grammar of Assent* informs us, Newman's characteristic doctrine on the illative sense developed out of his scrutiny of some texts in Aristotle dealing with prudential judgment. Newman felt that Aristotle came closest to the truth that counts in his treatment of moral and poetic judgments, and that out of this restricted analysis could be generalized a broader view of human knowledge serving as a corrective for Locke's nonempirically generated doubts about certitude in faith.

Unfortunately, Newman did not read the medieval sources with anything like the thoroughness marking his study of Locke and Aristotle. At the time of his conversion, there was not sufficient encouragement even in Rome for reading the medieval theologians and philosophers in depth. Newman did thumb over and underscore his copy of the *Contra Gentiles* and *Summa Theologiae* of St. Thomas, mainly at those passages where the Common Doctor is treating of faith and reason, the reasonableness of the act of faith, and the nature of conscience and the moral act. He was also careful to read the manuals in moral theology, to consult current theological opinion on his positions, and even to submit his book on assent to a philosophy professor for private criticism. But on the whole, we cannot count the medieval doctors and the later Scholastics among the formative influences on Newman's mind in philosophy. He did not want to stand in contradiction to them; he tried to take every advantage of their distinctions and to find in them an equivalent for his own terminology; yet he always found these sources to be somewhat alien to his mind and to be terminating a philosophical discussion just at the point where he saw the difficulties and the need for some fresh investigations.

2. *Newman's Philosophical Achievement*

In keeping with his fundamental aim of showing the reasonableness of the ordinary Christian's act of faith, Newman holds that the vocation of the religious thinker today is to describe and attempt to heal the alienations of modern personal and social existence. "In such circumstances, to speak the word evolving order and peace, and to restore the multitude of men to themselves and to each other, by a reassertion of what is old with a luminousness of explanation which is new, is a gift inferior only to that of revelation itself."[10] This is an ideal shared by theologians and philosophers in the Christian tradition, and comes close to expressing that combination of traditional and modern factors required by Pope Leo XIII as the basis for renewing Christian philosophy. In his own work, Newman sought to overcome the separation of philosophy and the Christian faith, not by resorting to some variety of fideism but by showing that the analysis of our experience accords with our assent of faith. He found it highly unrealistic to maintain either that faith is somehow corrupted by submitting the grounds of theistic conviction to careful philosophical inspection or that philosophy loses its integrity unless we methodically exclude every influence of faith upon our study of data.

Without devoting himself primarily to philosophical inquiries, Newman nevertheless is keenly aware of their distinctive nature and their demand upon the conscientious investigator. The method which he accepts is that of "contemplating the mind as it moves in fact, by whatever hidden mechanism."[11] This is close to Newton's standpoint and to Locke's historical plain method of descriptive analysis of the human mind in action, without any controlling assertions about its intrinsic nature. Yet Newman often criticizes Locke for advancing an unphilosophical argument or for overlooking the properly philosophical treatment of a question. These remarks indicate how carefully Newman tries

17

to respect the philosophical order, when he is arguing within that context. For instance, he submits his analysis of assent to the test of the public canons of evidence. To show that inference and the act of assent remain distinct, he applies in turn each of the rules of induction proposed by Bacon and reworked by Mill. Furthermore, he distinguishes explicitly between the theological account of faith and the philosophical analysis of "those ordinary laws of thought, which alone have a place in my [present] discussion." Thus when we say that Newman is primarily a religious thinker, we do not imply that he is either incapable of seeking rigor at the philosophical level or unwilling to use the accepted means of assuring it in his own thought.

Newman often stated that his bent of mind was not toward metaphysics but toward the logical, ethical, and practical approaches in philosophy. He did keep a private notebook on metaphysical topics treated in his own tentative way, but refrained from publishing the contents. He regarded classical metaphysics as a treatment of the real being of cause, substance, matter, and God, without having primary concern for our human mode of coming to know and assent to these realities. His reluctance to do metaphysics in this classical manner did not stem from any sympathy with Hume's plan of consigning all metaphysics books to the flames, but rather from a blending of other considerations. For one thing, he felt that his own competence lay in examining "that minute, continuous, experimental reasoning, which shows baldly on paper, but which drifts silently into an overwhelming cumulus of proof, and, when our start is true, brings us on to a true result."[12] His own contributions were most needed in this province of the actual uses of our mind to attain certitude through the personal mode of thinking. Newman used Lockean language in referring to his approach as an adherence to the psychological point of view, by which he meant a careful description of our human interiority or the concrete life of personal acts and their real objects. He was aware of breaking new ground for the descriptive analysis of human intelligence and the ways in which it actually establishes principles, weighs evidence, and makes the proofs which win our firm assent. By exploring the ways of personal reasoning, and thus moving beyond the limits of formalization, it might be possible to discover a new basis for overcoming the great chasm between Aristotelian metaphysics and the critical standpoints of the empiricists and Kant. Without claiming to have the special competence to complete such a task, Newman was nevertheless convinced that any metaphysics in the modern manner would have to ground itself thoroughly in a careful study of our concrete manner of knowing.

Newman did not encourage the rationalistic illusion that philosophers are brightly uniformed soldiers, drawn up in neatly separated lines of the true versus the false and carrying out their well planned manoeuvers in the clarity of high noon. Groping around for a more appropriate metaphor to convey the philosophers' condition, he called it a night battle in which the footing is terribly slippery and where the darkness does not enable us to distinguish friend and foe with any ease. Ten thousand intermixtures of the true, the probable, and the false are to be expected in such a situation of human investigation. Consequently, one of Newman's favorite axioms was that in philosophical matters egotism is the only true modesty. This is a warning that it is all too easy for the philosopher to slip out beyond his depth, and hence that he should carefully restrict his work to the method and questions for which his own mind is suited. That is why Newman never claimed omnicompetence for his own standpoint of concrete investigation or the psychological point of view. He did not regard his method as the only valid one to use in philosophy, but did recommend it as attaining some quite determinate results in the areas of his own interest.

The English Oratorian prefers to cut a furrow that is relatively narrow, but also one that is deep and fertile in its study of how men actually use their minds in making inferences and reaching assents. The present Selections make no effort to gather together all of his contributions in the philosophical order. Instead, they concentrate upon four major areas where Newman's approach has yielded some valuable results, which can furnish something new to traditional minds and something relevant to contemporary minds. These four broad regions are: the concrete way of knowing, human knowledge of the personal God, religion and social development, and the relation of reason and faith. These are not isolated themes but, as they are worked out in Newman's mind, are closely interrelated and furnish a basis of synthesis for outlying matters.

Newman's view of knowledge is more emphatically centered around judgment and assent than around the analysis of concepts. In this respect, he realizes that his *Grammar of Assent* differs from the standard Scholastic manuals of his day and moves beyond the standpoints of Locke and Hume. He does not set up a rivalry between notional and real assents, but distinguishes them carefully in order that he may find a reliable way of synthesizing them. Both notional and real assent agree in being an intellectually certain acceptance of some proposed object, taken in its own right. Assent is a distinctive act which can be reduced neither to the conclusion in a syllogistic inference nor to the correlative act of concluding. The mind concludes to something on the basis of its steps of argument and only in reference to the strength of those steps, whereas it assents directly and unconditionally to the presented object. Where notional and real assent differ is in regard to the precise object under acceptance. Notional assent is given to the proposition as such, whereas real assent is made to the individual fact or the existent being which is intended by the proposition. By means of the concrete image, our real assent directs us to the real thing in its own being. In order to achieve definite intellectual content and critical control in our human commitments, we must have notional assents. This is Newman's basis for requiring the creed or doctrinal factor in religious belief. Yet when the mind is concerned with the world of real existents, it cannot remain satisfied with notional assent to a proposition but must acknowledge the very being which is ultimately meant in our statements. Hence the plenary knowledge of an actuality must include a synthesis of notional and real assents, a requirement which must be strictly met in our religious acceptance of God.

Human assent can never be divorced from the inferences by which we examine our experience and work out its implications. Yet here again, Newman's mission is to distinguish between kinds of inference, so as to assure us of the maximal use of our intelligence. He discriminates between the formal inference recommended by the logicians and the Noetics of every age and the modes of natural and informal inference, cultivated also in every age by ordinary men or by all of us in our ordinary moments. We are all

21

familiar with the natural inference whereby, in the unconscious depths of our life, we arrive at conclusions spontaneously and implicitly, without being aware of having gone through any process of inquiry. Newman did not have to await Freud's analysis before describing this natural probing of the mind and the strength of the convictions which it generates, without our attending to the fact.

There is also a deliberate but informal type of inference which we use in dealing with concrete matters of fact. Newman instances the procedures followed by lawyers and physicians, judges and historians, as they sift a maze of contingent facts and details in order to reach some conclusion. But whereas contemporary analysts tend to regard this informal reasoning as applicable only in nontheoretical questions, Newman perceives a germ of generality in the informal mode of inference. Regardless of whether our interest is purely speculative or practical as well, we have to employ implicit reasoning or informal inference in treating of existential fact bearing on the world of real individuals. Newman's illative sense is not another hypostasized faculty but a way of describing what the mind actually does in trying to interpret the realm of existents, processes, and values. There is nothing privileged about illative reasoning, since it merely signifies the ordinary capacity we all have for weighing concrete evidence and finding our way to a conclusion about real things. For us all, truth lies in a deep-shafted well. Newman's recommendation is that the philosopher should recognize this common predicament and also acknowledge the validity of our informal inferring and concluding, as the human way of meeting the common predicament.

This theory of assent and inference is Newman's chief

instrument for explaining how the human person reaches certainty about the existent actuality of the material world, God, and other persons. He is familiar with Hume's critical dissolution of the knowledge of one's own self, but rejects it as an instance of artificial axioms being imposed to obscure a certitude. He remains closer to Locke and Descartes in defending our certitudinal apprehension of our own individual being and personal identity, or what he likes to refer to as "the home of our own minds."[13] But Newman does recognize a problem in trying to enlarge the luminous evidence about oneself to include evidential assent to other personal realities and the material world. In every such instance, an inductive informal inference is made from what we directly experience to these other existents. Newman does no more than sketch the moments in the several inferences to the material world and other selves. His limited concern is to show that we regard our mind as reliable when it does make existential inferences and reach existentially significant assents. Thus our inference and assent to God are not odd exceptions, but retain their solidarity with the other uses of concrete intelligence.

Newman draws another important parallel between the other cases of informal inference and the particular inference and assent leading to God: they all require some priming factor drawn from our experience. Theistic inference is not a self-sufficient rational exercise or ontological proof, but must work out the implications of our experience. Newman enumerates several aspects of experience capable of serving as the point of departure for an inference to God: causal action, order in the world, physical design, the course of history, and the obligation of conscience. He concedes the validity of theistic proofs taken from causality and

23

order, without himself developing in any detail arguments of this sort. As for the arguments from physical design and history, he remarks that they have some weight but are too involved in difficulties in our age to serve as the primary bases for a natural assent to God.

His own effort concentrates upon showing that conscience and the moral life furnish a powerful priming factor for an inference to God and an assent to His real being. Newman defends both the distinctive nature of conscience and its intentional reference to a personal, good God. After reflecting on the commanding act of conscience, we can infer the presence of a transcendent lawgiver and judge, can assent in a notional way to the proposition that God exists, and then can give our real assent to the actuality of God Himself. And if real assent is strongest when it involves the relation of person with person, then the moral link between ourselves and the divine lawgiver is central for a theism culminating in real assent and personal devotion to God.

What Newman says about educational, historical, and political affairs belongs for the most part within these respective disciplines. But his observations are made from a general philosophical standpoint that can be described as interpretative, developmental, and integrative. He holds that intellect is sovereign, not in the sense intended by absolute idealism, but as stressing that we assimilate particular problems and experiences to some comprehensive frame of meaning. Thus his concern for the idea of a university is understandable, for the university expresses in visible form the tensions generated between the broad interpretative principles of an age and the ever new problems and evidences which challenge their validity. The aim of

24

Newman's lectures on the *Idea of a University* is to under-line the powerful influence of the general context of mean-ing and antecedent probability within which the special modes of teaching operate, and to suggest that there is a responsibility for assuring that students will pursue human learning within a theistic and Christian climate. Yet he also wants plenty of elbow room for the inquiring mind, as it makes tentative starts and explores new regions.

There is a striking similarity between Newman's treat-ment of the university and his theory of the development of Christian doctrine. In both instances, his major purpose is to present a guiding idea for understanding the institutional and historical realities confronting us. The actual university and the actual condition of Christian dogma remain opaque to us, until we view them in the light of these guiding ideas or centers of interpretation and development. Their organ-izing ideals are not abstractly evolved but develop by prov-ing their relevance to the new issues which constantly arise. Both the continuity of tradition and the fresh thrust of prog-ress are needed for authentic development, as Newman conceives it. Hence a Christian, theistic center of inter-pretation is not static and removed from all difficulties, but develops and remains open to the problem-and-mystery aspects of human life. As Newman tartly phrases it, "it is not the way to learn to swim in troubled waters, never to have gone into them."[14] Integration in education and in religious existence cannot be achieved at the cost of elimi-nating all the risks of investigation or ignoring any aspects of our human reality, including the ever-present troubled waters.

Significantly, Newman makes no abrupt shift in method

when he comes to examine the relations between reason, faith, and religious existence. He practices a continuity of analysis, since his logic of concrete reasoning is designed for analogous uses. His previous stress upon the real assent to God prepares the way for regarding the religious response as its normal fruit. It also inclines him to take a descriptive and person-centered approach to the religious life, while respecting the reality of the Church as a developing religious society and interpretative context for our personal religious acts.

Because of his early apprenticeship to Butler and the Alexandrine Fathers, Newman remains remarkably free from the usual anxiety lest a philosophy of natural religion lead to deism and indifferentism. He studies the structure of natural religion in far greater detail than is permitted by the rapid mention of it at various spots in dogmatic theology. Although he does not have the advantage of modern techniques and comparative materials, he does grasp the essential human significance of belief, prayer, and sacrifice, as constituting the heart of religious existence. And his sense of the analogous manifestations of God in nature, human conscience, and the economy of salvation, prepares him to expect certain likenesses among the particular religions of mankind, without understating their sharp differences. In investigating the pattern of religious existence, Newman is animated by his constant purpose of arousing "the supreme homage of the heart to the Unseen, which really does but sanctify and exalt, not jealously destroy what is of earth."[15] It is in this spirit of religious humanism shared with his patron, St. Philip Neri, and with St. Francis de Sales that he undertakes all of his philosophically relevant inquiries and prepares us to reflect upon and perhaps accept the word of Christ.

3. *Contemporary Relevance*

Perhaps more than any other eminent Christian thinker of the past two centuries, Newman has suffered from extravagant admirers. They have felt free to invoke his support of their favorite philosophical or theological causes, usually on the basis of a highly selective reading and comparison with their own positions. The best way to prevent such abuses being perpetuated is to do Newman the honor of a careful reading along the lines required for the understanding of other major writers. Like them, he has to be given a critical study which respects the contour and context of his own thought. As he said in a letter to a friend: "You must consider me, as I am, investigatory."[16] For all his flowing periods, he remains in good control of both his ideas and his language, and thus deserves a precise analysis. His prose is the delicately calibrated instrument of his investigatory mind, and calls for a proportionate effort on our part. When we do acquire a solid grounding in Newman himself, it is time enough to consider comparisons with other thinkers and particularly with current tendencies in philosophy.

Thus the present collection of readings rests upon two convictions. First, it is better at the outset to assimilate a few basic themes in Newman than to attempt a fast expedition through all his writings. He cannot be mastered in a hurry; but we can appreciate him if we learn gradually to walk at his own pace and along his own path. He asks us to reflect along with him on a few central questions and to test his remarks by our own experience. In the second place, rather than run the risk of wild comparisons, it is safer for us to focus upon Newman's own text studied for its own sake. We can accept the paradox that Newman's contemporary relevance lies precisely in being himself and inviting us to study his thought in its own shape and texture.

Once we obtain a firm grounding in the thought of Newman himself, we are then able to notice his significance for such contemporary philosophies as naturalism and analytic philosophy, phenomenology and existentialism. Whatever his stress upon the interior personal life, Newman is perhaps the first major Christian thinker to be familiarly at home in the unbounded developing universe of modern science, in what he himself refers to as "the immeasurable ages and spaces of the universe."[17] He brings theism and Christianity unreservedly into the modern frame of reference or interpretative perspective which regards nature as vastly complex, endlessly evolving in time and space, and not neatly centered around man or specially responsive to his wishes. But Newman also measures out the distance separating this prevailing scientific world-image and the theoretical claims of philosophical naturalism.

The insistent pressure of morally indifferent physical events and the technological successes obtained within the limits of scientific thinking affect our imagination very powerfully, in favor of the naturalistic thesis that the objects thus attained constitute the entire range of reality. Even though he does not have a sophisticated philosophy of science, Newman does make us critically aware of this tug upon our real assent, and asks us to retain a firm distinction

28

between the current scientific and cultural image of the universe and the theoretical overclaims made by philosophical naturalism. He does this in order to distinguish between the intensity of the holistic image and the weakness of the metaphysical thesis of naturalism. Along with Bacon and Locke, Newman invites us to persist in the essentially human task of a double interrogation, instead of conforming to the single interest of naturalism. We must interrogate the natural world in order to understand, control, and enjoy it together; we must also examine the human heart in order to become aware of God's personal presence and our duty of religious response together to Him.

Newman's philosophical ancestry in Aristotle and the British empiricists is seen in his notable concern for linguistic usage. He has a keen ear for the philosophical import of our common conversation, whether it be ordinary discourse or the habitual talk of experts about their own field. His attentiveness to language-in-use is not geared to any argument from fantastic etymologies or any simple correlation of the structures of speech and of things. Rather, it is a means of access to our actual convictions, as well as to the mental acts, methodological premises, and intended distinctions which remain obscure until our discourse is carefully analyzed.

Newman's observation that "the logical evolutions of science, (induction etc.) are a rule of the game, not in the nature of things," indicates that the notion of a language game and the problem of constructural methods in science and mathematics are not foreign to his outlook.[18] His appeal to our actual modes of reasoning and discourse, taken in conjunction with his criticism of any universal claims for formalism in logic, bears a definite relationship with certain current tendencies in analytic philosophy. Newman would have comprehended the distinction which the contemporary British analytic philosopher, Stephen Toulmin, draws between our working logic and the formal patterns of idealized logic, as well as Toulmin's project of using the analogy of jurisprudence to show how we actually weigh the case in many instances of substantial argument.

In critical discussions with Locke and Hume and his own scientist-friends, Newman often appeals to the working language in favor of his views on probability and certitude, assent and inference, law and causality, conscience and God. Yet the ultimate aim of his linguistic and conceptual analysis is to reach thereby the living acts of the inferring and assenting mind. "Great as are the services of language in enabling us to extend the compass of our inferences, to test their validity, and to communicate them to others, still the mind itself is more versatile and vigorous than any of its works, of which language is one, and it is only under its penetrating and subtle action that the margin disappears, which I have described as intervening between verbal argumentation and conclusions in the concrete."[19] The theory of illative or concrete reasoning accounts for the fact that the human mind does close this margin, through a grasp and evaluation of meanings. Thus Newman would assimilate the analytic techniques for language and concept formation into the wider context of the inference and the judgment.

Very little is gained by attributing to Newman a phenomenology of this or that. The term "phenomenology" is currently being employed so loosely that it frequently serves only as a philosophical slogan. If we confine ourselves to its meaning for Husserl and the classical phenomenologists, however, we can observe some counterpart elements

30

in Newman's procedure. He regards a subjective psychologism as an unreal approach to our personal experience of reality. He tries to overcome the impasse of empiricism and rationalism by making a direct inspection of the acts in which the evidence is presented and the beliefs formed. His theme of implicit or informal inference involves a careful description of mental acts and their objects, the growth of ideas toward their meaningful realization in history, and the structural relations which characterize our temporal and contingent activities. Especially in the general theory of the development of ideas, Newman recognizes the intentional relationship between human acts and their objects, between particular profiles or temporal aspects of meaning and the plenary significance of a leading intentional principle. He also offers careful descriptions of the intentional acts and feelings of the religious mind. Yet the comparison cannot be pressed to the point of reading into Newman's account of the luminous evidence of the self and God something corresponding to Husserl's transcendental reduction or Scheler's unification of life by reference to an evolving cosmic deity. Newman remains alien to these doctrines because of his reflective acceptance of the primary and irreducible nature of the evidence for the contingently existing human self, the existing material world, and the religious bond holding between the finite person and the personal, transcendent God.

On these latter points, he anticipates some typical themes of existentialism. Newman grants that the experienced situation inclines men to make ambivalent interpretations of our dual relationship with the world and God. Like Kierkegaard, his interest centers upon the *how* or personal way of apprehending a truth. He foreshadows the existentialist analysis of the power of concrete images over our assents and our passions, the impact of the "ethos" or cultural situation upon our beliefs and moral decisions, and the need for an interpretative principle in attempting to understand human history. The human self is structured and morally qualified precisely by the kind of view it develops concerning the material world, history, and God. For reaching some certitude on this issue, Newman asks us to attend to the reflective individual in his responsible concern for his own being and freedom. "It is his gift to be the creator of his own sufficiency; and to be emphatically self-made. . . . No one outside of him can really touch him, can touch his soul, his immortality; he must live with himself for ever. He has a depth within him unfathomable, an infinite abyss of existence."[20] In that depth, Newman discerns the co-presence of the personal God and the need for existing in a visible world along with other selves or centers of moral freedom. To exist in the human manner is to work constantly along with other men toward a sharing in eternal life.

The Selections are arranged in four Parts, corresponding to four major regions in which Newman has done some philosophically significant work. Each Part begins with a brief editorial comment on the background, aim, and interrelation of the individual readings. The source materials are drawn from every period in Newman's long intellectual career, enabling us to see the remarkable persistence of his leading doctrines. There is also found here a wide range of literary forms, including expository chapters from Newman's books, articles first published in journals, a book review, letters, an extempore address, sermons, and a prayer. In all these forms, Newman finds an appropriate way of communicating his distinctive teaching. I have tried to choose continuous and relatively self-contained passages, and the source is given for every Selection. Wherever possible, I have used the text found in the books of Newman edited by Charles F. Harrold and published by Longmans, Green.

These readings could not have been brought together without the kind permission received from the several publishers and authors mentioned in the Acknowledgment. In addition, I have been aided in a special way by three people interested in Newman's thought. Father C. Stephen Dessain, present superior of the Oratory in Birmingham, has readily allowed me to use the manuscript materials from Newman's papers and letters. During his stay in England, Father Walter E. Stokes, S.J., graciously did some transcribing and checking in the Oratory sources as a friendly help. And my publisher, Mr. Henry Regnery, has given encouraging support to the entire project.

Normandy, Missouri
March, 1961

JAMES COLLINS

THE CONCRETE WAY

OF KNOWING

THE CONCRETE WAY OF KNOWING

SELECTION (1) contains Newman's own testimony in the *Apologia* to the influence of Butler and Keble, especially in regard to analogy and probability. He points out the need to save analogical thinking from becoming fanciful, and probability from leading to skepticism. For him, analogy is not only a theory of predication and inference, but a way of perceiving the similarity and instrumental function of the material universe in relation to the moral and spiritual universe. In Butler's hands, analogy was basically a negative argument stating that the same difficulties found in our study of nature may be expected to be present in our study of revealed and natural religion. Newman gives it a more positive significance by regarding material things as means whereby God conveys to us an awareness of His presence and powerful purpose. Thus he is able to accept the reality of matter, against Berkeley, since it must have an actuality of its own in order to serve as a sign or sacrament of the spiritual order. Newman agrees with Keble that moral and religious evidence is probable, not because it is lacking in certainty but because it concerns the mind's relation to a personal actuality as the object of its cognition and love.

37

Incidentally, Newman distinguishes between a person taken in his own mode of being and taken precisely as an object of our knowledge, which therefore can be objective even when it bears upon a personal reality.

In 1821, even before he had won his fellowship at Oriel, Newman contributed to *The Christian Observer* what is probably his earliest published writing, Selection (2). It was the first fruit of the "mathematical studies" (mathematics and Newtonian natural philosophy) into which he plunged after failing to gain first honors in the Trinity College examinations of 1820. He sharpened Butler's comparison between the scientific and religious views of the world, and then shifted the analysis to an analogy between the two types of reasoning involved. In both religious and scientific inquiries, we must be ready to tame the motives of passion and self-interest, live patiently with constantly arising difficulties, and follow the evidence wherever it leads us. Newman's immediate target was Thomas Paine's attempt to defend religious rationalism by modelling it after his simplistic notion of science as a procedure from which all difficulties, unlikely conclusions, and mysteries are banished. As a schoolboy, Newman had been troubled by reading the rationalistic criticism of Paine and Voltaire, but he had found a remedy in a more careful examination of the actual ways of the scientific mind. Newman's self-continuity can be seen in the fact that this essay and a companion piece were reissued in a private printing of 1871, within a year after the publication of the *Grammar of Assent,* which also deals with the analogous difficulties in scientific and religious reasoning.

It may seem surprising that Selection (3) should consist of some letters to Newman rather than of something by him.

But these letters are our best route for appreciating why Newman concentrated on the question of probability and certitude in his analysis of faith, as well as why he regarded the *Grammar of Assent* as his way of discharging a solemn intellectual obligation to his own generation. His closest friend in the Tractarian Movement at Oxford had been Richard Hurrell Froude, who died untimely in 1836. The latter's younger brother, William Froude, entered Oriel College in 1828 and began a lifelong friendship with Newman. Professionally, William Froude attained scientific eminence in hydrodynamics research for the British Navy, being the first to design experimental tanks for studying the effect of wave properties on model ships of various constructions. Largely through Newman's influence, Mrs. Froude and four of their children (one daughter later married Baron von Hügel) became Catholics, but William remained an agnostic. From 1844 until his death in 1879, he corresponded regularly with Newman on personal and religious matters. He was also one of Newman's main channels (along with St. George Mivart) for obtaining firsthand information about the trends in nineteenth-century science and the agnostic outlook accepted by so many scientists of the day. Froude stated as strongly as possible the position of scientific probabilism as extended into a complete outlook, which Charles Peirce in America was calling the principle of fallibilism. Froude maintained that anyone aiming at intellectual integrity must forego certitudinal assent to the teachings of religion, since they must be qualified by the same notes of tentativeness and revisability which attach to our scientific propositions.

Newman regarded Froude as his whetstone, particularly when the latter suggested that the stress on probability in

Newman's *Apologia* implied that our assent of faith is uncertain and conditional. Newman's response to this challenge was only gradually hammered out, resulting in the characteristic argument of the *Grammar of Assent*. Selections (4) through (9) chart the stages in his reply, whereas Selection (10) is Newman's last letter to Froude and a recapitulation of his defense of certitude in the assent of faith. Taken in this synoptic way, the Froude-Newman exchange is one of the most crucial intellectual dialogues transpiring during the past century on the relation between scientific and religious knowledge.

In Selection (4), Newman makes a preliminary survey of the field of knowledge, keeping the proposition at the center of his focus. His interest centers upon the mental act whereby we grasp and affirm the significance of the judgment, as stated in a proposition. He calls that act an apprehension, when he wants to stress the interpretation which we place upon the terms constituting the proposition, especially the term functioning as a predicate. There is a fundamental distinction between notional and real apprehension, depending upon whether the mind interprets the terms in the proposition as signifying respectively some abstract generality or some individual fact of existence. Since notional apprehension interprets the terms in a more abstract and general way, it bears a closer kinship with inference and reasoning than does real apprehension. The latter treats the terms of the proposition as referring to the individual existent, and one of Newman's great problems is to show how the inferential process can lead us to a real apprehension of terms and not simply to a notional apprehension of them. When he wants to characterize the mental act of grasping the significance of the proposition, taken now not

40

analytically in its separate terms but holistically as an assertion of the entire judgmental meaning, Newman calls it an act of assent. Thus apprehension and assent differ only in the way that a restricted interpretation of terms differs from an inclusive interpretation and acceptance of the whole proposition containing those terms.

Whereas inference is concerned with the particular grounds and steps leading to acceptance of some proposition about an object, assent is the direct and unconditioned acceptance of that propositionally stated object. Assent is a mental act wherein we adhere with certitude to an object in its own content, whatever the inferential process leading us to that object. There are two main kinds of assent: notional and real. Notional assent is the certitudinal acceptance of a proposition as such, whereas real assent is the certitudinal acceptance of the real fact or individual existent intended by the proposition. To achieve real assent, we must develop a concrete, living image wherein the individual reality is realized for our own mind. Newman does not distinguish between notional and real assent, or between inference and assent, in order to set them in mutual opposition but in order to synthesize them for obtaining the maximum human knowledge of the world and the works of the mind. The perfection of human knowledge is only reached in a complex act which joins the critical work of inference with the certitude of assent, and the breadth of notional assent with the existential fullness of real assent.

With Selection (5), he probes into the types of notional assents by a technique that is both descriptively close to our experience and attentive to our ways of speech. Instead of proposing an abstract definition of each kind of assent, Newman briefly sketches its salient trait and then seeks to provoke our insight inductively into its nature by describing its operations in many different spheres of life and talk. And in almost every class of notional assent, he considers its relation with the assent of faith. Here is an unobtrusive reminder that this entire grammar of assent aims at clarifying the act of religious faith, and that there is an indispensable notional factor in our religious assent.

He focuses our attention specially upon presumption or the assent which we give to principles. As Aristotle and the empirical thinkers hold, principles are not self-generating axioms but rest upon an intellectual generalization or inductive penetration of particular, experienced facts. The most important feature to note in Newman's treatment of the various principles is his sharp contrast between the principle of causality and that of the uniformity of natural law. In making this distinction, he remains faithful to Newton himself by treating physical laws as formulas about the uniform sequence among phenomena, rather than as real causal agencies. At the same time, Newman removes the causal principle from the criticism made by Hume and Mill, since they are concerned about uniform sequence and not about causality or what is actively produced through an effective will and purposive mind. Causality has a personal basis in the communication of being through an act of intelligence and generous love, which should not be confused with the description of mechanical relations. Newman's view of uniform natural law, as stating a general regularity rather than an inviolable necessity and causal agency, is basic to his subsequent criticism of Hume's stand on miracle, and is compatible with a statistical interpretation of scientific laws.

The intent of Selections (6) and (7) is to compare notional and real assents and to show our need for both kinds.

The process of human inquiry describes a sort of circular route, which begins with initial real assents about particular facts, generalizes the notional principles for inference, and eventually refers back to the existential order through our terminal real assents. Newman remains critically wary about real assents, since they do not furnish a warrant for themselves simply by their intensity, intentional reference, and sharp detail. Under the conditions of human knowing, the work of inference and notional assent is indispensable for sifting and controlling our real assents. On the other hand, Newman rejects the rationalistic assumption that a mind can be brought to give its real assent to something merely on the basis of the logical demonstrations and notional assents. This is the burden of the long excerpt which he makes in Selection (7) from his 1841 "Tamworth Reading Room" paper, which questions the sufficiency of a purely abstract statement of moral principles and scientific recommendations to insure our personal grasp of truth and the practical transformation of society. This paper is not an anti-intellectual plea but is simply an incisive way of showing the need to include our inferences and notional assents within the context of real assents and the complexus of images and passions leading to action. Incidentally, Newman's skillful choice of passages from the Tamworth paper suggests that he would have been his own best editor for a book of philosophically interesting readings.

The theme of a personal search for truth leads to the theory of the illative sense presented in Selection (8). We must agree to take human intelligence as we actually find it, not as we may ideally define it. Reasoning involves more than an impersonal use of syllogistic rules and truth tables, since it leads to the insight and judgment of some living mind. Moreover, we do not deal solely with general problems but also with questions about individual existents. Real reasoning in the realm of contingent, individual facts forces our mind to consider complex evidences, to make involved inferences, to notice converging probabilities, and to determine when it is safe to give our assent to some concrete matter. Whereas recent logicians use logical models and axioms for stating objective and subjective probabilities in regard to random physical phenomena, Newman examines the personal and nonformalized use of our mind which enables us to conduct inquiries into existential particulars and their human significance. He appeals to the practice of historians, jurists, generals, and everyman in coming to a practical decision or making a definite interpretation of a Gestalt figure. His example of the letters of the alphabet anticipates the famous figure of the "duck-rabbit" used in recent analysis.

The illative sense is nothing other than the use of our mind when it engages in such informal inference bearing upon contingent and concrete affairs, and seeks to arrive at a certitudinal assent. Newman acknowledges a debt to Aristotle's teaching on sound prudential judgment and practical wisdom. But the illative sense concerns our attainment of truth as well as opinion, and truth in the general speculative order rather than in practical decisions alone. And lest the Scholastics take alarm at a further multiplication of the mind's powers, Newman assures them that he is describing a perfective habit of our reasoning power itself in its natural and nonformalized condition.

With the aid of these analyses of knowledge, Newman now feels that he can make a reply to Locke and Froude on some important issues which affect the meaning of the act of faith. From the time when he first read Locke's *Essay* during an Oxford Long Vacation, he had wrestled with the contention that assent is conditional upon reasoning, that reasoning in concrete matters can only yield probability and not certitude, and therefore that the assent of faith can only be noncertitudinal, conditional, and confined to some degree of probability. Selection (9) offers Newman's reasons for rejecting this line of argument, with its "pretentious axiom that probable reasoning can never lead to certitude."[1] He appeals to our own experience, the canons of induction, and linguistic usage in support of the distinctive nature of assent, its certitudinal character in some matters of concrete fact, and hence the reasonableness of assenting to the teachings of revealed religion as being unconditionally true, even though they concern historical and existential matters. In criticizing Locke for not being experiential enough, Newman calls for "treating the subject, then, not according to *a priori* fitness, but according to the facts of human nature, as they are found in the concrete action of life."[2] When our mind does act in a real, illative way, it can attain certitude even in matters not included within Locke's antecedent schema of intuitions and abstract demonstrations. This is also Newman's reply to timid Catholics who forbade a rational study of the motive of credibility in the act of faith.

When Newman went to Rome in the spring of 1879 to receive the cardinal's hat, he reserved time in his busy schedule to draft his final letter to William Froude, Selection (10). Whereas Froude treats of probability and certainty mainly in reference to the propositional statement, Newman does so in respect to the mind's act of judging. He often distinguishes between "certainty" as bearing on propositions and "certitude" as bearing on the mind's assent.

We can have certitude even about the probability-value of a proposition. Newman does not contrast probability with certitude but rather with abstract, formalized demonstration. Probable reasoning is used by our mind in dealing with contingent facts and individual existents, apart from the formalized modes of mathematics and logic. We can obtain certitude in this way by attending to the convergence of particular arguments, but this does not mean that we always do attain it. Newman allows a function for will in faith and other acts of assent, but he rejects the will-to-believe approach later associated with William James. The personal, real reasoning or illative use of the mind can tell us that the evidence does *not* justify a passage from inferential inquiry to certitudinal assent, as well as that such a passage is valid. In Selection (11), Newman uses the metaphor of the weaving of a strong cable to convey to us the meaning of the mind's use of probable reasoning or informal, illative inference. This metaphor is also found in Charles Peirce who, however, did not allow that the mind attains to truth in an unconditional way.

CHAPTER I

THE UNIVERSE OF
ANALOGY AND PROBABILITY[1]

FOR MYSELF, if I may attempt to determine what I most gained from it [an early reading of Joseph Butler's *Analogy of Religion*], it lay in two points, which I shall have an opportunity of dwelling on in the sequel; they are underlying principles of a great portion of my teaching. First, the very idea of an analogy between the separate works of God leads to the conclusion that the system which is of less importance is economically or sacramentally connected with the more momentous system,[2] and of this conclusion the theory, to which I was inclined as a boy, viz. the unreality of material phenomena, is an ultimate resolution. At this time I did not make the distinction between matter itself and its phenomena, which is so necessary and so obvious in discussing the subject. Secondly, Butler's doctrine that Probability is the guide of life, led me, at least under the teaching to which a few years later I was introduced, to the question of the logical cogency of Faith, on which I have written so much. Thus to Butler I trace those two principles of my teaching, which have led to a charge against me both of fancifulness and of scepticism.

I think I am not wrong in saying, that the two main intellectual truths which it [John Keble's *Christian Year*] brought home to me, were the same two, which I had learned from Butler, though recast in the creative mind of my new master. The first of these was what may be called, in a large sense of the word, the Sacramental system; that is, the doctrine that material phenomena are both the types and the instruments of real things unseen,—a doctrine, which embraces in its fulness, not only what Anglicans, as well as Catholics, believe about Sacraments properly so called; but also the article of "the Communion of Saints"; and likewise the Mysteries of the faith. The connexion of this philosophy of religion with what is sometimes called "Berkeleyism" has been mentioned; I knew little of Berkeley at this time except by name; nor have I ever studied him.

On the second intellectual principle which I gained from Mr. Keble, I could say a great deal; if this were the place for it. It runs through very much that I have written, and has gained for me many hard names. Butler teaches us that probability is the guide of life. The danger of this doctrine, in the case of many minds, is, its tendency to destroy in them absolute certainty, leading them to consider every conclusion as doubtful, and resolving truth into an opinion, which it is safe indeed to obey or to profess, but not possible to embrace with full internal assent. If this were to be allowed, then the celebrated saying, "O God, if there be a God, save my soul, if I have a soul!" would be the highest measure of devotion:—but who can really pray to a Being, about whose existence he is seriously in doubt?

I considered that Mr. Keble met this difficulty by ascribing the firmness of assent which we give to religious doctrine, not to the probabilities which introduced it, but to the living power of faith and love which accepted it. In

matters of religion, he seemed to say, it is not merely probability which makes us intellectually certain, but probability
as it is put to account by faith and love. It is faith and love
which give to probability a force which it has not in itself.
Faith and love are directed towards an Object; in the vision
of that Object they live; it is that Object, received in faith
and love, which renders it reasonable to take probability as
sufficient for internal conviction. Thus the argument from
Probability, in the matter of religion, became an argument
from Personality, which in fact is one form of the argument
from Authority.

49

CHAPTER II

SCIENTIFIC AND RELIGIOUS INQUIRY[1]

MATHEMATICAL studies, it has been often said, prepare the mind for scepticism in religion. If however such be the fact, it may serve to strengthen our conviction of the existence of that fatal distemper of the soul which can convert the most salutary things into poison; for no science perhaps is more adapted to confirm our belief in the truth of Christianity than that of mathematics, when cultivated with a proper disposition of mind.

It is calculated to humble us, by making us sensible of the contracted range of our imagination and judgment; by shewing us how little we know, how little we can comprehend, and how erroneous oftentimes are the conclusions to which *a priori* speculations would lead us.

In studying the mathematics, passions and feelings and prejudices are excluded: there is nothing to excite hope, or gratify desire; nothing to be gained or to be lost. Whether the system of Ptolemy or that of Newton be the true one, our actual situation is the same; our rule of life is not altered; we are not personally interested in the event. And yet even here, when there is no temptation to be dissatisfied with truth, or to be afraid to avow it (as, often unhappily, is the case in matters of religion), many things occur, at which we cannot but wonder, and for which we can give no reason; nay, we are perhaps sometimes disposed to think, that had we the power to effect any alterations which might appear to us expedient, the arrangements of nature could be rendered far more regular, and its machinery less complicated.

For instance: the earth, in shape a *spheroid,* describes an *ellipse* round the sun, with an *irregular* motion, in three hundred and sixty-five days and a *fraction.* The attraction of the sun and moon, acting upon the earth, occasions *a precession of the equinoxes,* and the motion of that precession is *not uniform.* The ecliptic *cuts* the equator; nay the angle of obliquity is not *constant,* but is always *diminishing.* It were easy to add various seeming defects. "Why," it might be said, "is not every thing regular? Why is there this variation, this want of order, this apparent caprice? Why are not the properties of matter so contrived that the earth may be a sphere, that it may move in the simplicity of a circular orbit; that its motion may be uniform; that it may complete its revolution in an entire number of days without an additional fraction; that it may be undisturbed in its course by the action of the moon? Why has its axis this gradual cone-describing motion on its centre? Why must its poles be oblique to the plane in which it moves?" Who will not confess the rashness and arrogance of such objections, and of our attempting to give an opinion respecting the propriety of the plan approved by the Creator, while our judgment is in its present feeble state, and our knowledge of the system of the universe, and of the adaptation of its parts, is even more limited than that of the fly in the fable, who saw fit to find fault with the architectural proportions of one of the noblest buildings in the world?

51

Apply this confession to religion—how little do we know of the ways of God, and how unequal are our faculties to judge of what we *do* know! Shall we then presume to say, why was man allowed to fall? Why did not God forgive sin without an atonement? Why could not an atonement be made without the Son of God stooping to human nature and submitting to a painful death? Why did not God, instead of separating the Jews as a peculiar people to preserve the true religion, reveal his will at once to the whole world? Why is the truth of Christianity allowed to rest so much on historical evidence rather than the sensible perception of miracles; on moral rather than direct mathematical demonstrations?[2] "If the Gospel were written on the sun," said Paine, "it would be believed by all." To these and similar suggestions of unbelief, how striking is the answer of the Apostle: "Nay but, oh man! who art thou that repliest against God?"

Besides the objections arising from the *difficulties* of revelation, a second species of objections may be answered from the same analogy; for we may extend our argument to a defence of those mysteries which have been said to involve *contradictions* and *impossibilities*. How can the Divine Being exist in three Persons? How can God be the Creator of all things and not the author of evil? How can he "will not the death of a sinner," and yet punish him with everlasting death? How can God be omniscient and yet man a free agent? To these questions it will be time enough to reply when we are informed how many apparently contradictory propositions in science are reconciled; how, for example, space can be proved ever divisible, and yet it be proved that no straight line can be drawn from the tangent point dividing the space between the circumference of a circle and a line touching it; how again two lines, the

52

assymptotes of curves for instance, may be always drawing nearer to each other, yet never meet, with many other illustrations.

If persons would but consider this analogy, if they would but apply something of the same temper and calm judgment to religion which they do not refuse to science, there would be but few objections to the truths of the Bible. But their passions are brought into play: they fear lest the Gospel should be true; they hate the light, their heart is not inclined to spiritual duties, and therefore they approach the examination of the Scriptures with prejudice; they decide superficially, and turn away in disgust. The conclusions of Newton are implicitly believed, because the arguments which prove their truth are sound. The nature of those conclusions makes no difference in our belief; we acknowledge them whatever they may turn out to be; be they difficult, mysterious, incomprehensible, seemingly contradictory, it matters not,—they are *proved*.[3] Their peculiarity may indeed make us more particular and cautious in examining the proof; but if we detect no error *there,* we acquiesce in the truth of the proposition.

What would be said to that man, who, instead of sifting the proofs on which these propositions are built, and beginning with the demolition of the premises, should commence with asserting the falsity of the conclusion from some a priori conception of his own fancy, and then proceed, by the help of this assumption of error in the conclusions, to overthrow the reasonings on which it is founded? Yet this very thing is done daily with the Bible. Men begin at the wrong end of the scale of reasoning; and having refuted, as they conceive, a doctrine by arguments resting on the basis of preconceived ideas, they proceed up the ladder and arrive at once at the portentous determination, that all the proofs which have been advanced in support of that doctrine, and the book which contains an avowal of that doctrine, must be erroneous. It is in this spirit they lay down the unphilosophical axiom, that "a true religion can have no mysteries"; and then infer either that Christianity is not a true religion, because it contains mysteries—or that it contains no mysteries, because it is a true religion. Nothing can be more illogical, more unworthy of a person of science than such conclusions; but where the passions of men are roused, and their interests concerned, little regard is paid to consistency or impartiality.

CHAPTER III

SCIENCE AS EVERLASTINGLY TENTATIVE: TWO LETTERS FROM WILLIAM FROUDE TO NEWMAN[1]

December 29, 1859

My dear Newman,

It may indeed be as you tell me that I "do not really hold what I seem to hold," and "do not master my own views"— but to me it seems as if, different as are many of my opinions (if indeed I can be said to hold positive opinions) from those you would teach me, there is underlying all such differences, and irrespective of them or undercutting them, a source of disagreement between us indefinitely stronger than they, seated in the very principle of "thinking" and of "concluding" and in the very nature of thoughts and conclusions—and pervading the laws, which govern the various states of mind included in the various senses of the term "belief," and which fix the duties attached to them.

In reference to these subjects, my convictions so to call them, are the growth of a life, I seem to hold them or be held by them, very completely, and to see my way through them as clearly as I can see my way through anything—they first were reared, I am confident, under the mental training I received from my Brother Hurrell, and I am persuaded they have since been legitimately developed. The substance

55

of their nourishment has been derived chiefly from the circumstances of active life which have operated on them the more directly and more forcibly from the fact that they have lain so much in the domain of practical science, where, more than elsewhere, the principles and results of reasonings are confronted with the test of direct experiment, and where to be divested of prejudices and to arrive at truth simply, is the object most directly before the eyes, and is less difficult to pursue straight forward, than in any other departments of thought. By slow—(but only by slow) degrees the convictions I refer to become masters of my whole mind, mastering the dogmatic habit of thought, first in its relation to professional knowledge and scientific enquiry, (for when I was an under-graduate the general tone of Oxford teaching was at least as dogmatic in relation to sciences as in relation to Theology and had laid strong hold on me, there), and then penetrating at length into the region of Theology and altering my views in reference to it, so as to produce results which I fully admit to be at variance with Hurrell's direct teaching.

That in preference to the conclusions which he had drawn from his principles of thought, I should adhere to those which I have myself drawn from them, exposes me, I admit to the charge of presupposition. And in reply to this all I have to say (and what in part at least satisfies me) is, that his own mind was, as he himself felt, in many respects in a state of transition, and it is at least possible that he should have arrived at the same conclusions as those at which I have arrived, and there are many reasons which incline me to think he would have done so. But the consciousness that this surmise may be an error, does not at all shake my confidence that the principles of thought by which I am guided are not merely those which the experience of life has fully verified to me, but are also those which he was the first to develop in my mind.

I have no skill of saying much in few words and the profusion of words into which I sum my thoughts tends oftener to mystify than to explain. But I will at least endeavour to convey to you as distinctly as I can that rule or principle of thought which (irrespective of all differences of opinion) seems to hold my mind in the most complete antagonism to Catholicism. More strongly than I believe anything else I believe this—that no subject whatever—distinctly not in the region of the ordinary facts with which our daily experience is consonant—distinctly not in the domain of history or of politics, and yet again a fortiori, not in that of Theology, is my mind, (or as far as I can take the mind of any human being,) capable of arriving at an absolutely certain conclusion. That though of course some conclusions are far more certain than others, there is an element of uncertainty in all.

That though any probability however faint, may in its place make it a duty to act as if the conclusion to which it points were absolutely certain, yet that even the highest attainable probability does not justify the mind in discarding the residuum of doubt; and that the attempt (by any other means than a reiterated (and if [it] be improved) examination of all the bases of the whole probability) to enhance or intensify the sense of the preponderance of the probabilities in either scale, is distinctly an immoral use of faculties. And then, whereas on concluding that it is one's duty to act on such and such a degree of probability (whether great or small) the mind is very strongly drawn and inclined, to overrate the degree of probability in reference to which we proceed to act, this inclination is a temptation to be resisted, not an intimation to be relied on.

But when with integrity of heart anyone is conscious that he has done his very best to arrive at a true conclusion, whether by careful examination of the facts and investigation of their relations or by taking the advice of them, though he is not only bound to be guided in his conduct by such a conclusion but also ought to be "confident" that this is, for him, "the best" and "to have faith" in his cause, it is at the same time not less religiously his duty to keep before his eyes his knowledge of the fallibility of his processes of thought and those of advisers, and to maintain as vivid a recollection of the probabilities which lie against his conclusion, however small they may seem, as of the preponderating mass of probabilities in favor of it. And instead of saying "this is my honest belief and so help me God it ever shall be"—he ought to say "this is for the present the best conclusion I can come to, but in the sight of God I declare that I shall be at all times ready to reconsider it, if reasonably called on to do so, either in the score of errors of fact, or errors of judgment. Nay, I shall be anxious to reconsider it, exactly in proportion as I have grave reason to expect that honest reconsideration will lead me to abandon it." Our "doubts" in fact appear to me as sacred, and I think deserve to be cherished as sacredly as our beliefs; and our "will" has no function in reference to the formation or maintenance of our "Belief," but that of insisting that all probabilities on either side shall be honestly regarded, and weighed and borne in mind.

You will therefore readily understand that the fixedness of purpose with which Hurrell[2] has taken this step does not, to me at least, convey an enhanced impression of the soundness of judgment or the rightness of mind evinced by it. Had he been steering his boat at a regatta with baffling winds and intricate tides, or had he been riding a steeple-chase in difficult country, and judged that he should do better by "taking a line of his own" than by sticking to the course which he had been originally taught to follow—then if in taking the line he had said to himself "Though I think I see my way clearly, it is nevertheless possible that I may be wrong. I will therefore continue to be on the look-out for whatever may show whether I have been right or wrong" and had he said this with an honest intention of as readily admitting a proof that he had been wrong as of being satisfied he had been right—I think my brother Hurrell would have said (as I say) that thus and thus only he has wisely given effect to the dictum "To us, probability is the very guide of life."

When then, in starting on the race of life, he sets out by choosing his own line, the fact that he chooses it without misgiving and without reservation, impresses me the more unfavorably, in proportion as the stakes are more important and the choice of a course turns on considerations more really difficult of solution.

I do not overlook the view that "Spiritual insight is granted as the reward of Faith," nor do I venture to judge that (in some shape) it is an impossible or even an improbable one. Yet I feel it to be one in the highest degree improbable if the merit of Faith be measured as the Theologians seem to measure it, directly as the positiveness of the Belief and inversely as the strength of the evidence. Thus measured Faith seems to be but another word for "prejudice"—i.e., as the formation of a judgment, irrespective of, or out of proportion to the evidence on which it rests and I regard it as an instance of an immoral temper or an immoral use of the faculties. While on the other hand the only pattern of Faith which I can conceive to be meritorious, is the temper which, while it realizes as carefully as possible the exact degree of doubtfullness which attaches to its conclusions, acts nevertheless confidently on the best and wisest conclusion it can form—in confidence that the best and wisest use of every faculty we possess must be that use which will be most pleasing to Him by whom these faculties, whether perfect or imperfect, have been given us "to be exercised therewith."

It is but of late years that this temper has been thoroughly appreciated in the pursuit of scientific truth and in the cultivation of the mechanical arts, though here, earlier than elsewhere, its want was felt, and there were fewest obstacles to its growth. Its thorough appreciation however, even in these departments of thought seems confined to the higher class of minds (if I feel that it is pretty thoroughly appreciated by myself, I attribute it to the peculiar manner in which the development of principles first cultivated in my mind by Hurrell was assisted and disentangled by my interview[s] with Brunel—a man of singular grasp of thought, and truthfulness and honesty of purpose, and whose views have often seemed to me to be most remarkably supplemental to or explanatory of Hurrell's). And if year by year, Physical science and the mechanical arts, have of late, made progress with increasing rapidity and security, it is only by virtue of the wider and freer scope of action which this principle has conquered for itself in those districts of thought. The principle is making some progress even in Politics. Bye and bye I hope it will master men's minds in the province of religion.

For myself, in every province of thought and action, I am content to take as my motto the words "Ever learning and never able to come to a knowledge of the Truth." So long as I am able honestly to claim for myself the former characteristic, I am ready to submit contentedly to the reproach (if anyone choose to consider it a reproach) implied in the latter as a condition inherent in imperfect faculties—I will not bury the talent in the earth on the plea that the Master "is a hard one and gathers when he has not strewed."

You tell me indeed that "I do not really hold what I seem to hold, nor master my own thoughts"—and you say that some day or other I shall admit the truth of the observation—so be it! it is my principle to catch at any honest proof that I am in error and whenever you will help me to accomplish this, the reversal of my fundamental principle of universal doubt, it shall honestly exert its last effort on itself, in virtue of itself it shall destroy itself, and shall commit suicide when it has landed me at the threshold of certainty. But till that is accomplished, the principle would continue to hold me in universal scepticism, [even] were you to show me and were I to admit, and act on the admission, that there is an enormously preponderating probability of the truth of every proposition of Catholic Theology.

October 8, 1864

The *Apologia* has been very much read by men of Science and with a feeling of great interest, a feeling which couples the perception of extreme power of mind in the writer with an anxious and (wondering) curiosity to know how he substantiates the bridge by which he steps so freely from the state of doubt which (as they feel) inevitably attaches to

these results of probabilities, to the state of absolute certainty which he seems to substitute for this. I travelled with
Sir C. Lyell the other day to London on his return from the
British Association Meeting at Bath,[3] and without my leading the conversation in that direction the subject came
naturally to the surface, and he expressed the feeling which
I have mentioned not indeed as having a misgiving that you
would be able to turn the stream back but as knowing that
what you would have to say would deserve very serious
consideration.

It will be curious indeed if you should be brought to write
on the subject from Oxford.

It seems to me that the question has to be dealt with at
two successive steps or levels. First, is the principle that
belief is always to be tempered by or to leave room for,
doubt when it is founded on probability, the rightful and
logical application of "Probability" as the "guide of life" in
relation to life in its ordinary human aspect.

Second, supposing the first question answered in the
affirmative is the principle equally applicable in dealing
with those probabilities on which religious belief is
founded.

At least it seems to be a tenable view, a priori, that men
are intended to deal differently with their conclusions when
these lead up into Religion from that way in which they
deal with conclusions relating to the ordinary affairs of
life—as if instinct were to guide them in one case, logic in
the other; though an abundant crop of intractable difficulties arise when one attempts to reduce the distinction into
a rule of practical application, and though your grounds of
demur seem to make themselves felt towards the view itself,
when its corollaries are looked into.[4] For in the first place, it

is extremely difficult if not impossible to draw a clear and available line between the probabilities which lead up into Religion and those which belong to Common life so interwoven the two classes of questions are, when one really looks into them. And in the second place, if the distinction is regarded as sound, it seems at once necessary to assume that men are gifted with an instinctive faculty which enables them to perceive with certainty the facts of a super-natural occurrence, and to recognize it as super-natural at once and by a conscious act of unerring recognition instead of by intricate (and to a man of science impossible) process of determining in the first place that it is not natural.

CHAPTER IV

THE INTERPRETING MIND[1]

By our apprehension of propositions I mean our imposition of a sense on the terms of which they are composed. Now what do the terms of a proposition, the subject and predicate, stand for? Sometimes they stand for certain ideas existing in our own minds, and for nothing outside of them; sometimes for things simply external to us, brought home to us through the experiences and informations we have of them. All things in the exterior world are unit and individual, and are nothing else; but the mind not only contemplates those unit realities, as they exist, but has the gift, by an act of creation, of bringing before it abstractions and generalizations, which have no existence, no counterpart, out of it.

Now there are propositions, in which one or both of the terms are common nouns, as standing for what is abstract, general, and non-existing, such as "Man is an animal, some men are learned, an Apostle is a creation of Christianity, a line is length without breadth, to err is human, to forgive divine." These I shall call notional propositions, and the apprehension with which we infer or assent to them, notional.

64

And there are other propositions, which are composed of singular nouns, and of which the terms stand for things external to us, unit and individual, as "Philip was the father of Alexander," "the earth goes round the sun," "the Apostles first preached to the Jews"; and these I shall call real propositions, and their apprehension real.

There are then two kinds of apprehension or interpretation to which propositions may be subjected, notional and real.

Next, I observe, that the same proposition may admit of both of these interpretations at once, having a notional sense as used by one man, and a real as used by another. Thus a schoolboy may perfectly apprehend, and construe with spirit, the poet's words, "Dum Capitolium scandet cum tacita Virgine Pontifex"; he has seen steep hills, flights of steps and processions; he knows what enforced silence is; also he knows all about the Pontifex Maximus, and the Vestal Virgins; he has an abstract hold upon every word of the description, yet without the words therefore bringing before him at all the living image which they would light up in the mind of a contemporary of the poet, who had seen the fact described, or of a modern historian who had duly informed himself in the religious phenomena, and by meditation had realized the Roman ceremonial, of the age of Augustus. Again, "Dulce et decorum est pro patria mori," is a mere commonplace, a terse expression of abstractions in the mind of the poet himself, if Philippi is to be the index of his patriotism, whereas it would be the record of experiences, a sovereign dogma, a grand aspiration, inflaming the imagination, piercing the heart, of a Wallace or a Tell.

As the multitude of common nouns have originally been singular, it is not surprising that many of them should so remain still in the apprehension of particular individuals. In the proposition "Sugar is sweet," the predicate is a common noun as used by those who have compared sugar in their thoughts with honey or glycerine; but it may be the only distinctively sweet thing in the experience of a child, and may be used by him as a noun singular. The first time that he tastes sugar, if his nurse says, "Sugar is sweet" in a notional sense, meaning by sugar, lump-sugar, powdered, brown, and candied, and by sweet, a specific flavour or scent which is found in many articles of food and many flowers, he may answer in a real sense, and in an individual proposition, "Sugar is sweet," meaning "This sugar is this sweet thing."

Thirdly, in the same mind and at the same time, the same proposition may express both what is notional and what is real. When a lecturer in mechanics or chemistry shows to his class by experiment some physical fact, he and his hearers at once enunciate it as an individual thing before their eyes, and also as generalized by their minds into a law of nature. When Virgil says, "Varium et mutabile semper foemina," he both sets before his readers what he means to be a general truth, and at the same time applies it individually to the instance of Dido. He expresses at once a notion and a fact.

Of these two modes of apprehending propositions, notional and real, real is the stronger; I mean by stronger the more vivid and forcible. It is so to be accounted for the very reason that it is concerned with what is either real or is taken for real; for intellectual ideas cannot compete in effectiveness with the experience of concrete facts. Various proverbs and maxims sanction me in so speaking, such as "Facts are stubborn things," "Experientia docet," "Seeing

66

is believing"; and the popular contrast between theory and practice, reason and sight, philosophy and faith. Not that real apprehension, as such, impels to action, any more than notional; but it excites and stimulates the affections and passions, by bringing facts home to them as motive causes. Thus it indirectly brings about what the apprehension of large principles, of general laws, or of moral obligations, never could effect.

We may call it the normal state of Inference to apprehend propositions as notions:—and we may call it the normal state of Assent to apprehend propositions as things. If notional apprehension is most congenial to Inference, real apprehension will be the most natural concomitant on Assent. An act of Inference includes in its object the dependence of its thesis upon its premises, that is, upon a relation which is an abstraction; but an act of Assent rests wholly on the thesis as its object, and the reality of the thesis is almost a condition of its unconditionality.

An act of assent, it seems, is the most perfect and highest of its kind, when it is exercised on propositions, which are apprehended as experiences and images, that is, which stand for things; and, on the other hand, an act of inference is the most perfect and highest of its kind, when it is exercised on propositions which are apprehended as notions, that is, which are creations of the mind. An act of Inference indeed may be made with either of these modes of apprehension; so may an act of assent; but, when inferences are exercised on things, they tend to be conjectures or presentiments, without logical force; and when assents are exercised on notions, they tend to be mere assertions without any personal hold on them on the part of those who make them. If this be so, the paradox is true, that, when Inference is clearest, Assent may be least forcible, and, when Assent is most intense, Inference may be least distinct;—for, though acts of assent require previous acts of inference, they require them, not as adequate causes, but as *sine qua non* conditions: and, while the apprehension strengthens Assent, Inference often weakens the apprehension.

CHAPTER V

THE IMPORTANCE OF NOTIONAL ASSENT[1]

I SHALL consider Assent made to propositions which express abstractions or notions under five heads; which I shall call Profession, Credence, Opinion, Presumption, and Speculation.

1. *Profession.* There are assents so feeble and superficial, as to be little more than assertions. I class them all together under the head of Profession. Such are the assents made upon habit and without reflection; as when a man calls himself a Tory or a Liberal, as having been brought up as such; or again, when he adopts as a matter of course the literary or other fashions of the day, admiring the poems, or the novels, or the music, or the personages, or the costume, or the wines, or the manners, which happen to be popular, or are patronized in the higher circles. Such again are the assents of men of wavering restless minds, who take up and then abandon beliefs so readily, so suddenly, as to make it appear that they had no view (as it is called) on the matter they professed, and did not know to what they assented or why.

Then, again, when men say they have no doubt of a thing, this is a case, in which it is difficult to determine whether they assent to it, infer it, or consider it highly probable. There are many cases, indeed, in which it is impossible to discriminate between assent, inference, and assertion, on account of the otiose, passive, inchoate character of the act in question. If I say that tomorrow will be fine, what does this enunciation mean? Perhaps it means that it ought to be fine, if the glass tells truly; then it is the inference of a probability. Perhaps it means no more than a surmise, because it is fine to-day, or has been so for the week past. And perhaps it is a compliance with the word of another, in which case it is sometimes a real assent, sometimes a polite assertion or a wish.

Many a disciple of a philosophical school, who talks fluently, does but assert, when he seems to assent to the dicta of his master, little as he may be aware of it. Nor is he secured against this self-deception by knowing the arguments on which those *dicta* rest, for he may learn the arguments by heart, as a careless schoolboy gets up his Euclid. This practice of asserting simply on authority, with the pretence and without the reality of assent, is what is meant by formalism. To say "I do not understand a proposition, but I accept it on authority," is not formalism, but faith; it is not a direct assent to the proposition, still it is an assent to the authority which enunciates it; but what I here speak of is professing to understand without understanding. It is thus that political and religious watchwords are created; first one man of name and then another adopts them, till their use becomes popular, and then every one professes them, because every one else does. Such words are "liberality," "progress," "light," "civilization"; such are "justification by faith only," "vital religion," "private judgment," "the Bible and nothing but the Bible." Such again are "Rationalism," "Gallicanism," "Jesuitism," "Ultramontanism"—all of which, in the mouths of conscientious thinkers, have a definite meaning, but are used by the multitude as war-cries, nicknames, and shibboleths, with scarcely enough of the scantiest grammatical apprehension of them to allow of their being considered in truth more than assertions.

Thus, instances occur now and then, when, in consequence of the urgency of some fashionable superstition or popular delusion, some eminent scientific authority is provoked to come forward and to set the world right by his "ipse dixit." He, indeed, himself knows very well what he is about; he has a right to speak, and his reasonings and conclusions are sufficient, not only for his own, but for general assent, and, it may be, are as simply true and impregnable, as they are authoritative; but an intelligent hold on the matter in dispute, such as he has himself, cannot be expected in the case of men in general. They, nevertheless, one and all, repeat and retail his arguments, as suddenly as if they had not to study them, as heartily as if they understood them, changing round and becoming as strong antagonists of the error which their master has exposed, as if they had never been its advocates. If their word is to be taken, it is not simply his authority that moves them, which would be sensible enough and suitable in them, both apprehension and assent being in that case grounded on the maxim "Cuique in arte sua credendum"; but so far forth as they disown this motive, and claim to judge in a scientific question of the worth of arguments which require some real knowledge, they are little better, not of course in a very serious matter, than pretenders and formalists.

Not only Authority, but Inference also may impose on us assents which in themselves are little better than assertions, and which, so far as they are assents, can only be notional assents, as being assents, not to the propositions inferred, but to the truth of those propositions. For instance, it can be proved by irrefragable calculations, that the stars are not less than billions of miles distant from the earth; and the process of calculation, upon which such statements are made, is not so difficult as to require authority to secure our acceptance of both it and of them; yet who can say that he has any real, nay, any notional apprehension of a billion or a trillion? We can, indeed, have some notion of it, if we analyze it into its factors, if we compare it with other numbers, or if we illustrate it by analogies or by its implications; but I am speaking of the vast number in itself. We cannot assent to a proposition of which it is the predicate; we can but assent to the truth of it.

This leads me to the question, whether belief in a mystery can be more than an assertion. I consider it can be an assent, and my reasons for saying so are as follows:—A mystery is a proposition conveying incompatible notions, or is a statement of the inconceivable. Now we can assent to propositions (and a mystery is a proposition), provided we can apprehend them; therefore we can assent to a mystery, for, unless we in some sense apprehend it, we should not recognize it to be a mystery, that is, a statement uniting incompatible notions. The same act, then, which enables us to discern that the words of the proposition express a mystery, capacitates us for assenting to it. Words which make nonsense, do not make a mystery. No one would call Warton's line—"Revolving swans proclaim the welkin near"—an inconceivable assertion. It is equally plain, that the assent which we give to mysteries, as such, is notional assent; for, by the supposition, it is assent to propositions which we cannot conceive, whereas, if we had had experience of them, we should be able to conceive them, and without experience assent is not real.

But the question follows, Can processes of inference end in a mystery? that is, not only in what is incomprehensible, that the stars are billions of miles from each other, but in what is inconceivable, in the co-existence of (seeming) incompatibilities? For how, it may be asked, can reason carry out notions into their contradictories? since all the developments of a truth must from the nature of the case be consistent both with it and with each other. I answer, certainly processes of inference, however accurate, can end in mystery; and I solve the objection to such a doctrine thus:—our notion of a thing may be only partially faithful to the original; it may be in excess of the thing, or it may represent it incompletely, and, in consequence, it may serve for it, it may stand for it, only to a certain point, in certain cases, but no further. After that point is reached, the notion and the thing part company; and then the notion, if still used as the representative of the thing, will work out conclusions, not inconsistent with itself, but with the thing to which it no longer corresponds.

2. *Credence.* What I mean by giving credence to propositions is pretty much the same as having "no doubt" about them. It is the sort of assent which we give to those opinions and professed facts which are ever presenting themselves to us without any effort of ours, and which we commonly take for granted, thereby obtaining a broad foundation of thought for ourselves, and a medium of intercourse between ourselves and others. This form of notional assent comprises a great variety of subject-matters; and is, as I have implied, of an otiose and passive character, accepting whatever

73

comes to hand, from whatever quarter, warranted or not, so that it convey nothing on the face of it to its own disadvantage. From the time that we begin to observe, think, and reason, to the final failure of our powers, we are ever acquiring fresh and fresh informations by means of our senses, and still more from others and from books. The friends or strangers whom we fall in with in the course of the day, the conversations or discussions to which we are parties, the newspapers, the light reading of the season, our recreations, our rambles in the country, our foreign tours, all pour their contributions of intellectual matter into the storehouses of our memory; and, though much may be lost, much is retained. These informations, thus received with a spontaneous assent, constitute the furniture of the mind, and make the difference between its civilized condition and a state of nature. They are its education, as far as general knowledge can so be called; and, though education is discipline as well as learning, still, unless the mind implicitly welcomes the truths, real or ostensible, which these informations supply, it will gain neither formation nor a stimulus for its activity and progress. Besides, to believe frankly what it is told, is in the young an exercise of teachableness and humility.

Credence is the means by which, in high and low, in the man of the world and in the recluse, our bare and barren nature is overrun and diversified from without with a rich and living clothing. It is by such ungrudging, prompt assents to what is offered to us so lavishly, that we become possessed of the principles, doctrines, sentiments, facts, which constitute useful, and especially liberal knowledge. These various teachings, shallow though they be, are of a breadth which secures us against those *lacunae* of knowledge which are apt to befall the professed student, and keep us up to the mark in literature, in the arts, in history, and in public matters. They give us in great measure our morality, our politics, our social code, our art of life. They supply the elements of public opinion, the watchwords of patriotism, the standards of thought and action; they are our mutual understandings, our channels of sympathy, our means of co-operation, and the bond of our civil union. They become our moral language; we learn them as we learn our mother tongue; they distinguish us from foreigners; they are, in each of us, not indeed personal, but national characteristics.

This account of them implies that they are received with a notional, not a real assent; they are too manifold to be received in any other way. Even the most practised and earnest minds must needs be superficial in the greater part of their attainments. They know just enough on all sub-jects, in literature, history, politics, philosophy, and art, to be able to converse sensibly on them, and to understand those who are really deep in one or other of them. This is what is called, with a special appositeness, a gentleman's knowledge, as contrasted with that of a professional man, and is neither worthless nor despicable, if used for its proper ends; but it is never more than the furniture of the mind, as I have called it; it never is thoroughly assimilated with it. Yet of course there is nothing to hinder those who have even the largest stock of such notions from devoting them-selves to one or other of the subjects to which those notions belong, and mastering it with a real apprehension; and then their general knowledge of all subjects may be made vari-ously useful in the direction of that particular study or pur-suit which they have selected.

I have been speaking of secular knowledge; but religion may be made a subject of notional assent also, and is especially so made in our own country. Theology, as such always is notional, as being scientific: religion, as being personal, should be real; but, except within a small range of subjects, it commonly is not real in England. As to Catholic populations, such as those of mediaeval Europe, or the Spain of this day, or quasi-Catholic as those of Russia, among them assent to religious objects is real, not notional. To them the Supreme Being, our Lord, the Blessed Virgin, Angels and Saints, heaven and hell, are as present as if they were objects of sight, but such a faith does not suit the genius of modern England. There is in the literary world just now an affectation of calling religion a "sentiment"; and it must be confessed that usually it is nothing more with our own people, educated or rude.

3. *Opinion.* That class of assents which I have called Credence, being a spontaneous acceptance of the various informations, which are by whatever means conveyed to our minds, sometimes goes by the name of Opinion. When we speak of a man's opinions, what do we mean, but the collection of notions which he happens to have, and does not easily part with, though he has neither sufficient proof nor firm grasp of them? This is true; however, Opinion is a word of various significations, and I prefer to use it in my own. Besides standing for Credence, it is sometimes taken to mean Conviction, as when we speak of the "variety of religious opinions," or of being "persecuted for religious opinions," or of our having "no opinion on a particular point," or of another having "no religious opinions." And sometimes it is used in contrast with Conviction, as synonymous with a light and casual, though genuine assent; thus, if a man was every day changing his mind, that is, his assents, we might say, that he was very changeable in his opinions.

76

I shall here use the word to denote an assent, but an assent to a proposition, not as true, but as probably true, that is, to the probability of that which the proposition enunciates; and, as that probability may vary in strength without limit, so may the cogency and moment of the opinion. This account of opinion may seem to confuse it with Inference; for the strength of an inference varies with its premisses, and is a probability; but the two acts of mind are really distinct. Opinion, as being an assent, is independent of premisses. We have opinions which we never think of defending by argument, though, of course, we think they can be so defended. We are even obstinate in them, or what is called "opinionated," and may say that we have a right to think just as we please, reason or no reason; whereas Inference is in its nature and by its profession conditional and uncertain. To say that "we shall have a fine hay-harvest if the present weather lasts," does not come of the same state of mind as, "I am of opinion that we shall have a fine hay-harvest this year."

Opinion, thus explained, has more connexion with Credence than with Inference. It differs from Credence in these two points, viz. that, while Opinion explicitly assents to the probability of a given proposition, Credence is an implicit assent to its truth. It differs from Credence in a third respect, viz. in being a reflex act;—when we take a thing for granted, we have credence in it; when we begin to reflect upon our credence, and to measure, estimate, and modify it, then we are forming an opinion.

It is in this sense that Catholics speak of theological opinion, in contrast with faith in dogma. It is much more than an inferential act, but it is distinct from an act of certitude. And this is really the sense which Protestants give to the word, when they interpret it by Conviction; for their highest opinion in religion is, generally speaking, an assent to a probability—as even Butler has been understood or misunderstood to teach,—and therefore consistent with toleration of its contradictory.

Opinion, being such as I have described, is a notional assent, for the predicate of the proposition, on which it is exercised, is the abstract word "probable."

4. *Presumption.* By presumption I mean an assent to first principles; and by first principles I mean the propositions with which we start in reasoning on any given subject matter. They are in consequence very numerous, and vary in great measure with the persons who reason, according to their judgment and power of assent, being received by some minds, not by others, and only a few of them received universally. They are all of them notions, not images, because they express what is abstract, not what is individual and from direct experience.

(1) Sometimes our trust in our powers of reasoning and memory, that is, our implicit assent to their telling truly, is treated as a first principle; but we cannot properly be said to have any trust in them as faculties. At most we trust in particular acts of memory and reasoning. We are sure there was a yesterday, and that we did this or that in it; we are sure that three times six is eighteen, and that the diagonal of a square is longer than the side. So far as this we may be said to trust the mental act, by which the object of our assent is verified; but, in doing so, we imply no recognition of a general power or faculty, or of any capability or affection of our minds, over and above the particular act. We know indeed that we have a faculty by which we remember, as we know we have a faculty by which we breathe; but we

gain this knowledge by abstraction or inference from its particular acts, not by direct experience. Nor do we trust in the faculty of memory or reasoning as such, even after that we have inferred its existence; for its acts are often inaccurate, nor do we invariably assent to them.

However, if I must speak my mind, I have another ground for reluctance to speak of our trusting memory or reasoning, except indeed by a figure of speech. It seems to me unphilosophical to speak of trusting ourselves. We are what we are, and we use, not trust our faculties. To debate about trusting in a case like this, is parallel to the confusion implied in wishing I had had a choice if I would be created or no, or speculating what I should be like, if I were born of other parents. "Proximus sum egomet mihi." Our consciousness of self is prior to all questions of trust or assent. We act according to our nature, by means of ourselves, when we remember or reason. We are as little able to accept or reject our mental constitution, as our being. We have not the option; we can but misuse or mar its functions. We do not confront or bargain with ourselves; and therefore I cannot call the trustworthiness of the faculties of memory and reasoning one of our first principles.

(2) Next, as to the proposition, that there are things existing external to ourselves, this I do consider a first principle, and one of universal reception. It is founded on an instinct; I so call it, because the brute creation possesses it.[2] This instinct is directed towards individual phenomena, one by one, and has nothing of the character of a generalization; and, since it exists in brutes, the gift of reason is not a condition of its existence, and it may justly be considered an instinct in man also. What the human mind does is what brutes cannot do, viz. to draw from our ever-recurring expe-

riences of its testimony in particulars a general proposition, and, because this instinct or intuition acts whenever the phenomena of sense present themselves, to lay down in broad terms, by an inductive process, the great aphorism, that there is an external world, and that all the phenomena of sense proceed from it. This general proposition, to which we go on to assent, goes (*extensivè*, though not *intensivè*) far beyond our experience, illimitable as that experience may be, and represents a notion.

(3) I have spoken, and I think rightly spoken, of instinct as a force which spontaneously impels us, not only to bodily movements, but to mental acts. It is instinct which leads the quasi-intelligent principle (whatever it is) in brutes to perceive in the phenomena of sense a something distinct from and beyond those phenomena. It is instinct which impels the child to recognize in the smiles or the frowns of a countenance which meets his eyes, not only a being external to himself, but one whose looks elicit in him confidence or fear. And, as he instinctively interprets these physical phenomena, as tokens of things beyond themselves, so from the sensations attendant upon certain classes of his thoughts and actions he gains a perception of an external being, who reads his mind, to whom he is responsible, who praises and blames, who promises and threatens. As I am only illustrating a general view by examples, I shall take this analogy for granted here.

As then we have our initial knowledge of the universe through sense, so do we in the first instance begin to learn about its Lord and God from conscience; and, as from particular acts of that instinct, which makes experiences, mere images (as they ultimately are) upon the retina, the means of our perceiving something real beyond them, we go on to draw the general conclusion that there is a vast external world, so from the recurring instances in which conscience acts, forcing upon us importunately the mandate of a Superior, we have fresh and fresh evidence of the existence of a Sovereign Ruler, from whom those particular dictates which we experience proceed; so that, with limitations which cannot here be made without digressing from my main subject, we may, by means of that induction from particular experiences of conscience, have as good a warrant for concluding the Ubiquitous Presence of One Supreme Master, as we have, from parallel experience of sense, for assenting to the fact of a multiform and vast world, material and mental.[3]

However, this assent is notional, because we generalize a consistent, methodical form of Divine Unity and Personality with Its attributes, from particular experiences of the religious instinct, which are themselves, only *intensivè* not *extensivè*, and in the imagination, not intellectually, notices of Its Presence; though at the same time that assent may become real of course, as may the assent to the external world, viz. when we apply our general knowledge to a particular instance of that knowledge, as, according to a former remark, the general "varium et mutabile" was realized in Dido. And in thus treating the origin of these great notions, I am not forgetting the aid which from our earliest years we received from teachers, nor am I denying the influence of certain original forms of thinking or formative ideas, connatural with our minds, without which we could not reason at all. I am only contemplating the mind as it moves in fact, by whatever hidden mechanism; as a locomotive engine could not move without steam, but still, under whatever number of forces, it certainly does start from Birmingham and does arrive in London.

(4) And so again, as regards the first principles expressed in such propositions as "There is a right and a wrong," "a true and a false," "a just and an unjust," "a beautiful and a deformed"; they are abstractions to which we give a notional assent in consequence of our particular experiences of qualities in the concrete, to which we give a real assent. As we form our notion of whiteness from the actual sight of snow, milk, a lily, or a cloud, so after experiencing the sentiment of approbation which arises in us on the sight of certain acts one by one, we go on to assign to that sentiment a cause, and to those acts a quality, and we give to this notional cause or quality the name of virtue, which is an abstraction, not a thing. And in like manner, when we have been affected by a certain specific admiring pleasure at the sight of this or that concrete object, we proceed by an arbitrary act of the mind to give a name to the hypothetical cause or quality in the abstract, which excites it. We speak of it as beautifulness, and henceforth, when we call a thing beautiful, we mean by the word a certain quality of things which creates in us this special sensation.

These so-called first principles, I say, are really conclusions or abstractions from particular experiences; and an assent to their existence is not an assent to things or their images, but to notions, real assent being confined to the propositions directly embodying those experiences. Such notions indeed are an evidence of the reality of the special sentiments in particular instances, without which they would not have been formed; but in themselves they are abstractions from facts, not elementary truths prior to reasoning.

I am not of course dreaming of denying the objective existence of the Moral Law, nor our instinctive recognition of the immutable difference in the moral quality of acts, as elicited in us by one instance of them. Even one act of cruelty, ingratitude, generosity, or justice, reveals to us at once *intensivè* the immutable distinction between those qualities and their contraries; that is, in that particular instance and *pro hac vice*. From such experience—an experience which is ever recurring—we proceed to abstract and generalize; and thus the abstract proposition "There is a right and a wrong," as representing an act of inference, is received by the mind with a notional, not a real assent. However, in proportion as we obey the particular dictates which are its tokens, so are we led on more and more to view it in the association of those particulars, which are real, and virtually to change our notion of it into the image of that objective fact, which in each particular case it undeniably is.

(5) Another of these presumptions is the belief in causation. It is to me a perplexity that grave authors seems to enunciate as an intuitive truth, that every thing must have a cause. If this were so, the voice of nature would tell false; for why in that case stop short at One, who is Himself without cause? The assent which we give to the proposition, as a first principle, that nothing happens without a cause, is derived, in the first instance, from what we know of ourselves; and we argue analogically from what is within us to what is external to us. One of the first experiences of an infant is that of his willing and doing; and, as time goes on, one of the first temptations of the boy is to bring home to himself the fact of his sovereign arbitrary power, though it be at the price of waywardness, mischievousness, and disobedience. And when his parents, as antagonists of this wilfulness, begin to restrain him, and to bring his mind and conduct into shape, then he has a second series of experi-

ences of causes and effect, and that upon a principle or rule. Thus the notion of causation is one of the first lessons which he learns from experience, that experience limiting it to agents possessed of intelligence and will. It is the notion of power combined with a purpose and an end. Physical phenomena, as such, are without sense; and experience teaches us nothing about physical phenomena as causes. Accordingly, wherever the world is young, the movements and changes of physical nature have been and are spontaneously ascribed by its people to the presence and will of hidden agents, who haunt every part of it, the woods, the mountains and the streams, the air and the stars, for good or for evil;—just as children again, by beating the ground after falling, imply that what has bruised them has intelligence;—nor is there any thing illogical in such a belief. It rests on the argument from analogy.

As time goes on, and society is formed, and the idea of science is mastered, a different aspect of the physical universe presents itself to the mind. Since causation implies a sequence of acts in our own case, and our doing is always posterior, never contemporaneous or prior, to our willing, therefore, when we witness invariable antecedents and consequents, we call the former the cause of the latter, though intelligence is absent, from the analogy of external appearances. At length we go on to confuse causation with order; and, because we happen to have made a successful analysis of some complicated assemblage of phenomena, which experience has brought before us in the visible scene of things, and have reduced them to a tolerable dependence on each other, we call the ultimate points of this analysis, and the hypothetical facts in which the whole mass of phenomena is gathered up, by the name of causes, whereas they are really only the formula under which those phenomena are conveniently represented. Thus the constitutional formula, "The king can do no wrong," is not a fact, or a cause of the Constitution, but a happy mode of bringing out its genius, of determining the correlations of its elements, and of grouping or regulating political rules and proceedings in a particular direction and in a particular form. And in like manner, that all the particles of matter throughout the universe are attracted to each other with a force varying inversely with the square of their respective distances, is a profound idea, harmonizing the physical works of the Creator; but even could it be proved to be a universal fact, and also to be the actual cause of the movements of all bodies in the universe, still it would not be an experience, any more than is the mythological doctrine of the presence of innumerable spirits in those same physical phenomena.

Of these two senses of the world "cause," viz. that which brings a thing to be, and that on which a thing under given circumstances follows, the former is that of which our experience is the earlier and more intimate, being suggested to us by our consciousness of willing and doing. The latter of the two requires a discrimination and exactness of thought for its apprehension, which implies special mental training; else, how do we learn to call food the cause of refreshment, but day never the cause of night, though night follows day more surely than refreshment follows food? Starting, then, from experience, I consider a cause to be an effective will; and, by the doctrine of causation, I mean the notion, or first principle, that all things come of effective will; and the reception or presumption of this notion is a notional assent.

(6) As to causation in the second sense, viz. an ordinary succession of antecedents and consequents, or what is called

85

the Order of Nature, when so explained, it falls under the doctrine of general laws; and of this I proceed to make mention, as another first principle or notion, derived by us from experience, and accepted with what I have called a presumption. By natural law I mean the fact that things happen uniformly according to fixed circumstances, and not without them and at random: that is, that they happen in an order; and, as all things in the universe are unit and individual, order implies a certain repetition, whether of things or like things, or of their affections and relations. Thus we have experience, for instance, of the regularity of our physical functions, such as the beating of the pulse and the heaving of the breath; of the recurring sensations of hunger and thirst; of the alternation of waking and sleeping, and the succession of youth and age. In like manner we have experience of the great recurring phenomena of the heavens and earth, of day and night, summer and winter. Also, we have experience of a like uniform succession in the instance of fire burning, water choking, stones falling down and not up, iron moving towards a magnet, friction followed by sparks and crackling, an oar looking bent in the stream, and compressed steam bursting its vessel. Also, by scientific analysis, we are led to the conclusion that phenomena, which seem very different from each other, admit of being grouped together as modes of the operation of one hypothetical law, acting under varied circumstances. For instance, the motion of a stone falling freely, of a projectile, and of a planet, may be generalized as one and the same property, in each of them, of the particles of matter; and this generalization loses its character of hypothesis, and becomes a probability, in proportion as we have reason for thinking on other grounds that the particles of all matter really move and act towards

86

each other in one certain way in relation to space and time, and not in half a dozen ways; that is, that nature acts by uniform laws. And thus we advance to the general notion or first principle of the sovereignty of law throughout the universe.

There are philosophers who go farther, and teach, not only a general, but an invariable, and inviolable, and necessary uniformity in the action of the laws of nature, holding that everything is the result of some law or laws, and that exceptions are impossible; but I do not see on what ground of experience or reason they take up this position. Our experience, rather, is adverse to such a doctrine, for what concrete fact or phenomenon exactly repeats itself? Some abstract conception of it, more perfect than the recurrent phenomenon itself, is necessary before we are able to say that it has happened even twice, and the variations which accompany the repetition are of the nature of exceptions. The earth, for instance, never moves exactly in the same orbit year by year, but is in perpetual vacillation. It will, indeed, be replied that this arises from the interaction of one law with another, of which the actual orbit is only the accidental issue, that the earth is under the influence of a variety of attractions from cosmical bodies, and that, if it is subject to continual aberrations in its course, these are accounted for accurately or sufficiently by the presence of those extraordinary and variable attractions:—science, then, by its analytical processes sets right the *prima facie* confusion.

Of course; still let us not by our words imply that we are appealing to experience, when really we are only accounting, and that by hypothesis, for the absence of experience. The confusion is a fact, the reasoning processes are not facts. The extraordinary attractions assigned to account for our experience of that confusion are not themselves experienced phenomenal facts, but more or less probable hypotheses, argued out by means of an assumed analogy between the cosmical bodies to which those attractions are referred, and falling bodies on the earth. I say "assumed," because that analogy (in other words, the unfailing uniformity of nature) is the very point which has to be proved. It is true, that we can make experiment of the law of attraction in the case of bodies on the earth; but, I repeat, to assume from analogy that, as stones do fall to the earth, so Jupiter, if let alone, would fall upon the earth and the earth upon Jupiter, and with certain peculiarities of velocity on either side, is to have recourse to an explanation which is not necessarily valid, unless nature is necessarily uniform. Nor, indeed, has it yet been proved, nor ought it to be assumed, even that the law of velocity of falling bodies on the earth is invariable in its operation; for that again is only an instance of the general proposition, which is the very thesis in debate. It seems safer, then, to hold that the order of nature is not necessary, but general in its manifestations.

But, it may be urged, if a thing happens once, it must happen always; for what is to hinder it? Nay, on the contrary, why, because one particle of matter has a certain property, should all particles have the same? Why, because particles have instanced the property a thousand times, should the thousand and first instance it also? It is *prima facie* unaccountable that an accident should happen twice, not to speak of its happening always. If we expect a thing to happen twice, it is because we think it is not an accident, but has a cause. What has brought about a thing once, may bring it about twice. *What* is to hinder its happening?

rather, What is to make it happen? Here we are thrown back from the question of Order to that of Causation. A law is not a cause, but a fact; but when we come to the question of cause, then, as I have said, we have no experience of any cause but Will. If, then, I must answer the question, What is to alter the order of nature? I reply, That which willed it;—That which willed it, can unwill it; and the invariableness of law depends on the unchangeableness of that Will.

And here I am led to observe that, as a cause implies a will, so order implies a purpose. Did we see flint celts, in their various receptacles all over Europe, scored always with certain special and characteristic marks, even though those marks had no assignable meaning or final cause whatever, we should take that very repetition, which indeed is the principle of order, to be a proof of intelligence. The agency then which has kept up and keeps up the general laws of nature, energizing at once in Sirius and on the earth, and on the earth in its primary period as well as in the nineteenth century, must be Mind, and nothing else, and Mind at least as wide and as enduring in its living action, as the immeasurable ages and spaces of the universe on which that agency has left its traces.

5. *Speculation.* Speculation is one of those words which, in the vernacular, have so different a sense from what they bear in philosophy. It is commonly taken to mean a conjecture, or a venture on chances; but its proper meaning is mental sight, or the contemplation of mental operations and their results as opposed to experience, experiment, or sense, analogous to its meaning in Shakespeare's line, "Thou hast no speculation in those eyes." In this sense I use it here.

And I use it in this sense to denote those notional assents which are the most direct, explicit, and perfect of their kind, viz. those which are the firm, conscious acceptance of propositions, as true. This kind of assent includes the assent to all reasoning and its conclusions, to all general propositions, to all rules of conduct, to all proverbs, aphorisms, sayings, and reflections on men and society. Of course mathematical investigations and truths are the subjects of this speculative assent. So are legal judgments, and constitutional maxims, as far as they appeal to us for assent. So are the determinations of science; so are the principles, disputations, and doctrines of theology. That there is a God, that He has certain attributes, and in what sense He can be said to have attributes, that He has done certain works, that He has made certain revelations of Himself and of His will, and what they are, and the multiplied bearings of the parts of the teaching, thus developed and formed, upon each other, all this is the subject of notional assent, and of that particular department of it which I have called Speculation. As far as these particular subjects can be viewed in the concrete and represent experiences, they can be received by real assent also; but as expressed in general propositions they belong to notional apprehension and assent.

CHAPTER VI

THE PATH OF REAL ASSENT[1]

I HAVE IN A measure anticipated the subject of Real Assent by what I have been saying about Notional. In comparison of the directness and force of the apprehension, which we have of an object, when our assent is to be called real, Notional Assent and Inference seem to be thrown back into one and the same class of intellectual acts, though the former of the two is always an unconditional acceptance of a proposition, and the latter is an acceptance on the condition of an acceptance of its premisses. In its Notional Assents as well as in its inferences, the mind contemplates its own creations instead of things; in Real, it is directed towards things, represented by the impressions which they have left on the imagination. These images, when assented to, have an influence both on the individual and on society, which mere notions cannot exert.

I have already given various illustrations of Real Assent; I will follow them up here by some instances of the change of Notional Assent into Real.

1. For instance; boys at school look like each other, and pursue the same studies, some of them with greater success than others; but it will sometimes happen, that those who

acquitted themselves but poorly in class, when they come into the action of life, and engage in some particular work, which they have already been learning in its theory and with little promise of proficiency, are suddenly found to have what is called an eye for that work—an eye for trade matters, or for engineering, or a special taste for literature—which no one expected from them at school, while they were engaged on notions. Minds of this stamp not only know the received rules of their profession, but enter into them, and even anticipate them, or dispense with them, or substitute other rules instead. And when new questions are opened, and arguments are drawn up on one side and the other in long array, they with a natural ease and promptness form their views and give their decision, as if they have no need to reason, from their clear apprehension of the lie and issue of the whole matter in dispute, as if it were drawn out in a map before them. These are the reformers, systematizers, inventors, in various departments of thought, speculative and practical; in education, in administration, in social and political matters, in science. Such men indeed are far from infallible; however great their powers, they sometimes fall into great errors, in their own special department, while second-rate men who go by rule come to sound and safe conclusions. Images need not be true; but I am illustrating what vividness of apprehension is, and what is the strength of belief consequent upon it.

2. Again:—twenty years ago, the Duke of Wellington wrote his celebrated letter on the subject of the national defences. His authority gave it an immediate circulation among all classes of the community; none questioned what he said, nor as if taking his words on faith merely, but as intellectually recognizing their truth; yet few could be said

to see or feel that truth. His letter lay, so to say, upon the pure intellect of the national mind, and nothing for a time came of it. But eleven years afterwards, after his death, the anger of the French colonels with us, after the attempt upon Louis Napoleon's life, transferred its facts to the charge of the imagination. Then forthwith the national assent became in various ways an operative principle, especially in its promotion of the volunteer movement. The Duke, having a special eye for military matters, had realized the state of things from the first; but it took a course of years to impress upon the public mind an assent to his warning deeper and more energetic than the reception it is accustomed to give to a clever article in a newspaper or a review.

3. And so generally: great truths, practical or ethical, float on the surface of society, admitted by all, valued by few, exemplifying the poet's adage, "Probitas laudatur et alget," until changed circumstances, accident, or the continual pressure of their advocates, force them upon its attention. The iniquity, for instance, of the slave-trade ought to have been acknowledged by all men from the first; it was acknowledged by many, but it needed an organized agitation, with tracts and speeches innumerable, so to affect the imagination of men as to make their acknowledgment of that iniquitousness operative.

Let these instances suffice of Real Assent in its relation to Notional; they lead me to make three remarks in further illustration of its character.

1. The fact of the distinctness of the images which are required for real assent, is no warrant for the existence of the objects which those images represent. A proposition, be it ever so keenly apprehended, may be true or may be false. If we simply put aside all inferential information, such as

is derived from testimony, from general belief, from the concurrence of the senses, from common sense, or otherwise, we have no right to consider that we have apprehended a truth, merely because of the strength of our mental impression of it. Hence the proverb, "Fronti nulla fides." An image, with the characters of perfect veracity and faithfulness, may be ever so distinct and eloquent an object presented before the mind (or, as it is sometimes called, an "objectum internum," or a "subject-object"); but, nevertheless, there may be no external reality in the case, corresponding to it, in spite of its impressiveness. One of the most remarkable instances of this fallacious impressiveness is the illusion which possesses the minds of able men, those especially who are exercised in physical investigations, in favour of the inviolability of the laws of nature. Philosophers of the school of Hume discard the very supposition of miracles, and scornfully refuse to hear evidence in their behalf in given instances, from their intimate experience of physical order and of the ever-recurring connexion of antecedent and consequent. Their imagination usurps the functions of reason; and they cannot bring themselves even to entertain as a hypothesis (and this is all that they are asked to do) a thought contrary to that vivid impression of which they are the victims, that the uniformity of nature which they witness hour by hour, is equivalent to a necessary, inviolable law.

Yet it is plain, and I shall take it for granted here, that when I assent to a proposition, I ought to have some more legitimate reason for doing so, than the brilliancy of the image of which that proposition is the expression. That I have no experience of a thing happening except in one way, is a cause of the intensity of my assent, if I assent, but not a reason for my assenting. In saying this, I am not disposed to deny the presence in some men of an idiosyncratic sagacity, which really and rightly sees reasons in impressions which common men cannot see, and is secured from the peril of confusing truth with make-belief; but this is genius, and beyond rule. I grant too, of course, that accidentally impressiveness does in matter of fact, as in the instance which I have been giving, constitute the motive principle of belief; for the mind is ever exposed to the danger of being carried away by the liveliness of its conceptions, to the sacrifice of good sense and conscientious caution, and the greater and the more rare are its gifts, the greater is the risk of swerving from the line of reason and duty; but here I am not speaking of transgressions of rule any more than of exceptions to it, but of the normal constitution of our minds, and of the natural and rightful effect of acts of the imagination upon us, and this is, not to create assent, but to intensify it.

2. Next, Assent, however strong, and accorded to images however vivid, is not therefore necessarily practical. Strictly speaking, it is not imagination that causes action; but hope and fear, likes and dislikes, appetite, passion, affection, the stirrings of selfishness and self-love. What imagination does for us is to find a means of stimulating those motive powers; and it does so by providing a supply of objects strong enough to stimulate them. The thought of honour, glory, duty, self-aggrandisement, gain, or on the other hand of Divine Goodness, future reward, eternal life, perseveringly dwelt upon, leads us along a course of action corresponding to itself, but only in case there be that in our minds which is congenial to it. However, when there is that preparation of mind, the thought does lead to the act. Hence it is that the fact of a proposition being accepted with a real assent is accidentally an earnest of that proposition being carried

95

out in conduct, and the imagination may be said in some sense to be of a practical nature, inasmuch as it leads to practice indirectly by the action of its object upon the affections.

3. There is a third remark suggested by the view which I have been taking of real assents, viz. that they are of a personal character, each individual having his own, and being known by them. It is otherwise with notions; notional apprehension is in itself an ordinary act of our common nature. All of us have the power of abstraction, and can be taught either to make or to enter into the same abstractions; and thus to co-operate in the establishment of a common measure between mind and mind. And, though for one and all of us to assent to the notions which we thus apprehend in common, is a further step, as requiring the adoption of a common standpoint of principle and judgment, yet this too depends in good measure on certain logical processes of thought, with which we are all familiar, and on facts which we all take for granted. But we cannot make sure, for ourselves or others, of real apprehension and assent, because we have to secure first the images which are their objects, and these are often peculiar and special. They depend on personal experience; and the experience of one man is not the experience of another. Real assent, then, as the experience which it presupposes, is proper to the individual, and as such, thwarts rather than promotes the intercourse of man with man. It shuts itself up, as it were, in its own home, or at least it is its own witness and its own standard; and, as in the instances above given, it cannot be reckoned on, anticipated, accounted for, inasmuch as it is the accident of this man or that.

96

CHAPTER VII

BELIEF AND ACTION[1]

IT APPEARS from what has been said, that, though Real Assent is not intrinsically operative, it accidentally and indirectly affects practice. It is in itself an intellectual act, of which the object is presented to it by the imagination; and though the pure intellect does not lead to action, nor the imagination either, yet the imagination has the means, which pure intellect has not, of stimulating those powers of the mind from which action proceeds. Real Assent then, or Belief, as it may be called, viewed in itself, that is, simply as Assent, does not lead to action; but the images in which it lives, representing as they do the concrete, have the power of the concrete upon the affections and passions, and by means of these indirectly become operative. Still this practical influence is not invariable, nor to be relied on; for, given images may have no tendency to affect given minds, or to excite them to action. Thus, a philosopher or a poet may vividly realize the brilliant rewards of military genius or of eloquence, without wishing either to be a commander or an orator. However, on the whole, broadly contrasting Belief with Notional Assent and with Inference, we shall not, with this explanation, be very wrong in pronouncing that acts of Notional Assent and of Inference do not affect our conduct, and acts of Belief, that is, of Real Assent, do (not necessarily, but do) affect it.

I have said enough to admit of my introducing it [Inference] here in contrast with Real Assent or Belief, and that contrast is necessary in order to complete what I have been saying about the latter. Let me then, for the sake of the latter, be allowed here to say, that, while Assent, or Belief, presupposes some apprehension of the things believed, Inference requires no apprehension of the things inferred; that in consequence, Inference is necessarily concerned with surfaces and aspects; that it begins with itself, and ends with itself; that it does not reach as far as facts; that it is employed upon formulas; that, as far as it takes real objects of whatever kind into account, such as motives and actions, character and conduct, art, science, taste, morals, religion, it deals with them, not as they are, but simply in its own line as materials of argument or inquiry, that they are to it nothing more than major and minor premisses and conclusions. Belief, on the other hand, being concerned with things concrete, not abstract, which variously excite the mind from their moral and imaginative properties, has for its objects, not only directly what is true, but inclusively what is beautiful, useful, admirable, heroic; objects which kindle devotion, rouse the passions, and attach the affections; and thus it leads the way to actions of every kind, to the establishment of principles, and the formation of character, and is thus again intimately connected with what is individual and personal.

I insisted on this marked distinction between Beliefs on the one hand, and Notional Assents and Inferences on the other, many years ago in words which it will be to my purpose to use now.[2] I quote them, because, over and above their appositeness in this place, they present the doctrine which I have been insisting, from a second point of view, and with a freshness and force which I cannot now command, and, moreover, (though they are my own, nevertheless, from the length of time which has elapsed since their publication,) almost with the cogency of an independent testimony.

They occur in a protest which I had occasion to write in February, 1841, against a dangerous doctrine maintained, as I considered, by two very eminent men of that day, now no more—Lord Brougham and Sir Robert Peel. That doctrine was to the effect that the claims of religion could be secured and sustained in the mass of men, and in particular in the lower classes of society, by acquaintance with literature and physical science, and through the instrumentality of Mechanics' Institutes and Reading Rooms, to the serious disparagement, as it seemed to me, of direct Christian instruction. In the course of my remarks is found the passage which I shall here quote and which, with whatever differences in terminology, and hardihood of assertion, befitting the circumstances of its publication, nay, as far as words go, inaccuracy of theological statement, suitably illustrates the subject here under discussion. It runs thus:

"People say to me, that it is but a dream to suppose that Christianity should regain the organic power in human society which once it possessed. I cannot help that; I never said it could. I am not a politician; I am proposing no measures, but exposing a fallacy and resisting a pretence. Let Benthamism reign, if men have no aspirations; but do not tell them to be romantic and then solace them with 'glory:' do not attempt by philosophy what once was done by reli-

99

gion. The ascendency of faith may be impracticable, but the reign of knowledge is incomprehensible. The problem for statesmen of this age is how to educate the masses, and literature and science cannot give the solution.

Science gives us the grounds or premises from which religious truths are to be inferred; but it does not set about inferring them, much less does it reach the inference—that is not its province. It brings before us phenomena, and it leaves us, if we will, to call them works of design, wisdom, or benevolence; and further still, if we will, to proceed to confess an Intelligent Creator. We have to take its facts, and to give them a meaning, and to draw our own conclusions from them.[3] First comes knowledge, then a view, then reasoning, and then belief. This is why science has so little of a religious tendency; deductions have no power of persuasion. The heart is commonly reached, not through the reason, but through the imagination, by means of direct impressions, by the testimony of facts and events, by history, by description. Persons influence us, voices melt us, looks subdue us, deeds inflame us. Many a man will live and die upon a dogma: no man will be a martyr for a conclusion. A conclusion is but an opinion; it is not a thing which *is*, but which *we are 'quite sure about'*; and it has often been observed, that we never say we are sure and certain without implying that we doubt. To say that a thing *must* be, is to admit that it *may not* be.

No one, I say, will die for his own calculations: he dies for realities. This is why a literary religion is so little to be depended upon; it looks well in fair weather; but its doctrines are opinions, and when called to suffer for them it slips them between its folios, or burns them at its hearth. And this again is the secret of the distrust and raillery with

100

which moralists have been so commonly visited. They say and do not. Why? Because they are contemplating the fitness of things, and they live by the square, when they should be realizing their high maxims in the concrete. Now Sir Robert Peel thinks better of natural history, chemistry, and astronomy than of such ethics; but these too, what are they more than divinity *in posse?* He protests against 'controversial divinity:' is *inferential* much better?

I have no confidence, then, in philosophers who *cannot help* being religious, and are Christians by *implication.* They sit at home, and reach forward to distances which astonish us; but they hit without grasping, and are sometimes as confident about shadows as about realities. They have worked out by a calculation the lie of a country which they never saw, and mapped it by means of a gazetteer; and, like blind men, though they can put a stranger on his way, they cannot walk straight themselves, and do not feel it quite their business to walk at all.

Logic makes but a sorry rhetoric with the multitude; first shoot round corners, and you may not despair of converting by a syllogism. Tell men to gain notions of a Creator from His works, and, if they were to set about it (which nobody does) they would be jaded and wearied by the labyrinth they were tracing. Their minds would be gorged and surfeited by the logical operation. Logicians are more set upon concluding rightly, than on right conclusions. They cannot see the end for the process. Few men have that power of mind which may hold fast and firmly a variety of thoughts. We ridicule 'men of one idea;' but a great many of us are born to be such, and we should be happier if we knew it. To most men argument makes the point in hand only more doubtful, and considerably less impressive. After all, man

101

is *not* a reasoning animal; he is a seeing, feeling, contemplating, acting animal. He is influenced by what is direct and precise. It is very well to freshen our impressions and convictions from physics, but to create them we must go elsewhere. Sir Robert Peel 'never can think it possible that a mind can be so constituted, that, after being familiarized with the wonderful discoveries which have been made in every part of experimental science, it can retire from such contemplations without more enlarged conceptions of God's providence, and a higher reverence for His name!' If he speaks of religious minds, he perpetrates a truism; if of irreligious, he insinuates a paradox.

Life is not long enough for a religion of inferences; we shall never have done beginning, if we determine to begin with proof. We shall ever be laying our foundations; we shall turn theology into evidences, and divines into textuaries. We shall never get at our first principles. Resolve to believe nothing, and you must prove your proofs and analyze your elements, sinking farther and farther, and finding 'in the lowest depth a lower deep,' till you come to the broad bosom of scepticism. I would rather be bound to defend the reasonableness of assuming that Christianity is true, than demonstrate a moral governance from the physical world. Life is for action. If we insist on proofs for everything, we shall never come to action: to act you must assume, and that assumption is faith.

Let no one suppose, that in saying this I am maintaining that all proofs are equally difficult, and all propositions equally debatable. Some assumptions are greater than others, and some doctrines involve postulates larger than others, and more numerous. I only say, that impressions lead to action, and that reasonings lead from it. Knowledge of premises, and inferences upon them,—this is not to *live*. It is very well as a matter of liberal curiosity and of philosophy to analyze our modes of thought: but let this come second, and when there is leisure for it, and then our examinations will in many ways even be subservient to action. But if we commence with scientific knowledge and argumentative proof, or lay any great stress upon it as the basis of personal Christianity, or attempt to make man moral and religious by libraries and museums, let us in consistency take chemists for our cooks, and mineralogists for our masons.

Now I wish to state all this as matter of fact, to be judged by the candid testimony of any persons whatever. Why we are so constituted that faith, not knowledge or argument, is our principle of action, is a question with which I have nothing to do; but I think it is a fact, and, if it be such, we must resign ourselves to it as best we may, unless we take refuge in the intolerable paradox, that the mass of men are created for nothing, and are meant to leave life as they entered it.

So well has this practically been understood in all ages of the world, that no religion yet has been a religion of physics or of philosophy. It has ever been synonymous with revelation. It never has been a deduction from what we know; it has ever been an assertion of what we are to believe. It has never lived in a conclusion; it has ever been a message, a history, or a vision. No legislator or priest ever dreamed of educating our moral nature by science or by argument. There is no difference here between true religions and pretended. Moses was instructed not to reason

103

from the creation, but to work miracles. Christianity is a history supernatural, and almost scenic: it tells us what its Author is, by telling us what He has done.

Lord Brougham himself has recognized the force of this principle. He has not left his philosophical religion to argument; he has committed it to the keeping of the imagination. Why should he depict a great republic of letters, and an intellectual pantheon, except that he feels that instances and patterns, not logical reasonings, are the living conclusions which alone have a hold over the affections or can form the character?"

CHAPTER VIII

CONCRETE REASONING OR THE

ILLATIVE SENSE[1]

[1. *Factual Analysis of the Human Mind.*] We are in a world of facts, and we use them; for there is nothing else to use. We do not quarrel with them, but we take them as they are, and avail ourselves of what they can do for us. It would be out of place to demand of fire, water, earth, and air their credentials, so to say, for acting upon us, or ministering to us. We call them elements, and turn them to account, and make the most of them. We speculate on them at our leisure. But what we are still less able to doubt about or annul, at our leisure or not, is that which is at once their counterpart and their witness, I mean, ourselves. We are conscious of the objects of external nature, and we reflect and act upon them, and this consciousness, reflection, and action we call our own rationality. And as we use the (so called) elements without first criticizing what we have no command over, so is it much more unmeaning in us, to criticize or find fault with our own nature, which is nothing else than we ourselves, instead of using it according to the use of which it ordinarily admits. Our being, with its faculties, mind and body, is a fact not admitting of question, all things being of necessity referred to it, not it to other things.

If I may not assume that I exist, and in a particular way, that is, with a particular mental constitution, I have nothing to speculate about, and had better let speculation alone. Such as I am, it is my all; this is my essential stand-point, and must be taken for granted; otherwise, thought is but an idle amusement, not worth the trouble. There is no medium between using my faculties, as I have them, and flinging myself upon the external world according to the random impulse of the moment, as spray upon the surface of the waves, and simply forgetting that I am.

I am what I am, or I am nothing. I cannot think, reflect, or judge about my being, without starting from the very point which I aim at concluding. My ideas are all assumptions, and I am ever moving in a circle. I cannot avoid being sufficient for myself, for I cannot make myself any thing else, and to change me is to destroy me. If I do not use myself, I have no other self to use. My only business is to ascertain what I am, in order to put it to use. It is enough for the proof of the value and authority of any function which I possess, to be able to pronounce that it is natural. What I have to ascertain is the laws under which I live. My first elementary lesson of duty is that of resignation to the laws of my nature, whatever they are; my first disobedience is to be impatient at what I am, and to indulge an ambitious aspiration after what I cannot be, to cherish a distrust of my powers, and to desire to change laws which are identical with myself.

Truths such as these, which are too obvious to be called irresistible, are illustrated by what we see in universal nature. Every being is in a true sense sufficient for itself, so as to be able to fulfil its particular needs. It is a general law that, whatever is found as a function or an attribute of any class of beings, or is natural to it, is in its substance suitable to it, and subserves its existence, and cannot be rightly regarded as a fault or enormity. No being could endure, of which the constituent parts were at war with each other. And more than this; there is that principle of vitality in every being, which is of a sanative and restorative character, and which brings all its parts and functions together into one whole, and is ever repelling and correcting the mischiefs which befall it, whether from within or without, while showing no tendency to cast off its belongings as if foreign to its nature. The brute animals are found severally with limbs and organs, habits, instincts, appetites, surroundings, which play together for the safety and welfare of the whole; and, after all exceptions, may be said each of them to have, after its own kind, a perfection of nature. Man is the highest of the animals, and more indeed than an animal, as having a mind; that is, he has a complex nature different from theirs, with a higher aim and a specific perfection; but still the fact that other beings find their good in the use of their particular nature, is a reason for anticipating that to use duly our own is our interest as well as our necessity.

What is the peculiarity of our nature, in contrast with the inferior animals around us? It is that, though man cannot change what he is born with, he is a being of progress with relation to his perfection and characteristic good. Other beings are complete from their first existence, in that line of excellence which is allotted to them; but man begins with nothing realized (to use the word), and he has to make capital for himself by the exercise of those faculties which are his natural inheritance. Thus he gradually advances to the fulness of his original destiny. Nor is this progress mechanical, nor is it of necessity; it is committed to the personal efforts of each individual of the species; each of us has the prerogative of completing his inchoate and rudimental nature, and of developing his own perfection out of the living elements with which his mind began to be. It is his gift to be the creator of his own sufficiency; and to be emphatically self-made. This is the law of his being, which he cannot escape; and whatever is involved in that law he is bound, or rather he is carried on, to fulfil.

And here I am brought to the bearing of these remarks upon my subject. For this law of progress is carried out by means of the acquisition of knowledge, of which inference and assent are the immediate instruments. Supposing, then, the advancement of our nature, both in ourselves individually and as regards the human family, is to every one of us in his place a sacred duty, it follows that that duty is intimately bound up with the right use of these two main instruments of fulfilling it. And as we do not gain the knowledge of the law of progress by any *a priori* view of man, but by looking at it as the interpretation which is provided by himself on a large scale in the ordinary action of his intellectual nature, so too we must appeal to himself, as a fact, and not to any antecedent theory, in order to find what is the law of his mind as regards the two faculties in question. If then such an appeal does bear me out in deciding, as I have done, that the course of inference is ever more or less obscure, while assent is ever distinct and definite, and yet that what is in its nature thus absolute does, in fact, follow upon what in outward manifestation is thus complex, indirect, and recondite, what is left to us but to take things as they are, and to resign ourselves to what we find? that is, instead of devising, what cannot be, some sufficient science

of reasoning, which may compel certitude in concrete conclusions, to confess that there is no ultimate test of truth
besides the testimony borne to truth by the mind itself, and
that this phenomenon, perplexing as we may find it, is a
normal and inevitable characteristic of the mental constitution of a being like man on a stage such as the world. His
progress is a living growth, not a mechanism; and its instruments are mental acts, not the formulas and contrivances
of language.

We are accustomed in this day to lay great stress upon
the harmony of the universe; and we have well learned the
maxim so powerfully inculcated by our own English philosopher [Francis Bacon], that in our inquiries into its laws,
we must sternly destroy all idols of the intellect, and subdue
nature by co-operating with her. Knowledge is power, for
it enables us to use eternal principles which we cannot
alter. So also is it in that microcosm, the human mind. Let
us follow Bacon more closely than to distort its faculties
according to the demands of an ideal optimism, instead of
looking out for modes of thought proper to our nature, and
faithfully observing them in our intellectual exercises.

[2. *Implicit or Informal Reasoning.*] Reason, according
to the simplest view of it, is the faculty of gaining knowledge without direct perception, or of ascertaining one thing
by means of another. In this way it is able, from small beginnings, to create to itself a world of ideas, which do or do
not correspond to the things themselves for which they
stand, or are true or not, according as it is exercised soundly
or otherwise. One act may suffice for a whole theory; one
principle may create and sustain a system; one minute token
is a clue to a large discovery. The mind ranges to and fro,
and spreads out, and advances forward with a quickness

which has become a proverb, and a subtlety and versatility which baffle investigation. It passes on from point to point, gaining one by some indication; another on a probability; then availing itself of an association; then falling back on some received law; next seizing on testimony; then committing itself to some popular impression, or some inward instinct, or some obscure memory; and thus it makes progress not unlike a clamberer on a steep cliff, who, by quick eye, prompt hand, and firm foot, ascends how he knows not himself, by personal endowments and by practice, rather than by rule, leaving no track behind him, and unable to teach another. It is not too much to say that the stepping by which great geniuses scale the mountains of truth is as unsafe and precarious to men in general, as the ascent of a skilful mountaineer up a literal crag. It is a way which they alone can take; and its justification lies in their success. And such mainly is the way in which all men, gifted or not gifted, commonly reason,—not by rule, but by an inward faculty.

Reasoning, then, or the exercise of Reason, is a living spontaneous energy within us, not an art. But when the mind reflects upon itself, it begins to be dissatisfied with the absence of order and method in the exercise, and attempts to analyze the various processes which take place during it, to refer one to another, and to discover the main principles on which they are conducted, as it might contemplate and investigate its faculty of memory or imagination. The boldest, simplest, and most comprehensive theory which has been invented for the analysis of the reasoning process, is the well-known science for which we are indebted to Aristotle, and which is framed upon the principle that every act of reasoning is exercised upon neither more nor less than three terms. Short of this, we have many general words in familiar use to designate particular methods of thought, according to which the mind reasons (that is, proceeds from truth to truth), or to designate particular states of mind which influence its reasonings. Such methods are antecedent probability, analogy, parallel cases, testimony, and circumstantial evidence; and such states of mind are prejudice, deference to authority, party spirit, attachment to such and such principles, and the like. In like manner we distribute the Evidences of Religion into External and Internal; into *a priori* and *a posteriori;* into Evidences of Natural Religion and of Revealed; and so on. Again, we speak of proving doctrines either from the nature of the case, or from Scripture, or from history; and of teaching them in a dogmatic, or a polemical, or a hortatory way. In these and other ways we instance the reflective power of the human mind, contemplating and scrutinizing its own acts.

Here, then, are two processes, distinct from each other,— the original process of reasoning, and next, the process of investigating our reasonings. All men reason, for to reason is nothing more than to gain truth from former truth, without the intervention of sense, to which brutes are limited; but all men do not reflect upon their own reasonings, much less reflect truly and accurately, so as to do justice to their own meaning; but only in proportion to their abilities and attainments. In other words, all men have a reason, but not all men can give a reason. We may denote, then, these two exercises of mind as reasoning and arguing, or as conscious and unconscious reasoning, or as Implicit Reason and Explicit Reason. And to the latter belong the words, science, method, development, analysis, criticism, proof, system, principles, rules, laws, and others of a like nature.

That these two exercises are not to be confounded together would seem too plain for remark, except that they have been confounded. Clearness in argument certainly is not indispensable to reasoning well. Accuracy in stating doctrines or principles is not essential to feeling and acting upon them. The exercise of analysis is not necessary to the integrity of the process analyzed. The process of reasoning is complete in itself, and independent. The analysis is but an account of it; it does not make the conclusion correct; it does not make the inference rational. It does not cause a given individual to reason better. It does but give him a sustained consciousness, for good or for evil, that he is reasoning. How a man reasons is as much a mystery as how he remembers. He remembers better and worse on different subject-matters, and he reasons better and worse. Some men's reason becomes genius in particular subjects, and is less than ordinary in others. The gift or talent of reasoning may be distinct in different subjects, though the process of reasoning is the same. Now a good arguer or clear speaker is but one who excels in analyzing or expressing a process of reason, taken as his subject-matter. He traces out the connexion of facts, detects principles, applies them, supplies deficiencies, till he has reduced the whole into order. But his talent of reasoning, or the gift of reason as possessed by him, may be confined to such an exercise, and he may be as little expert in other exercises, as a mathematician need be an experimentalist; as little creative of the reasoning itself which he analyzes, as a critic need possess the gift of writing poems.

112

It is hardly too much to say, that almost all reasons formally adduced in moral inquiries, are rather specimens and symbols of the real grounds, than those grounds themselves. They do but approximate to a representation of the general character of the proof which the writer wishes to convey to another's mind. They cannot, like mathematical proof, be passively followed with an attention confined to what is stated, and with the admission of nothing but what is urged. Rather, they are hints towards, and samples of, the true reasoning, and demand an active, ready, candid, and docile mind, which can throw itself into what is said, neglect verbal difficulties, and pursue and carry out principles.

[3. *Nature of the Illative Sense.*] Even when argument is the most direct and severe of its kind, there must be those assumptions in the process which resolve themselves into the conditions of human nature; but how many more assumptions does that process in ordinary concrete matters involve, subtle assumptions, not directly arising out of these primary conditions, but accompanying the course of reasoning, step by step, and traceable to the sentiments of the age, country, religion, social habits and ideas, of the particular inquirers or disputants, and passing current without detection, because admitted equally on all hands! And to these must be added the assumptions which are made from the necessity of the case, in consequence of the prolixity and elaborateness of any argument which should faithfully note down all the propositions which go to make it up. We recognize this tediousness even in the case of the theorems of Euclid, though mathematical proof is comparatively simple.

Logic then does not really prove; it enables us to join issue with others; it suggests ideas; it opens views; it maps out for us the lines of thought; it verifies negatively; it determines when differences of opinion are hopeless; and when and how far conclusions are probable; but for genuine proof in concrete matter we require an *organon* more delicate, versatile, and elastic than verbal argumentation.

An object of sense presents itself to our view as one whole, and not in its separate details: we take it in, recognize it, and discriminate it from other objects, all at once. Such too is the intellectual view we take of the *momenta* of proof for a concrete truth; we grasp the full tale of premisses and the conclusion, *per modum unius,*—by a sort of instinctive perception of the legitimate conclusion in and through the premisses, not by a formal juxta-position of propositions; though of course such a juxta-position is useful and natural, both to direct and to verify, just as in objects of sight our notice of bodily peculiarities, or the remarks of others may aid us in establishing a case of disputed identity. And, as this man or that will receive his own impression of one and the same person, and judge differently from others about his countenance, its expression, its moral significance, its physical contour and complexion, so an intellectual question may strike two minds very differently, may awaken in them distinct associations, may be invested by them in contrary characteristics, and lead them to opposite conclusions;—and so, again, a body of proof, or a line of argument, may produce a distinct, nay, a dissimilar effect, as addressed to one or to the other.

Thus in concrete reasonings we are in great measure thrown back into that condition, from which logic proposed to rescue us. We judge for ourselves, by our lights, and on our own principles; and our criterion of truth is not so much the manipulation of propositions, as the intellectual and

114

moral character of the person maintaining them, and the ultimate silent effect of his arguments or conclusions upon our minds.

Certitude is a mental state: certainty is a quality of propositions. Those propositions I call certain, which are such that I am certain of them. Certitude is not a passive impression made upon the mind from without, by argumentative compulsion, but in all concrete questions (nay, even in abstract, for though the reasoning is abstract, the mind which judges of it is concrete) it is an active recognition of propositions as true, such as it is the duty of each individual himself to exercise at the bidding of reason, and, when reason forbids, to withhold. And reason never bids us be certain except on an absolute proof; and such a proof can never be furnished to us by the logic of words, for as certitude is of the mind, so is the act of inference which leads to it. Every one who reasons, is his own centre; and no expedient for attaining a common measure of minds can reverse this truth;—but then the question follows, is there any *criterion* of the accuracy of an act of inference, such as may be our warrant that certitude is rightly elicited in favour of the proposition inferred, since our warrant cannot, as I have said, be scientific? The sole and final judgment on the validity of an inference in concrete matter is committed to the personal action of the ratiocinative faculty, the perfection or virtue of which I call the Illative Sense, a use of the word "sense" parallel to our use of it in "good sense," "common sense," a "sense of beauty," etc.: and I own I do not see any way to go farther than this in answer to the question. However, I can at least explain my meaning more fully.

It is the mind that reasons, and that controls its own rea-

sonings, not any technical apparatus of words and propositions. This power of judging and concluding, when in its
perfection, I call the Illative Sense, and I shall best illustrate
it by referring to parallel faculties, which we commonly
recognize without difficulty.

For instance, how does the mind fulfil its function of
supreme direction and control, in matters of duty, social
intercourse, and taste? In all of these separate actions of
the intellect, the individual is supreme, and responsible to
himself, nay, under circumstances, may be justified in opposing himself to the judgment of the whole world; though
he uses rules to his great advantage, as far as they go, and
is in consequence bound to use them. As regards moral
duty, the subject is fully considered in the well-known
treatises of Aristotle.[2] He calls the faculty which guides the
mind in matters of conduct, by the name of *phronesis,* or
judgment. This is the directing, controlling, and determining principle in such matters, personal and social. What it
is to be virtuous, how we are to gain the just idea and
standard of virtue, how we are to approximate in practice
to our own standard, what is right and wrong in a particular case, for the answers in fulness and accuracy to these
and similar questions, the philosopher refers us to no code
of laws, to no moral treatise, because no science of life, applicable to the case of an individual, has been or can be
written. Such is Aristotle's doctrine, and it is undoubtedly
true.

An ethical system may supply laws, general rules, guiding
principles, a number of examples, suggestions, landmarks,
limitations, cautions, distinctions, solutions of critical or
anxious difficulties; but who is to apply them to a particular case? whither can we go, except to the living intellect,

our own, or another's? What is written is too vague, too negative for our need. It bids us avoid extremes; but it cannot ascertain for us, according to our personal need, the golden mean. The authoritative oracle, which is to decide our path, is something more searching and manifold than such jejune generalizations as treatises can give, which are most distinct and clear when we least need them. It is seated in the mind of the individual, who is thus his own law, his own teacher, and his own judge in those special cases of duty which are personal to him. It comes of an acquired habit, though it has its first origin in nature itself, and it is formed and matured by practice and experience; and it manifests itself, not in any breadth of view, any philosophical comprehension of the mutual relations of duty towards duty, or any consistency in its teachings, but it is a capacity sufficient for the occasion, deciding what ought to be done here and now, by this given person, under these given circumstances. It decides nothing hypothetical, it does not determine what a man should do ten years hence, or what another should do at this time. It may indeed happen to decide ten years hence as it does now, and to decide a second case now as it now decides a first; still its present act is for the present, not for the distant or the future.

I doubt whether it is correct, strictly speaking, to consider this *phronesis* as a general faculty, directing and perfecting all the virtues at once. So understood, it is little better than an abstract term, including under it a circle of analogous faculties, severally proper to the separate virtues. Properly speaking, there are as many kinds of *phronesis* as there are virtues; for the judgment, good sense, or tact which is conspicuous in a man's conduct in one subject-matter, is not necessarily traceable in another. As in the parallel cases of

117

memory and reasoning he may be great in one aspect of his character, and little-minded in another. He may be exemplary in his family, yet commit a fraud on the revenue; he may be just and cruel, brave and sensual, imprudent and patient. And if this be true of the moral virtues, it holds good still more fully when we compare what is called his private character with his public. A good man may make a bad king; profligates have been great statesmen, or magnanimous political leaders.

So, too, I may go on to speak of the various callings and professions which give scope to the exercise of great talents, for these talents also are matured, not by mere rule, but by personal skill and sagacity. They are as diverse as pleading and cross-examining, conducting a debate in Parliament, swaying a public meeting, and commanding an army; and here, too, I observe that, though the directing principle in each case is called by the same name,—sagacity, skill, tact, or prudence,—still there is no one ruling faculty leading to eminence in all these various lines of action in common, but men will excel in one of them, without any talent for the rest.

The parallel may be continued in the case of the Fine Arts, in which, though true and scientific rules may be given, no one would therefore deny that Phidias or Rafael had a far more subtle standard of taste and a more versatile power of embodying it in his works, than any which he could communicate to others in even a series of treatises. And here again genius is indissolubly united to one definite subject-matter; a poet is not therefore a painter, or an architect a musical composer.

And so, again, as regards the useful arts and personal accomplishments, we use the same word "skill," but proficiency in engineering or in ship-building, or again in engraving, or again in singing, in playing instruments, in acting, or in gymnastic exercises, is as simply one with its particular subject-matter, as the human soul with its particular body, and is, in its own department, a sort of instinct or inspiration, not an obedience to external rules of criticism or of science.

It is natural, then, to ask the question, why ratiocination should be an exception to a general law which attaches to the intellectual exercises of the mind; why it is held to be commensurate with logical science; and why logic is made an instrumental art sufficient for determining every sort of truth, while no one would dream of making any one formula, however generalized, a working rule at once for poetry, the art of medicine, and political warfare?

This is what I have to remark concerning the Illative Sense, and in explanation of its nature and claims; and on the whole, I have spoken of it in four respects,—as viewed in itself, in the subject-matter, in the process it uses, and in its function and scope.

First, viewed in its exercise, it is one and the same in all concrete matters, though employed in them in different measures. We do not reason in one way in chemistry or law, in another in morals or religion; but in reasoning on any subject whatever, which is concrete, we proceed, as far indeed as we can, by the logic of language, but we are obliged to supplement it by the more subtle and elastic logic of thought; for forms by themselves prove nothing.

Secondly, it is in fact attached to definite subject-matters, so that a given individual may possess it in one department of thought, for instance, history, and not in another, for instance, philosophy.

119

Thirdly, in coming to its conclusion, it proceeds, always in the same way, by a method of reasoning which is the elementary principle of that mathematical calculus of modern times, which has so wonderfully extended the limits of abstract science.

Fourthly, in no class of concrete reasonings, whether in experimental science, historical research, or theology, is there any ultimate test of truth and error in our inferences besides the trustworthiness of the Illative Sense that gives them its sanction; just as there is no sufficient test of poetical excellence, heroic action, or gentlemanlike conduct, other than the particular mental sense, be it genius, taste, sense of propriety, or the moral sense, to which those subject-matters are severally committed. Our duty in each of these is to strengthen and perfect the special faculty which is its living rule, and in every case as it comes to do our best. And such also is our duty and our necessity, as regards the Illative Sense.

[4. *Range of the Illative Sense*. In treating of the range of the Illative Sense,] I will mention under separate heads some of those elementary contrarieties of opinion, on which the Illative Sense has to act, discovering them, following them out, defending or resisting them, as the case may be.

As to the statement of the case. This depends on the particular aspect under which we view a subject, that is, on the abstraction which forms our representative notion of what it is. Sciences are only so many distinct aspects of nature; sometimes suggested by nature itself, sometimes created by the mind. (1) One of the simplest and broadest aspects under which to view the physical world, is that of a system of final causes, or, on the other hand, of initial or effective causes. Bacon, having it in view to extend our power over nature, adopted the latter. He took firm hold of the idea of causation (in the common sense of the word) as contrasted to that of design, refusing to mix up the two ideas in one inquiry, and denouncing such traditional interpretations of facts, as did but obscure the simplicity of the aspect necessary for his purpose. He saw what others before him might have seen in what they saw, but who did not see as he saw it. In this achievement of intellect, which has been so fruitful in results, lie his genius and his fame.

(2) So again, to refer to a very different subject-matter, we often hear of the exploits of some great lawyer, judge or advocate, who is able in perplexed cases, when common minds see nothing but a hopeless heap of facts, foreign or contrary to each other, to detect the principle which rightly interprets the riddle, and, to the admiration of all hearers, converts a chaos into an orderly and luminous whole. This is what is meant by originality in thinking: it is the discovery of an aspect of a subject-matter, simpler, it may be, and more intelligible than any hitherto taken.

(3) On the other hand, such aspects are often unreal, as being mere exhibitions of ingenuity, not of true originality of mind. This is especially the case in what are called philosophical views of history. Such seems to me the theory advocated in a work of great learning, vigour, and acuteness, Warburton's *Divine Legation of Moses*. I do not call Gibbon merely ingenious; still his account of the rise of Christianity is the mere subjective view of one who could not enter into its depth and power.

(4) The aspect under which we view things is often intensely personal; nay, even awfully so, considering that, from the nature of the case, it does not bring home its idiosyncrasy either to ourselves or to others. Each of us

looks at the world in his own way, and does not know that perhaps it is characteristically his own. This is the case even as regards the senses. Some men have little perception of colours; some recognize one or two; to some men two contrary colours, as red and green, are one and the same. How poorly can we appreciate the beauties of nature, if our eyes discern, on the face of things, only an Indian-ink or a drab creation!

(5) So again, as regards form: each of us abstracts the relation of line to line in his own personal way,—as one man might apprehend a curve as convex, another as concave. Of course, as in the case of a curve, there may be a limit to possible aspects; but still, even when we agree together, it is not perhaps that we learn one from another, or fall under any law of agreement, but that our separate idiosyncrasies happen to concur. I fear I may seem trifling, if I allude to an illustration which has ever had a great force with me, and that for the very reason it is so trivial and minute. Children, learning to read, are sometimes presented with the letters of the alphabet turned into the figures of men in various attitudes. It is curious to observe from such representations, how differently the shape of the letters strikes different minds. In consequence I have continually asked the question in a chance company, which way certain of the great letters look, to the right or the left; and whereas nearly every one present had his own clear view, so clear that he could not endure the opposite view, still I have generally found that one half of the party considered the letters in question to look to the left, while the other half thought they looked to the right.

These instances, because they are so casual, suggest how it comes to pass, that men differ so widely from each other in religious and moral perceptions. Here, I say again, it does not prove that there is no objective truth, because not all men are in possession of it; or that we are not responsible for the associations which we attach, and the relations which we assign, to the objects of the intellect. But this it does suggest to us, that there is something deeper in our differences than the accident of external circumstances; and that we need the interposition of a Power greater than human teaching and human argument to make our beliefs true and our minds one.

Next I come to the implicit assumption of definite propositions in the first start of a course of reasoning, and the arbitrary exclusion of others, of whatever kind. Unless we had the right, when we pleased, of ruling that propositions were irrelevant or absurd, I do not see how we could conduct an argument at all; our way would be simply blocked up by extravagant principles and theories, gratuitous hypotheses, false issues, unsupported statements, and incredible facts. There are those who have treated the history of Abraham as an astronomical record, and have spoken of our Adorable Saviour as the sun in *Aries*. Arabian Mythology has changed Solomon into a mighty wizard. Noah has been considered the patriarch of the Chinese people. The ten tribes have been pronounced still to live in their descendants, the Red Indians; or to be the ancestors of the Goths and Vandals, and thereby of the present European races. Some have conjectured that the Apollos of the Acts of the Apostles was Apollonius Tyaneus. Able men have reasoned out, almost against their will, that Adam was a negro. These propositions, and many others of various kinds, we should think ourselves justified in passing over, if we were engaged in a work of sacred history; and there are others, on the contrary, which we should assume as true by our own right, and without notice, and without which we could not set about or carry on our work.

However, the right of making assumptions has been disputed; but, when the objections are examined, I think they only go to show that we have no right in argument to make any assumption we please. Thus, in the historical researches which just now came before us, it seems fair to say that no testimony should be received, except such as comes from competent witnesses, while it is not unfair to urge, on the other side, that tradition, though unauthenticated, being (what is called) in possession, has a prescription in its favour, and may, *prima facie*, or provisionally, be received. Here are the materials of a fair dispute; but there are writers who seem to have gone far beyond this reasonable scepticism, laying down as a general proposition that we have no right in philosophy to make any assumption whatever, and that we ought to begin with a universal doubt.[3] This, however, is of all assumptions the greatest, and to forbid assumptions universally is to forbid this one in particular. Doubt itself is a positive state, and implies a definite habit of mind, and thereby necessarily involves a system of principles and doctrines all its own. Again, if nothing is to be assumed, what is our very method of reasoning but an assumption? and what our nature itself? The very sense of pleasure and pain, which is one of the most intimate portions of ourselves, inevitably translates itself into intellectual assumptions.

Of the two, I would rather have to maintain that we ought to begin with believing every thing that is offered to our acceptance, than that it is our duty to doubt of every thing. The former, indeed, seems the true way of learning.

In that case, we soon discover and discard what is contra-dictory to itself; and error having always some portion of truth in it, and the truth having a reality which error has not, we may expect, that when there is an honest purpose and fair talents, we shall somehow make our way forward, the error falling off from the mind, and the truth develop-ing and occupying it. Thus it is that the Catholic religion is reached, as we see, by inquirers from all points of the compass, as if it mattered not where a man began, so that he had an eye and a heart for the truth.

CHAPTER IX

THE INTEGRITY OF HUMAN ASSENT[1]

THE DOCTRINE which I have been enunciating requires such careful explanation, that it is not wonderful that writers of great ability and name are to be found who have put it aside for a doctrine of their own; but no doctrine on the subject is without its difficulties, and certainly not theirs, though it carries with it a show of common sense. The authors to whom I refer wish to maintain that there are degrees of assent, and that, as the reasons for a proposition are strong or weak, so is the assent. It follows from this that absolute assent has no legitimate exercise, except as ratifying acts of intuition or demonstration. What is thus brought home to us is indeed to be accepted unconditionally; but as to reasonings in concrete matters, they are never more than probabilities, and the probability in each conclusion which we draw is the measure of our assent to that conclusion. Thus assent becomes a sort of necessary shadow, following upon inference, which is the substance; and is never without some alloy of doubt, because inference in the concrete never reaches more than probability.

Such is what may be called the *a priori* method of regarding assent in its relation to inference. It condemns an unconditional assent in concrete matters on what may be called the nature of the case. Assent cannot rise higher than its source; inference in such matters is at best conditional, therefore assent is conditional also.

Abstract argument is always dangerous, and this instance is no exception to the rule; I prefer to go by facts. The theory to which I have referred cannot be carried out in practice. It may be rightly said to prove too much; for it debars us from unconditional assent in cases in which the common voice of mankind, the advocates of this theory included, would protest against the prohibition. There are many truths in concrete matter, which no one can demonstrate, yet every one unconditionally accepts; and though of course there are innumerable propositions to which it would be absurd to give an absolute assent, still the absurdity lies in the circumstances of each particular case, as it is taken by itself, not in their common violation of the pretentious axiom that probable reasoning can never lead to certitude.

Locke's remarks on the subject are an illustration of what I have been saying. This celebrated writer, after the manner of his school, speaks freely of degrees of assent, and considers that the strength of assent given to each proposition varies with the strength of the inference on which the assent follows; yet he is obliged to make exceptions to his general principle,—exceptions, unintelligible on his abstract doctrine, but demanded by the logic of facts. The practice of mankind is too strong for the antecedent theorem, to which he is desirous to subject it.

First he says, in his chapter "On Probability," "Most of the propositions we think, reason, discourse, nay, act upon, are such as we cannot have undoubted knowledge of their

127

truth; yet some of them *border so near* upon certainty, that we *make* no doubt at all about them, but *assent* to them *as firmly,* and act according to that assent as resolutely, *as if they were infallibly demonstrated,* and that our knowledge of them was perfect and certain."[2] Here he allows that inferences, which are only "near upon certainty," are so near, that we legitimately accept them with "no doubt at all," and "assent to them as firmly as if they were infallibly demonstrated." That is, he affirms and sanctions the very paradox to which I am committed myself.

Again; he says, in his chapter on "The Degrees of Assent," that "when any particular thing, consonant to the constant observation of ourselves and others in the like case, comes attested by the concurrent reports of all that mention it, we receive it as easily, and build as firmly upon it, as if it were certain knowledge, and we reason and act thereupon, *with as little doubt as if it were perfect demonstration.*"[3] And he repeats, "These *probabilities* rise so near to certainty, that they *govern our thoughts as absolutely,* and influence all our actions as fully, as *the most evident demonstration;* and in what concerns us, we make little or no difference between them and certain knowledge. *Our belief thus grounded, rises to assurance.*" Here again, "probabilities" may be so strong as to "govern our thoughts as absolutely" as sheer demonstration, so strong that belief, grounded on them, "rises to assurance," that is, to certitude.

I have so high a respect both for the character and the ability of Locke, for his manly simplicity of mind and his outspoken candour, and there is so much in his remarks upon reasoning and proof in which I fully concur, that I feel no pleasure in considering him in the light of an opponent to views which I myself have ever cherished as true, with

128

an obstinate devotion; and I would willingly think that in the passage which follows in his chapter on "Enthusiasm," he is aiming at superstitious extravagances which I should repudiate myself as much as he can do; but, if so, his words go beyond the occasion, and contradict what I have quoted from him above.

He that would seriously set upon the search of truth, ought in the first place, to prepare his mind with a love of it. For he that loves it not will not take much pains to get it, nor be much concerned when he misses it. There is nobody, in the commonwealth of learning, who does not profess himself a lover of truth,—and there is not a rational creature, that would not take it amiss, to be thought otherwise of. And yet, for all this, one may truly say, there are very few lovers of truth, for truth-sake, even amongst those who persuade themselves that they are so. How a man may know, whether he be so, in earnest, is worth inquiry; and I think, there is this one unerring mark of it, viz. *the not entertaining any proposition with greater assurance than the proofs it is built on will warrant.* Whoever goes beyond this measure of assent, it is plain, receives not truth in the love of it, loves not truth for truth-sake, but for some other by-end. For the evidence that any proposition is true (*except such as are self-evident*) lying only in the proofs a man has of it, whatsoever degrees of assent he affords it *beyond the degrees of that* evidence, it is plain *all that surplusage of assurance* is owing to some other affection, and not to the love of truth; it being as *impossible* that the love of truth should carry *my assent above the evidence* there is to me that it is true, as that the love of truth should make me assent to any proposition for the sake of that evidence which it has not that it is true; which is in effect to love it as a truth, because it is possible or probable that it may not be true.[4]

Here he says that it is not only illogical, but immoral to "carry our *assent above* the *evidence* that a proposition is true," to have "a surplusage of *assurance beyond* the degree of that evidence." And he excepts from this rule only self-evident propositions. How then is it not consistent with

129

right reason, with the love of truth for its own sake, to allow in his words, certain strong "probabilities" to "govern our thoughts as absolutely as the most evident demonstration"? how is there no "surplusage of assurance beyond the degrees of evidence" when in the case of those strong probabilities, we permit "our belief, thus grounded, to rise to assurance," as he pronounces we are rational in doing? Of course he had in view one set of instances, when he implied that demonstration was the condition of absolute assent, and another set when he said that it was no such condition; but he surely cannot be acquitted of slovenly thinking in thus treating a cardinal subject. A philosopher should so anticipate the application, and guard the enunciation of his principles, as to secure them against the risk of their being made to change places with each other, to defend what he is eager to denounce, and to condemn what he finds it necessary to sanction.

However, whatever is to be thought of his *a priori* method and his logical consistency, his *animus*, I fear, must be understood as hostile to the doctrine which I am going to maintain. He takes a view of the human mind, in relation to inference and assent, which to me seems theoretical and unreal. Reasonings and convictions which I deem natural and legitimate, he apparently would call irrational, enthusiastic, perverse, and immoral; and that, as I think, because he consults his own ideal of how the mind ought to act, instead of interrogating human nature, as an existing thing, as it is found in the world. Instead of going by the testimony of psychological facts, and thereby determining our constitutive faculties and our proper condition, and being content with the mind as God has made it, he would form men as he thinks they ought to be formed, into something better and higher, and calls them irrational and indefensible, if (so to speak) they take to the water, instead of remaining under the narrow wings of his own arbitrary theory.

1. Now the first question which this theory leads me to consider is, whether there is such an act of the mind as assent at all. If there is, it is plain it ought to show itself unequivocally as such, as distinct from other acts. For if a professed act can only be viewed as the necessary and immediate repetition of another act, if assent is a sort of reproduction and double of an act of inference, if when inference determines that a proposition is somewhat, or not a little, or a good deal, or very like truth, assent as its natural and normal counterpart says that it *is* somewhat, or not a little, or a good deal, or very like truth, then I do not see what we mean by saying, or why we say at all, that there is any such act. It is simply superfluous, in a psychological point of view, and a curiosity for subtle minds, and the sooner it is got out of the way the better. When I assent, I am supposed, it seems, to do precisely what I do when I infer, or rather not quite so much, but something which is included in inferring; for, while the disposition of my mind towards a given proposition is identical in assent and in inference, I merely drop the thought of the premisses when I assent, though not of their influence on the proposition inferred. This then, and no more after all, is what nature prescribes, and this, and no more than this, is the conscientious use of our faculties, so to assent forsooth as to do nothing else than infer. Then, I say, if this be really the state of the case, if assent in no real way differs from inference, it is one and the same thing with it. It is another name for inference, and to speak of it at all does but mislead. Nor can it fairly be urged as a parallel case that an act of con-

131

scious recognition, though distinct from an act of knowledge, is after all only its repetition. On the contrary, such a
recognition is a reflex act with its own object, viz. the act
of knowledge itself. As well might it be said that the hearing
of the notes of my voice is a repetition of the act of singing:—it gives no plausibility then to the anomaly I am
combating.

I lay it down, then, as a principle that either assent is
intrinsically distinct from inference, or the sooner we get rid
of the word in philosophy the better. If it be only the echo
of an inference, do not treat it as a substantive act; but, on
the other hand, supposing it be not such an idle repetition,
as I am sure it is not, supposing the word "assent" does hold
a rightful place in language and in thought, if it does not
admit of being confused with concluding and inferring, if
the two words are used for two operations of the intellect
which cannot change their character, if in matter of fact they
are not always found together, if they do not vary with each
other, if one is sometimes found without the other, if one
is strong when the other is weak, if sometimes they seem
even in conflict with each other, then, since we know perfectly well what an inference is, it comes upon us to consider what, as distinct from inference, an assent is, and we
are, by the very fact of its being distinct, advanced one
step towards that account of it which I think is the true one.[5]
The first step then towards deciding the point, will be to
inquire what the experience of human life, as it is daily
brought before us, teaches us of the relation to each other
of inference and assent.

(1) First, we know from experience that assents may
endure without the presence of the inferential acts upon
which they were originally elicited. It is plain, that, as life

goes on, we are not only inwardly formed and changed by the accession of habits, but we are also enriched by a great multitude of beliefs and opinions, and that, on a variety of subjects. These beliefs and opinions, held, as some of them are, almost as first principles, are assents, and they constitute, as it were, the clothing and furniture of the mind. I have already spoken of them under the head of "Credence" and "Opinion."[6] Sometimes we are fully conscious of them; sometimes they are implicit, or only now and then come directly before our reflective faculty. Still they are assents; and, when we first admitted them, we had some kind of reason, slight or strong, recognized or not, for doing so. However, whatever those reasons were, even if we ever realized them, we have long forgotten them. Whether it was the authority of others, or our own observation, or our reading, or our reflections, which became the warrant of our assent, any how we received the matters in question into our minds as true, and gave them a place there. We assented to them, and we still assent, though we have forgotten what the warrant was. At present they are self-sustained in our minds, and have been so for long years; they are in no sense conclusions; they imply no process of thought. Here then is a case in which assent stands out as distinct from inference.

(2) Again; sometimes assent fails, while the reasons for it and the inferential act which is the recognition of those reasons, are still present, and in force. Our reasons may seem to us as strong as ever, yet they do not secure our assent. Our beliefs, founded on them, were and are not; we cannot perhaps tell when they went; we may have thought that we still held them, till something happened to call our attention to the state of our minds, and then we found that

133

our assent had become an assertion. Sometimes, of course, a cause may be found why they went; there may have been some vague feeling that a fault lay at the ultimate basis, or in the underlying conditions, of our reasonings; or some misgiving that the subject-matter of them was beyond the reach of the human mind; or a consciousness that we had gained a broader view of things in general than when we first gave our assent; or that there were strong objections to our first convictions, which we had never taken into account. But this is not always so; sometimes our mind changes so quickly, so unaccountably, so disproportionately to any tangible arguments to which the change can be referred, and with such abiding recognition of the force of the old arguments, as to suggest the suspicion that moral causes, arising out of our condition, age, company, occupations, fortunes, are at the bottom. However, what once was assent is gone; yet the perception of the old arguments remains, showing that inference is one thing, and assent another.

(3) And as assent sometimes dies out without tangible reasons, sufficient to account for its failure, so sometimes, in spite of strong and convincing arguments, it is never given. We sometimes find men loud in their admiration of truths which they never profess. As, by the law of our mental constitution, obedience is quite distinct from faith, and men may believe without practising, so is assent also independent of our acts of inference. Again, prejudice hinders assent to the most incontrovertible proofs. Again, it not unfrequently happens, that while the keenness of the ratiocinative faculty enables a man to see the ultimate result of a complicated problem in a moment, it takes years for him to embrace it as a truth, and to recognize it as an item in the circle of his knowledge. Yet he does at last so accept it, and then we say that he assents.

(4) Again; very numerous are the cases, in which good arguments, and really good as far as they go, and confessed by us to be good, nevertheless are not strong enough to incline our minds ever so little to the conclusion at which they point. But why is it that we do not assent a little, in proportion to those arguments? On the contrary, we throw the full *onus probandi* on the side of the conclusion, and we refuse to assent to it at all, until we can assent to it altogether. The proof is capable of growth; but the assent either exists or does not exist.

(5) I have already alluded to the influence of moral motives in hindering assent to conclusions which are logically unimpeachable. According to the couplet,

> A man convinced against his will
> Is of the same opinion still,—

assent then is not the same as inference.

(6) Strange as it may seem, this contrast between inference and assent is exemplified even in the province of mathematics. Argument is not always able to command our assent, even though it be demonstrative. Sometimes of course it forces its way, that is, when the steps of the reasoning are few, and admit of being viewed by the mind altogether. Certainly, one cannot conceive a man having before him the series of conditions and truths on which it depends that the three angles of a triangle are together equal to two right angles, and yet not assenting to that proposition. Were all propositions as plain, though assent would not in consequence be the same act as inference, yet it would certainly follow immediately upon it. I allow then as much as this, that, when an argument is in itself and by itself conclusive of a truth, it has by a law of our nature the same command over our assent, or rather the truth which it has reached has the same command, as our senses have. Cer-

tainly our intellectual nature is under laws, and the correlative of ascertained truth is unreserved assent.

But I am not speaking of short and lucid demonstrations; but of long and intricate mathematical investigations; and in that case, though every step may be indisputable, it still requires a specially sustained attention and an effort of memory to have in the mind all at once all the steps of the proof, with their bearings on each other, and the antecedents which they severally involve; and these conditions of the inference may interfere with the promptness of our assent.

Hence it is that party spirit or national feeling or religious prepossessions have before now had power to retard the reception of truths of a mathematical character; which never could have been, if demonstrations were *ipso facto* assents. Nor indeed would any mathematician, even in questions of pure science, assent to his own conclusions, on new and difficult ground, and in the case of abstruse calculations, however often he went over his work, till he had the corroboration of other judgments besides his own. He would have carefully revised his inference, and would assent to the probability of his accuracy in inferring, but still he would abstain from an immediate assent to the truth of his conclusion. Yet the corroboration of others cannot add to his perception of the proof; he would still perceive the proof, even though he failed in gaining their corroboration. And yet again he might arbitrarily make it his rule, never to assent to his conclusions without such corroboration, or at least before the lapse of a sufficient interval. Here again inference is distinct from assent.

I have been showing that inference and assent are distinct acts of the mind, and that they may be made apart

136

from each other. Of course I cannot be taken to mean that there is no legitimate or actual connexion between them, as if arguments adverse to a conclusion did not naturally hinder assent; or as if the inclination to give assent were not greater or less according as the particular act of inference expressed a stronger or weaker probability; or as if assent did not always imply grounds in reason, implicit, if not explicit, or could be rightly given without sufficient grounds. So much is it commonly felt that assent must be preceded by inferential acts, that obstinate men give their own will as their very reason for assenting, if they can think of nothing better; "stat pro ratione voluntas." Indeed, I doubt whether assent is ever given without some preliminary, which stands for a reason; but it does not follow from this, that it may not be withheld in cases when there are good reasons for giving it to a proposition, or may not be withdrawn after it has been given, the reasons remaining, or may not remain when the reasons are forgotten, or must always vary in strength, as the reasons vary; and this substantiveness, as I may call it, of the act of assent is the very point which I have wished to establish.

2. And in showing that assent is distinct from an act of inference, I have gone a good way towards showing in what it differs from it. If assent and inference are each of them the acceptance of a proposition, but the special characteristic of inference is that it is conditional, it is natural to suppose that assent is unconditional. Again, if assent is the acceptance of truth, and truth is the proper object of the intellect, and no one can hold conditionally what by the same act he holds to be true, here too is a reason for saying that assent is an adhesion without reserve or doubt to the proposition to which it is given. And again, it is to be pre-

137

sumed that the word has not two meanings: what it has at one time, it has at another. Inference is always inference; even if demonstrative, it is still conditional; it establishes an introvertible conclusion on the condition of incontrovertible premisses. To the conclusion thus drawn, assent gives its absolute recognition. In the case of all demonstration, assent, when given, is unconditionally given. In one class of subjects, then, assent certainly is always unconditional; but if the word stands for an undoubting and unhesitating act of the mind once, why does it not denote the same always? what evidence is there that it ever means any thing else than that which the whole world will unite in witnessing that it means in certain cases? why are we not to interpret what is controverted by what is known? This is what is suggested on the first view of the question; but to continue:—

In demonstrative matters assent excludes the presence of doubt: now are instances producible, on the other hand, of its ever co-existing with doubt in cases of the concrete? As the above instances have shown, on very many questions we do not give an assent at all. What commonly happens is this, that, after hearing and entering into what may be said for a proposition, we pronounce neither for nor against it. We may accept the conclusion as a conclusion, dependent on premisses, abstract, and tending to the concrete; but we do not follow up our inference of a proposition by giving an assent to it. That there are concrete propositions to which we give unconditional assents, I shall presently show; but I am now asking for instances of conditional, for instances in which we assent a little and not much. Usually, we do not assent at all. Every day, as it comes, brings with it opportunities for us to enlarge our circle of assents. We read the newspapers; we look through debates in Parliament, pleadings in the law courts, leading articles, letters of correspondents, reviews of books, criticisms in the fine arts, and we either form no opinion at all upon the subjects discussed, as lying out of our line, or at most we have only an opinion about them. At the utmost we say that we are inclined to believe this proposition or that, that we are not sure it is not true, that much may be said for it, that we have been much struck by it; but we never say that we give it a degree of assent. We might as well talk of degrees of truth as of degrees of assent.

Yet Locke heads one of his chapters with the title "Degrees of Assent"; and a writer, of this century, who claims our respect from the tone and drift of his work, thus expresses himself after Locke's manner: "Moral evidence," he says, "may produce a variety of degrees of assents, from suspicion to moral certainty. For, here, the degree of assent depends upon the degree in which the evidence on one side preponderates, or exceeds that on the other. And as this preponderancy may vary almost infinitely, so likewise may the degrees of assent. For a few of these degrees, though but for a few, names have been invented. Thus, when the evidence on one side preponderates a very little, there is ground for suspicion, or conjecture. Presumption, persuasion, belief, conclusion, conviction, moral certainty,—doubt, wavering, distrust, disbelief,—are words which imply an increase or decrease of this preponderancy. Some of these words also admit of epithets which denote a further increase or diminution of the assent."[7]

Can there be a better illustration than this passage supplies of what I have been insisting on above, viz. that, in teaching various degrees of assent, we tend to destroy

139

assent, as an act of the mind, altogether? This author makes the degrees of assent "infinite," as the degrees of probability are infinite. His assents are really only inferences, and assent is a name without a meaning, the needless repetition of an inference. But in truth "suspicion, conjecture, presumption, persuasion, belief, conclusion, conviction, moral certainty," are not, "assents" at all; they are simply more or less strong inferences of a proposition; and "doubt, wavering, distrust, disbelief," are recognitions, more or less strong, of the probability of its contradictory.

There is only one sense in which we are allowed to call such acts or states of mind assents. They are opinions; and, as being such, they are, as I have already observed, when speaking of Opinion, assents to the plausibility, probability, doubtfulness, or untrustworthiness, of a proposition; that is, not variations of assent to an inference, but assents to a variation in inferences. When I assent to a doubtfulness, or to a probability, my assent, as such, is as complete as if I assented to a truth; it is not a certain degree of assent. And, in like manner, I may be certain of an uncertainty; that does not destroy the specific notion conveyed in the word "certain."

I do not know then when it is that we ever deliberately profess assent to a proposition without meaning to convey to others the impression that we accept it unreservedly, and that because it is true. Certainly, we familiarly use such phrases as a half-assent, as we also speak of half-truths; but a half-assent is not a kind of assent any more than a half-truth is a kind of truth. As the object is indivisible, so is the act. A half-truth is a proposition which in one aspect is a truth, and in another is not; to give a half-assent is to feel drawn towards assent, or to assent one moment and not the

140

next, or to be in the way to assent to it. It means that the proposition in question deserves a hearing, that it is probable or attractive, that it opens important views, that it is a key to perplexing difficulties, or the like.

3. Treating the subject then, not according to *a priori* fitness, but according to the facts of human nature, as they are found in the concrete action of life, I find numberless cases in which we do not assent at all, none in which assent is evidently conditional;—and many, as I shall now proceed to show, in which it is unconditional, and these in subject-matters which admit of nothing higher than probable reasoning. If human nature is to be its own witness, there is no medium between assenting and not assenting. Locke's theory of the duty of assenting more or less according to degrees of evidence, is invalidated by the testimony of high and low, young and old, ancient and modern, as continually given in their ordinary sayings and doings. Indeed, as I have shown, he does not strictly maintain it himself; yet, though he feels the claims of nature and fact to be too strong for him in certain cases, he gives no reason why he should violate his theory in these, and yet not in many more.

Now let us review some of those assents, which men give on evidence short of intuition and demonstration, yet which are as unconditional as if they had that highest evidence.[8]

First of all, starting from intuition, of course we all believe, without any doubt, that we exist; that we have an individuality and identity all our own; that we think, feel and act, in the home of our own minds; that we have a present sense of good and evil, of a right and a wrong, of a true and a false, of a beautiful and a hideous, however we analyze our ideas of them. We have an absolute vision before

141

us of what happened yesterday or last year, so as to be able without any chance of mistake to give evidence upon it in a court of justice, let the consequences be ever so serious. We are sure that of many things we are ignorant, that of many things we are in doubt, and that of many things we are not in doubt.

Nor is the assent which we give to facts limited to the range of self-consciousness. We are sure beyond all hazard of a mistake, that our own self is not the only being existing; that there is an external world; that it is a system with parts and a whole, a universe carried on by laws; and that the future is affected by the past. We accept and hold with an unqualified assent, that the earth, considered as a phenomenon, is a globe; that all its regions see the sun by turns; that there are vast tracts on it of land and water; that there are really existing cities on definite sites, which go by the names of London, Paris, Florence, and Madrid. We are sure that Paris or London, unless suddenly swallowed up by an earthquake or burned to the ground, is to-day just what it was yesterday, when we left it.

We laugh to scorn the idea that we had no parents, though we have no memory of our birth; that we shall never depart this life, though we can have no experience of the future; that we are able to live without food, though we have never tried; that a world of men did not live before our time, or that that world has had no history; that there has been no rise and fall of states, no wars, no revolutions, no art, no science, no literature, no religion.

We should be either indignant or amused at the report of our intimate friend being false to us; and we are able sometimes, without any hesitation, to accuse certain parties of

142

hostility and injustice to us. We may have a deep consciousness, which we never can lose, that we on our part have
been cruel to others, and that they have felt us to be so, or
that we have been, and have been felt to be, ungenerous to
those who love us. We may have an overpowering sense of
our moral weakness, of the precariousness of our life, health,
wealth, position, and good fortune. We may have a clear
view of the weak points of our physical constitution, of
what food or medicine is good for us, and what does us
harm. We may be able to master, as least in part, the course
of our past history; its turning-points, our hits, and our
great mistakes. We may have a sense of the presence of a
Supreme Being, which never has been dimmed by even a
passing shadow, which has inhabited us ever since we can
recollect any thing, and which we cannot imagine our
losing. We may be able, for others have been able, so to
realize the precepts and truths of Christianity, as deliberately to surrender our life, rather than transgress the one or
to deny the other.

On all these truths we have an immediate and an unhesitating hold, nor do we think ourselves guilty of not loving
truth for truth's sake, because we cannot reach them
through a series of intuitive propositions. Assent on reasonings not demonstrative is too widely recognized an act to be
irrational, unless man's nature is irrational, too familiar to
the prudent and clear-minded to be an infirmity or an
extravagance. None of us can think or act without the acceptance of truths, not intuitive, not demonstrated, yet
sovereign. If our nature has any constitution, any laws, one
of them is this absolute reception of propositions as true,
which lie outside the narrow range of conclusions to which

logic, formal or virtual, is tethered; nor has any philosophical theory the power to force on us a rule which will not work for a day.

When, then, philosophers lay down principles, on which it follows that our assent, except when given to objects of intuition or demonstration, is conditional, that the assent given to propositions by well-ordered minds necessarily varies with the proof producible for them, and that it does not and cannot remain one and the same while the proof is strengthened or weakened,—are they not to be considered as confusing together two things very distinct from each other, a mental act or state and a scientific rule, an interior assent and a set of logical formulas? When they speak of degrees of assent, surely they have no intention at all of defining the position of the mind itself relative to the adoption of a given conclusion, but they are recording their perception of the relation of that conclusion towards its premisses. They are contemplating how representative symbols work, not how the intellect is affected towards the thing which those symbols represent.

In real truth they as little mean to assert the principle of measuring our assents by our logic, as they would fancy they could record the refreshment which we receive from the open air by the readings of the graduated scale of a thermometer. There is a connexion doubtless between a logical conclusion and an assent, as there is between the variation of the mercury and our sensations; but the mercury is not the cause of life and health, nor is verbal argumentation the principle of inward belief. If we feel hot or chilly, no one will convince us to the contrary by insisting that the glass is at 60°. It is the mind that reasons and assents, not a diagram on paper. I may have difficulty in the management of a proof, while I remain unshaken in my adherence to the conclusion. Supposing a boy cannot make his answer to some arithmetical or algebraical question tally with the book, need he at once distrust the book? Does his trust in it fall down a certain number of degrees, according to the force of his difficulty? On the contrary, he keeps to the principle, implicit but present to his mind, with which he took up the book, that the book is more likely to be right than he is; and this mere preponderance of probability is sufficient to make him faithful to his belief in its correctness, till its incorrectness is actually proved.

My own opinion is, that the class of writers of whom I have been speaking, have themselves as little misgiving about the truths which they pretend to weigh out and measure as their unsophisticated neighbours; but they think it a duty to remind us, that since the full etiquette of logical requirements has not been satisfied, we must believe those truths at our peril. They warn us, that an issue which can never come to pass, in matter of fact, is nevertheless in theory a possible supposition. They do not, for instance, intend for a moment to imply that there is even the shadow of a doubt that Great Britain is an island, but they think we ought to know, if we do not know, that there is no proof of the fact, in mode and figure, equal to the proof of a proposition of Euclid; and that in consequence they and we are all bound to suspend our judgment about such a fact, though it be in an infinitesimal degree, lest we should seem not to love truth for truth's sake. Having made their protest, they subside without scruple into that same absolute assurance of only partially-proved truths, which is natural to the illogical imagination of the multitude.

4. It remains to explain some conversational expressions,

at first sight favourable to that doctrine of degrees in assent, which I have been combating.[9]

(1) We often speak of giving a modified and qualified, or a presumptive and *prima facie* assent, or (as I have already said) a half-assent to opinions or facts; but these expressions admit of an easy explanation. Assent, upon the authority of others is often, as I have noticed, when speaking of notional assents, little more than a profession or acquiescence or inference, not a real acceptance of a proposition. I report, for instance, that there was a serious fire in the town in the past night; and then perhaps I add, that at least the morning papers say so;—that is, I have perhaps no positive doubt of the fact; still, by referring to the newspapers I imply that I do not take on myself the responsibility of the statement. In thus qualifying my apparent assent, I show that it was not a genuine assent at all. In like manner a *prima facie* assent is an assent to an antecedent probability of a fact, not to the fact itself; as I might give a *prima facie* assent to the Plurality of worlds or to the personality of Homer, without pledging myself to either absolutely. "Half-assent," of which I spoke above, is an inclination to assent, or again, an intention of assenting, when certain difficulties are surmounted. When we speak without thought, assent has as vague a meaning as half-assent; but when we deliberately say, "I assent," we signify an act of the mind so definite as to admit of no change but that of its ceasing to be.

(2) And so, too, though we sometimes use the phrase "conditional assent," yet we only mean thereby to say that we will assent under certain contingencies. Of course we may, if we please, include a condition in the proposition to which our assent is given; and then, that condition en-

ters into the matter of the assent, but not into the assent itself. To assent to "If this man is in a consumption, his days are numbered," is as little a conditional assent, as to assent to "Of this consumptive patient the days are numbered," which (though without the conditional form), is an equivalent proposition. In such cases, strictly speaking, the assent is given neither to antecedent nor consequent of the conditional proposition, but to their connexion, that is, to the enthymematic *inferentia*. If we place the condition external to the proposition, then the assent will be given to "That 'his days are numbered' is conditionally true"; and of course we can assent to the conditionality of a proposition as well as to its probability. Or again, if so be, we may give our assent not only to the *inferentia* in a complex conditional proposition, but to each of the simple propositions, of which it is made up, besides. "There will be a storm soon, for the mercury falls";—here, besides assenting to the connexion of the propositions, we may assent also to "The mercury falls," and to "There will be a storm." This is assenting to the premiss, *inferentia*, and thing inferred, all at once;—we assent to the whole syllogism, and to its component parts.

(3) In like manner are to be explained the phrases, "deliberate assent," a "rational assent"; "a sudden," "impulsive," or "hesitating" assent. These expressions denote, not kinds or qualities, but the circumstances of assenting. A deliberate assent is an assent following upon deliberation. It is sometimes called a conviction, a word which commonly includes in its meaning two acts, both the act of inference, and the act of assent consequent upon the inference. On the other hand, a hesitating assent is an assent to which we have been slow and intermittent in coming; or an assent which, when given is thwarted and obscured by external

147

and flitting misgivings, though not such as to enter into the act itself, or essentially to damage it.

There is another sense in which we speak of a hesitating or uncertain assent; viz. when we assent in act, but not in the habit of our minds. Till assent to a doctrine or fact is my habit, I am at the mercy of inferences contrary to it; I assent to-day, and give up my belief, or incline to disbelief, to-morrow. I may find it my duty, for instance, after the opportunity of careful inquiry and inference, to assent to another's innocence, whom I have for years considered guilty; but from long prejudice I may be unable to carry my new assent well about me, and may every now and then relapse into momentary thoughts injurious to him.

(4) A more plausible objection to the absolute absence of all doubt or misgiving in an act of assent is found in the use of the terms firm and weak assent, or in the growth of belief and trust. Thus, we assent to the events of history, but not with that fulness and force of adherence to the received account of them with which we realize a record of occurrences which are within our own memory. And again, we assent to the praise bestowed on a friend's good qualities with an energy which we do not feel, when we are speaking of virtue in the abstract: and if we are political partisans, our assent is very cold, when we cannot refuse it, to representations made in favour of the wisdom or patriotism of statesmen whom we dislike. And then as to religious subjects, we speak of strong faith and feeble faith; of the faith which would move mountains, and of the ordinary faith "without which it is impossible to please God." And as we can grow in graces, so surely can we inclusively in faith. Again we rise from one work on Christian evidences with our faith enlivened and invigorated;

148

from another perhaps with the distracted father's words in our mouth, "I believe, help my unbelief."

Now it is evident, first of all, that habits of mind may grow, as being a something permanent and continuous; and by assent growing, it is often only meant that the habit grows and has greater hold upon the mind.

But again, when we carefully consider the matter, it will be found that this increase or decrease of strength does not lie in the assent itself, but in its circumstances and con-comitants; for instance, in the emotions, in the ratiocinative faculty, or in the imagination.

For instance, as to the emotions, this strength of assent may be nothing more than the strength of love, hatred, interest, desire, or fear, which the object of the assent elicits, and this is especially the case when that object is of a religious nature. Such strength is adventitious and accidental; it may come, it may go; it is found in one man, not in another; it does not interfere with the genuineness and perfection of the act of assent. Balaam assented to the fact of his own intercourse with the supernatural, as well as Moses; but, to use religious language, he had light without love; his intellect was clear, his heart was cold. Hence his faith would popularly be considered wanting in strength. On the other hand, prejudice implies strong assents to the disadvantage of its object; that is, it encourages such assents, and guards them from the chance of being lost.

Again, when a conclusion is recommended to us by the number and force of the arguments in proof of it, our recognition of them invests it with a luminousness, which in one sense adds strength to our assent to it, as it certainly does protect and embolden that assent. Thus we assent to a review of recent events, which we have studied from original documents, with a triumphant peremptoriness which it neither occurs to us, nor is possible for us, to exercise, when we make an act of assent to the assassination of Julius Caesar, or to the existence of the Abipones, though we are as securely certain of these latter facts as of the doings and occurrences of yesterday.

And further, all that I have said about the apprehension of propositions is in point here. We may speak of assent to our Lord's divinity as strong or feeble, according as it is given to the reality as impressed upon the imagination, or to the notion of it as entertained by the intellect.

(5) Nor, lastly, does this doctrine of the intrinsic integrity and indivisibility (if I may so speak) of assent interfere with the teaching of Catholic theology as to the pre-eminence of strength in divine faith, which has a supernatural origin, when compared with all belief which is merely human and natural. For first, that pre-eminence consists, not in its differing from human faith, merely in degree of assent, but in its being superior in nature and kind, so that the one does not admit of a comparison with the other; and next, its intrinsic superiority is not a matter of experience, but is above experience. Assent is ever assent; but in the assent which follows on a divine announcement, and is vivified by a divine grace, there is, from the nature of the case, a transcendent adhesion of mind, intellectual and moral, and a special self-protection, beyond the operation of those ordinary laws of thought, which alone have a place in my discussion.

CHAPTER X

THE CERTITUDE OF FAITH[1]

Rome
April 29, 1879

[My dear William,]

I have been touched by your consideration for me in writing to me, when you would put into shape your thoughts upon religion, thus putting me in your affection and regard on a level with dear Hurrell; and I wish I had just now leisure enough and vigour of mind enough to answer your letter so thoroughly as I think it could be answered, and as its delicacy and tenderness for me deserves. But I will set down just as it strikes me on reading, having no books and depending mainly on my memory.

My first and lasting impression is that in first principles we agree together more than you allow; and this is a difficulty in my meeting you, that I am not sure you know what I hold and what I don't; otherwise why should [you] insist so strongly on points which I maintain as strongly as you?

Thus you insist very strongly on knowledge mainly depending upon the experience of facts, as if I denied it; whereas, as a general truth and when experience is attainable, I hold it more fully than you. I say "more fully," be-

151

cause, whereas you hold that "to *select,* square, and to fit together materials which experience has supplied is the very function of the intellect," I should [not] allow the intellect to select, but only to estimate them.

I will set down dicta of mine, which I think you do not recollect, which are to be found in my University Sermons, Essay on Development of Doctrine, and Essay on Assent.

"No one can completely define things which exist externally to the mind, and which are known to him by experience."

"Our notions of things are never simply commensurate with the things themselves."

"It is as easy to create as to define."

"This distinction between inference and assent is exemplified even in mathematics."

"Argument is not always able to command our assent though it be demonstration."

"Concrete matter does not admit of demonstration."

"It is to me a perplexity that grave authors seem to enunciate as an intuitive truth, that everything must have a cause."

"The notion of causation is one of the first lesson which we learn from experience."

"Starting from experience, I call a cause an effective will."

"There are philosophers who teach an invariable uniformity in the laws of nature; I do not see on what ground of experience or reason they take up this position."

"Gravitation is not an experience any more than is the mythological doctrine of the presence of innumerable spirits in physical phenomena."

"Because we have made a successful analysis of some complicated assemblage of phenomena, which experience has brought before us, in the visible scene of things, and have reduced them to a tolerable dependence on each other, we call the ultimate points of this analysis and the hypothetical facts in which the whole mass of phenomena is gathered up by the name of causes, whereas they are really only formulae under which these phenomena are conveniently represented" etc., and so on.

You say "I doubt whether it is really possible to give a blind man a common idea of a star." I have drawn out elaborately in one of my University Sermons the necessity of experience from the case of a blind man attempting to write upon colours, how he might go on swimmingly at first—but before long—in spite of his abstract knowledge would be precipitated into some desperate mistake.

I can't think you would write as you have written had you recollected in my volumes passages such as these. Therefore you must let me state what, according to my own view of the matter, I consider to be our fundamental difference, and it is certainly so considerable and accompanied with so [much that is] simply *a priori* and personal, that, if you really hold firmly all you say, I must with great grief consider I shall have done all that I can do, when I have clearly stated what I conceive it to be.

We differ in our sense and our use of the word "certain." I use it of minds, you of propositions. I fully grant the uncertainty of all conclusions in your sense of the word, but I maintain that minds may in my sense be certain of conclusions which are uncertain in yours.

Thus, when you say that "no man of high scientific position but bears in mind that a residue of doubt attaches to the most thoroughly established scientific truths," I am glad at all times to learn of men of science, as of all men, but I

153

did not require their help in this instance, since I have myself laid it down, as I had already quoted my words, [that] "concrete matter does not admit of demonstration." That is, in your sense of the word "doubt," viz. a recognition and judgment that the proof is not wholly complete, attaches to all propositions; this I would maintain as well as you. But if you mean that the laws of the human mind do not command and force it to accept as true and to assent absolutely to propositions which are not logically demonstrated, this I think so great a paradox, that all the scientific philosophers in Europe would be unable by their united testimony to make me believe it. That Great Britain is an island is a geographical, scientific truth. Men of science are certain of it; they have in their intellects no doubt at all about it; they would hold and rightly that a residuum of defectiveness of proof attaches to it as a thesis; and, in consequence they would admit some great authority, who asserted that it was geographically joined to Norway, tho' a canal was cut across it, to give them his reasons, but they would listen without a particle of sympathy for the great man or doubt as to his hallucination, and all this, while they allowed it had not been absolutely and fully proved impossible that he was right.

Then I go on to say, that [it is] just this, which scientific men believe of Great Britain, viz. that its insularity is an absolute truth, that we believe of the divinity of Christianity; and, as men of science nevertheless would give a respectful attention and a candid and careful though not a sympathetic hearing to any man of name and standing who proposes to prove to them that Great Britain is not an island, so we too, did men in whom we confide come to us stating their conviction that Christianity was not true, we should indeed feel drawn to such men as little as professors of science to the man who would persuade them that Great Britain was joined to the continent, but we should, if we acted rightly, do our utmost, as I have ever tried to do, in the case of unbelievers, to do justice to their arguments. Of course it may be said that I could not help being biassed, but that may be said of men of science too.

I hold, then, and I certainly do think that scientific philosophers must, if they are fair, confess too, that there are truths of which they are certain, tho' they are not logically proved; which are to be as cordially accepted as if they were absolutely proved, which are to be accepted beyond their degree of probability, considered as conclusions from premisses. You yourself allow that there are cases in which we are forced and have a duty to act, as if what is but possible were certainly true, as in our precautions against fire; I go further so much, not as to say that in merely possible, or simply probable cases, but in particular cases of the highest probability, as in that of the insularity of Great Britain, it is a law of human intellect to accept with an inward assent as absolutely true, what is not yet demonstrated. We all observe this law; science may profess to ignore it; but men of science observe it every day of their lives, just as religious men observe it in their own province.

In opposition then to what you assume without proof, which you don't seem to know that I have denied, even to throwing down the gauntlet in denying, I maintain that an act of inference is distinct from an act of assent, and that [the latter's] strength does not vary with the strength of the inference. A hundred and one eye witnesses add strength to the inference drawn from the evidence of a hundred, but not to the assent which that evidence creates.

155

There is a faculty in the mind which I think I have called the inductive sense, which, when properly cultivated and used, answers to Aristotle's *phronesis*, its province being, not virtue, but the "inquisitio veri," which decides for us, beyond any technical rules, when, how, etc. to pass from inference to assent, and when and under what circumstances, etc. etc. not. You seem yourself to admit this faculty, when you speak of the intellect not only as adjusting, but as selecting the results of experience. Indeed I cannot understand how you hold certain opinions with such strength of conviction, as you[r] view of divine justice, of the inutility, if not worse, of prayer, ("it seems to me *impossible* that I should *ever*" etc.) against eternal punishment, against the Atonement, unless you were acting by means of some mental faculty (rightly or wrongly used) which brought you on to assents far more absolute than could be reached by experience and the legitimate action of logic upon its results.

I am led to conclude then that you grant or rather hold two principles most important to my view of this great matter:—first that there is a mental faculty which reasons in a far higher way than that of merely measuring the force of conclusions by the force of premisses: and next, that the mind has a power of determining ethical questions, which serve as major premisses to syllogisms, without depending upon experience. And now I add a third, which is as important as any: the gradual process by which great conclusions are forced upon the mind, and the confidence of their correctness which the mind feels from the fact of that gradualness.

This too you feel as much as I should do. You say, "the communication of mind with mind cannot be effected by any purely abstract process." I consider, when I sum up the course of thought by which I am landed in Catholicity, that it consists in three propositions: that there has been or will be a Revelation; that Christianity is that Revelation; and that Catholicity is its legitimate expression; and that these propositions naturally strengthen the force of each. But this is only how I should sum up in order to give outstanders an idea of my line of argument, not as myself having been immediately convinced by abstract propositions. Nothing surely have I insisted on more earnestly in my Essay on Assent, than on the necessity of thoroughly subjecting abstract propositions to concrete. It is in the experience of daily life that the power of religion is learnt. You will say that deism or scepticism is learnt by that experience. Of course; but I am not arguing, but stating what I hold, which you seem to me not to know.

And I repeat, it is not by syllogisms or other logical process that trustworthy conclusions are drawn, such as command our assent, but by that minute, continuous, experimental reasoning, which shows baldly on paper, but which drifts silently into an overwhelming cumulus of proof, and, when our start is true, brings us on to a true result. Thus it is that a man may be led on from scepticism, deism, methodism, anglicanism, into the Catholic Church, God being with him all through his changes, and a more and more irresistible assent to the divinity of the Catholic Church being wrought out by those various changes; and he will simply laugh and scoff at your doctrine that his evidence is necessarily defective and that scientific authorities are agreed that he can't be certain. And here I must digress a moment to give expression to a marvel that you should think I do not hold with [Hurrell].[2] "There is another point in

157

which etc. etc. he used to feel that, whoever was heartily doing his best to do God's will, as far as he knew it, would be divinely guided to a clear knowledge of theological truth." Why, this is what I have enunciated or implied in all that I have written:—but to return.

You continue:—"The consciousness that they mean the same thing by the same words is a consciousness growing out of experience or daily experiment." This I have virtually insisted on in a whole chapter in my Essay on Assent, in which, among other instances in point, I refer to the difference of the aspects under which the letters of the alphabet present themselves to different minds, asking "which way does B look? to the right or to the left?" Moreover, it is the principle of my Essay on Doctrinal Development, and I consider it emphatically enforced in the history of the Catholic Schools. You must not forget that, though we maintain the fact of a Revelation as a first principle, as firmly as you can hold that nature has its laws, yet, when the matter of the Revelation [given] comes to be considered, very little is set down as the original doctrine which alone is *de fide,* and within which the revealed truth lies and is limited. As Newton's theory is the development of the laws of motion and the first principles of geometry, so the corpus of Catholic doctrine is the outcome of Apostolic preaching. That corpus is the slow working out of conclusions by means of meditation, prayer, analytical thought, argument, controversy, through a thousand minds, through eighteen centuries and the whole of Europe. There has been a continual process in operation of correction, refinement, adjustment, revision, enucleation, etc., and this from the earliest times, as recognized by Vincent of Lerins. The arguments by which the prerogatives of the Blessed Virgin are proved may be scorned as insufficient by mechanicians, but in fact they are beyond their comprehension, and I claim for theologians that equitable concession that they know their own business better than others do which you claim for mechanical philosophers. *Cuique in arte sua credendum:* I do not call your friends "technical" in their mechanics, tho' you do call me "technical" in my theology; but I go so far as to take for my own friends what I grant to yours, and should ever do (so); I have long thought your great men in science to be open to the charge of superciliousness, and I will never indulge them in it.

Our teaching, as well as yours, requires the preparation and exercise of long thought and of a thorough imbuing in religious ideas. Even were those ideas not true, still a long study would be necessary for understanding them; [when such a study is given,] what you call the random reasonings of theologians will be found to have as clear a right to be treated with respect as those proceedings of mechanical philosophers who you say are so microscopic in their painstaking. Words are but the symbols of ideas, and the microscopic reasoner, who is not only so painstaking, but so justly successful in his mechanics, is simply an untaught child in questions of theology. Hence it is that we, as well as you, make such account of authority, even though it be not infallible. Athanasius, Gregory, Augustine, Leo, Thomas Aquinas, Suarez, Francis de Sales, Petavius, Lambertini, and a host besides have, from our estimate of their theological instinct that honour with us, which, on account of their mechanical and physical instincts, you accord to your men of material science.

You say that an ordinary man would think it his duty to listen to any great mechanical philosopher who should

159

bring reasons for even so great a paradox as the possibility of perpetual motion; why should such personal reverence be reserved for mechanicians alone? why not for theologians? To none indeed of the opinions of the schools, nor to the reasonings even of Councils and Popes, are we bound; none are *de fide;* none but may be changed. I think there was a day when the whole body of divines was opposed to the doctrine of the Immaculate Conception; two great men, St. Bernard and St. Thomas, threw back the reception of it for 600 years. The Jesuits have reversed the long dominant opinion of St. Augustine of absolute predestination, and have been confirmed by two saints, St. Francis de Sales and St. Alfonso. On the other hand sometimes a doctrine of the schools has been made a dogma, that is, has been pronounced a portion of the original revelation, but this, when it has occurred, has been no sudden extempore procedure, but the issue of long examination and the controversy of centuries. There were circumstances in the mode of conducting the Vatican Council which I could not like, but its definition of the Pope's Infallibility was nothing short of the upshot of numberless historical facts looking that way, and of the multitudinous mind of theologians acting upon them.

What then you say of mechanical science, I say emphatically of theology, viz. that it "makes progress by being always alive to its own fundamental uncertainties." We may allowably argue, and do argue, against everything but what has been ruled to be Apostolic; we do (thus argue), and I grant sometimes with far less temper, and sometimes with far less freedom of mind than mechanical philosophers (argue) in their own province, and for a plain reason, because theology involves more questions which may be called burning than physics; but if you [who] are modest before Newton and Faraday may be fierce with table-turners, and the *schola astronomicorum* with that poor man who some years ago maintained that the moon did not rotate, I think it no harm to extend an indulgence towards the *prejudicium* or the *odium theologicum,* in religious writers.

And now I go on to the relation of the will to assent, in theological matters, as to which, perhaps from my own fault, I have not made my doctrine quite clear to you in the passage in [my novel,] Loss and Gain. You seem to think that I hold that in religion the will is simply to supersede the intellect, and that we are to force ourselves to believe against evidence, or at least in some way or other not to give the mind fair play in the question of accepting or rejecting Christianity. I will say then what I really meant. Now, as far as I recollect, [in that novel] Reding says, "I see the truth as tho' seen thro' clouds. I have real grounds for believing, and only floating imaginations against it; is this enough for faith?"

First of all, then, I had fancied that every one granted that in practical matters our wishes were apt to bias our judgments and decisions, how then is it strange that a Catholic Priest, as in that story, who was quite sure that there was but one truth and that he possessed it, should be urgent with a youth who was within grasp of this pearl of great price, lest, under the strong secular motives against his acting, he might through faintheartedness miss it? But he would hold, and I hold most distinctly that, tho' faith is the result of will, itself ever follows intellectual judgment.

But again; it must be recollected, that since nothing concrete admits of demonstration, and there is always a residuum of imperfection in the proof, it is always also possible,

161

perhaps even plausibly to resist a conclusion, even tho' it be one which all sensible men consider beyond question. Thus, in this day especially, new lights are thrown upon historical events and characters, sometimes important, sometimes, as the world agrees, clever, ingenious, but not likely to have a permanent value. Now here it is the common sense, good judgment, *phronesis*, which sweeps away the aggressive theory. But there are cases in which judgment influences the will. Thus a tutor might say to his pupil, "I advise you not to begin your historical studies with Niebuhrism or you will end by knowing nothing; depend upon it the world is not mistaken in the grand outline of events. When objections come before you, consider them fairly, but don't begin with doubting," and his pupil might, by an act of the will, put from his mind, at least for the time, real difficulties.[3]

Still more [does this apply] to the cases, not a few, in which excited, timid, narrow, feeble, or over-sensitive minds have their imaginations so affected by a one single difficulty connected with a received truth that [it] decides for them their rejection of it against reason, evidence, authority, and general reception. They cannot get over what so distresses them, and after a thousand arguments for the truth, return with full confidence to their objection. Thus if a man said he was fully convinced of the divinity of the Catholic Church, if he judged her by her rights, her doctrines, her history, or her fruits, but that he could not get over the fact that in the Apocalypse the dragon was red and red was the colour of the Cardinal's cassocks, I should (think) it would be the duty of a friend to tell him to put this difficulty aside by a vigorous act of the will, and to become a Catholic.

This is an extreme case; there are others more intelligible and to the point. Wives may be unfaithful, but Othello ought by a strong act of the will to have put aside his suspicions. Do you mean to say that a man can feel any doubt whatever of the truth and affection of an old friend? is he not in his inward heart fully confident and certain of him, while he will willingly own that there is a residue of doubt looking at the fact as a matter of inference and proof? Will it be anything to him that a stranger who has not his experience does not feel the force of them, when put into words? That stranger will of course disbelieve, but that is not reason against his own believing. You will say that cases of perfidy are possible, and a man may at length be obliged to pronounce against his friend; certainly, and (false) arguments may overcome the Christian and he may give up his faith, but, till such a strong conclusion has overtaken him, he will by an act of the will reject, it will be his duty, as well as his impulse to reject, all doubts, as a man rejects doubts about his friend's truth. And if it be said that his friend is visibly present, and the object of faith invisible, there the action of supernatural grace comes in, which I cannot enter upon here. It brings us into a leading question of premisses, not of proof. I have said much on this point in my Essay on Assent.

CHAPTER XI

THE STRENGTH OF MORAL REASONING[1]

July 6, 1864

THE BEST illustration of what I hold is that of a cable, which is made up of a number of separate threads, each feeble, yet together as sufficient as an iron rod.

An iron rod represents mathematical or strict demonstration; a cable represents moral demonstration, which is an assemblage of probabilities, separately insufficient for certainty, but, when put together, irrefragable. A man who said "I cannot trust a cable, I must have an iron bar," would *in certain given* cases, be irrational and unreasonable:— so too is a man who says I must have a rigid demonstration, not moral demonstration, of religious truth.

KNOWLEDGE AND THE

PERSONAL GOD

KNOWLEDGE AND THE PERSONAL GOD

THE TEXTS gathered in Part Two apply the theory of inference and assent to our natural knowledge of God, the clari-
fication of which is Newman's main purpose in treating of
the various acts of the mind. His analysis concentrates upon
the theistic appeal to design and conscience, with the aim
of dethroning the former from its place of primacy and
making the latter more central for our acceptance of God.
Newman concedes that these are not the only considerations that lead men to God. "Is not the being of God reported to us by testimony, handed down by history, inferred by an inductive process, brought home to us by
metaphysical necessity, urged on us by the suggestions of
our conscience? It is a truth in the natural order, as well as
in the supernatural."[1] Within his own intellectual situation,
however, the pressing task is to make a comparison between
the way of design and that of conscience.

Newman was acquainted with the argument for God from
the evidences of design in nature, as set forth in Paley's
Natural Theology and the thought of the Noetic School at
Oxford. But he also belonged to that Victorian generation
which witnessed Mill's confession of serious reservations

about the probative force of this reasoning and Darwin's rejection of it in favor of the natural selection mechanism. He recognized this criticism and advised against basing one's theistic conviction primarily upon the design argument. Selection (12) sets forth his four main objections. (a) The design argument narrows unduly the point of departure for inferences to God, since our mind can begin with causality, conscience, and history, as well as with physical evidences. Hence Newman deliberately calls this argument a "physical theology" rather than a "natural theology," since the latter would include all the natural ways to God. Newman always respected metaphysics and natural theology as the paramount philosophical sciences aiding our faith in a positive way. (b) We should not confuse design, which rests upon impersonal natural adaptations in the inorganic and organic worlds, with the more general argument from order. The latter approach stresses the purposive intelligence at work in the world and the meaningful finality toward which the material world is tending. (c) A theism grounded only upon the design argument is unsatisfactory both for morality and natural religion and for revealed religion. At the most, it tells us about God's power, wisdom, and goodness, insofar as they are principles required by an artisan (perhaps even a finite one, as Hume had suggested) to fashion our physical universe. This approach does not transform our conduct by presenting a moral demand, or lead us to the holy and merciful God of natural religion, or uncover any special evidence in man for expecting a redeemer from sin. (d) Thus physico-theology is not a distinctive kind of knowledge, but a compromise which is unsatisfactory for scientist, philosopher, and theologian alike. It fails to move the scientist who is aware of being limited by his method to phenomenal and immanent principles of explanation; it leads the philosopher no farther than to a divinized view of nature; and it diverts attention away from those distinctively human and moral phenomena which aid the theologian in his description of fallen man and the need for grace. Selection (13) recapitulates these objections against a trend of thought which, if given the primacy, leads to a pantheistic or a finitist conception of God. Newman adds, of course, that if one already believes in God, then he can profit by studying nature and the reports of scientific work and interpreting the findings in terms of a divine presence.

The constructive part of his theism begins in Selection (14) with some private manuscript notes, composed during the germinal year 1859, when the leading themes of the *Grammar of Assent* were first taking shape in Newman's mind. These notes are written in his own exploratory and experiential style of metaphysics, and reveal his preoccupation with the epistemological problem as it develops from Descartes to Kant (at least, the version of Kantian philosophy presented in the history written by Chalybäus). Newman agrees with Locke in maintaining the two sources of experience for the formation of the mind: the operation of the senses, and reflection upon our own thoughts or intellectual operations. But he stresses more than does Locke the unifying and interpretative role of the mind in bringing our sensations to a meaningful order. There is also a self-correction of some of Newman's own earlier expressions about trusting our knowing powers. He now sets a definite limit to both natural faith and skepticism, which Hume had used dialectically to reduce our human certitudes.

We have experiential certitude about our own personal

existence and its primary modalities, consciousness and reasoning. In a characteristic way, Newman broadens out the Cartesian Cogito (I am thinking) into the affirmation: *Sentio, ergo sum:* "I am conscious that I exist in that I feel."[2] And he concedes for the occasion to Kant that there is a certain inference involved in moving from awareness of my feeling to knowledge of my existence. From this it follows, however, that my mind is intrinsically sound in its other existential inferences, especially its inference to the existence of a material world and God. Awareness of the moral phenomena of conscience can lead to knowledge of God's real being, which we then interpret on the analogy of a person placed in a position of moral command over us. Our natural ability to grasp an experienced being as a unified whole, especially in the case of the human person, is basic for Newman's approach to God.

A decade later, in the summer of 1869, Newman submitted the galleys of the *Grammar of Assent* to Rev. Dr. Charles Meynell, who taught Scholastic philosophy at Oscott Seminary. Newman's side of the correspondence is given in Selection (15). He had been apprehensive about presenting his writings for criticism to any Scholastic philosophers, whom he described in this caustic way:

What an *irritabile genus* Catholic philosophers are—they think they do the free Church of God service by subjecting it to an etiquette as grievous as that which led to the King of Spain being burned to cinders. . . . Our theological philosophers are like the old nurses who wrap the unhappy infant in swaddling bands or boards—put a lot of blankets over him—and shut the windows that not a breath of fresh air may come to his skin as if he were not healthy enough to bear wind and water in due measure.[3]

Newman himself was engaged in opening a few philosophical windows and allowing some fresh winds to sweep into the halls of the mind. And he was fortunate enough to find in Meynell a sympathetic yet conscientious critic, quite unlike some of the Scholastics who tried to smother the *Grammar of Assent* with objections upon its publication. Meynell made useful references to Maine de Biran, Kant, Mill, Hamilton, and Darwin. The correspondence with Meynell also shows us how genuinely concerned Newman was to achieve some communication and understanding with the more traditional philosophers and theologians, as well as his sturdy confidence in the main line of his argument. Meynell's queries helped him to clarify the key distinction between instinct and intuition on the basis of their respective realization of particular and general facts, as well as to defend a realism of perception that is inferential yet certitudinal. What Newman said here about the experiential and inductive basis of many physical and moral principles, along with our perception of real existents, served as a long-range preparation for his central doctrine on the inference and assent to God.

In Selection (16), we find Newman writing an intimate note to one of his oldest friends, Lord Blachford (Frederick Rogers), in which he distinguishes between knowing that matter exists and not knowing its internal nature. He makes an only half-playful suggestion that the philosophical differences between himself, Blachford, and Thomas Huxley over the material world were deep enough to renew Kant's moratorium on every noncritical metaphysics. He also makes an acid comment on Huxley's intolerance of theistic arguments. Newman defends our knowledge of an existent material world to the point of securing the human mind's basic ability to make some valid existential inferences from the phenomena of consciousness. But he is too strongly aware of the prevailing phenomenalism and the limitations of a scientific description of matter to claim any essential insight into the particular natures in the material world. Hence he does not base his own natural conviction about God upon the design argument or advance any theses about the essential structure of material things. Even in Selection (17), a letter of spiritual and intellectual advice, Newman stresses how harrowing it is to inquire about the springs of theistic assent. His recommendation that the inquirer should look to the enabling facts of conscience indicates the path which he himself finds intellectually most fruitful.

In Selection (18), we return once more to Newman's manuscript notations for his preliminary account of the proof of theism from conscience. This text brings out most of the elements involved in his treatment of moral facts as leading men to accept God. There is a direct link between the epistemological issues already treated in Selection (14) and the present analysis of conscience. For Newman now regards the commanding act of conscience as one of those irreducible forms or modalities of personal self-awareness, bound up with the certitude about one's own existence. And by underlining the fact that the mind is carried out beyond itself in search of a superior personal reality and moral guide, he sets out the rational grounds for the inference to God from conscience, instead of restricting himself to the transition from a notional to a real mode of assent to God. Yet the question of the real theistic assent is not forgotten, since the inference itself is connected with facts bearing upon the moral agent's own existence. Newman also spells out for us here the four main reasons for his preference for the moral approach to God through conscience. This way to God is available to us all, is adapted to a moral and religious response in the practical order, provides an interpretative basis for understanding nature and overcoming skepticism, and encourages us to make a humanly meaningful and responsible use of sensible experience.

Newman's next goal is to show in more detail that his foundation in conscience is not reducible to some other components in human existence. Selection (19) systematically reviews the main substitutes for conscience proposed by the British moralists: civil law, utility, fine taste, and self-esteem. He does not deny that these factors can have a moral aspect and thus share in the activity of conscience, but only that conscience can be dissolved without remainder into one or all of them. Thus Newman is ready to accept the traditional British description of conscience as a moral sense, as long as this term applies only to that function of conscience which declares the right and the wrong, leaving intact the other distinctive function of conscience to command authoritatively and to convey acts of approval or blame. Lord Shaftesbury's naturalizing reduction of conscience to a taste or sentiment about man's internal feelings and gentlemanly manner is criticized here; it also underlies Newman's famous description of the fastidious gentleman given in the *Idea of a University*. What Newman opposes is a transformation of the commanding act of conscience into an appraisal of esthetic fitness, good breeding, and social sympathy.

Conscience in its full integrity furnishes us with the image or concrete realization of God as a loving provider, a personal lawgiver, and the just judge of human actions. This image is required, if we are ever to move from a notional to a real assent to God. Selection (20) deals precisely with this transition, rather than with the basis in inference for the notional assent to God. Newman is not using his analysis of conscience here to furnish a proof of God's existence (although a proof can be drawn from this source), but to account reasonably for our accepting God with a real assent. He examines the basis for assenting not only to the proposition stating that God is, but also to His very being as a personal reality. We do not see God in the present life, and yet we gain a personal knowledge of Him in the mode of a real assent and respond morally and religiously to Him as a vividly apprehended person. How we can do this even with respect to the natural truth about God is Newman's distinctive problem, and he does not find it recognized, let alone adequately handled, in most treatises on natural theology.

His solution is found in his theory of the passage from notional to real assent. The transition can be made, provided that we have an image whereby the entire content of the notional signification (both inference and assent in the notional mode) can be related with one's own selfhood. In trying to gain a concrete realization of the transcendent yet personal and good being of God, we can reflect upon our conscience considered precisely in its commanding function, as having a sanction, and as entailing emotions of fear and satisfaction. Conscience serves as the interior principle supplying the individual with the intimate image of a moral lawgiver, a just and holy judge, and a providential ruler distinct from the whole world and yet personally concerned for our welfare. Wordsworth expresses this personal significance of conscience in words that Newman would make his own:

> Conscience reverenced and obeyed,
> As God's most intimate presence in the soul,
> And His most perfect image in the world.[4]

174

By referring the evidence for our notional apprehension of God to this concrete personal image, resulting from our reflective interpretation of the acts of conscience, we can establish the sort of connection between the abstract reasoning about God and the existence of our personal self which enables us to give a real assent to God in His moral and religious significance.

CHAPTER XII

DESIGN, A FINITE GOD, AND NATURALISM[1]

[I WILL NOT] fall into the fashion of the day, of identifying Natural Theology with Physical Theology; which said Physical Theology is a most jejune study, considered as a science, and really is no science at all, for it is ordinarily nothing more than a series of pious or polemical remarks upon the physical world viewed religiously, whereas the word "Natural" properly comprehends man and society, and all that is involved therein, as the great Protestant writer, Dr. Butler, shows us.

The school of Physics, from its very drift and method of reasoning, has nothing to do with Religion. However, there is a science which avails itself of the phenomena and laws of the material universe, as exhibited by that school, as a means of establishing the existence of Design in their construction, and thereby the fact of a Creator and Preserver. This science has, in these modern times, at least in England, taken the name of Natural Theology[2]; and, though absolutely distinct from Physics, yet Physical Philosophers, having furnished its most curious and interesting data, are apt to claim it as their own, and to pride themselves upon it accordingly.

177

I have no wish to speak lightly of the merits of this so-called Natural, or, more properly, Physical Theology. There are a great many minds so constituted that, when they turn their thoughts to the question of the existence of a Supreme Being, they feel a comfort in resting the proof mainly or solely on the Argument of Design which the Universe furnishes. To them this science of Physical Theology is of high importance. Again, this science exhibits, in great prominence and distinctness, three of the more elementary notions which the human reason attaches to the idea of a Supreme Being, that is, three of His simplest attributes, Power, Wisdom, and Goodness.

These are great services rendered to faith by Physical Theology, and I acknowledge them as such. Whether, however, Faith on that account owes any great deal to Physics or Physicists, is another matter. The Argument from Design is really in no sense due to the philosophy of Bacon. [In his essay on von Ranke, Lord Macaulay] has a striking passage on this point. "As respects Natural Religion," he says, "it is not easy to see that the philosopher of the present day is more favourably situated than Thales or Simonides. He has before him just the same evidences of design in the structure of the universe which the early Greeks had. We say, just the same; for the discoveries of modern astronomers and anatomists *have really added nothing* to the force of that argument which a reflecting mind finds in every beast, bird, insect, fish, leaf, flower, and shell. The reasoning by which Socrates, in Xenophon's hearing, confuted the little atheist, Aristodemus, is exactly the reasoning of Paley's Natural Theology. Socrates makes precisely the same use of the statutes of Polycletus and the pictures of Zeuxis, which Paley makes of the watch."[3]

178

Physical Theology, then, is pretty much what it was two thousand years ago, and has not received much help from modern science: but now, on the contrary, I think it has received from it a positive disadvantage,—I mean, it has been taken out of its place, has been put too prominently forward, and thereby has almost been used as an instrument against Christianity,—as I will attempt in a few words to explain.

I confess, in spite of whatever may be said in its favour, I have ever viewed it [Physical Theology] with the greatest suspicion. As one class of thinkers has substituted what is called a scriptural Religion, and another a Patristical or Primitive Religion, for the theological teaching of Catholicism, so a Physical Religion or Theology is the very gospel of many persons of the Physical School, and therefore, true as it may be in itself, still under the circumstances is a false gospel. Half of the truth is a falsehood:—consider what this so-called Theology teaches, and then say whether what I have asserted is extravagant.

Any one divine attribute of course virtually includes all; still if a preacher always insisted on the Divine Justice, he would practically be obscuring the Divine Mercy, and if he insisted only on the incommunicableness and distance from the creature of the Uncreated Essence, he would tend to throw into the shade the doctrine of a Particular Providence. Observe, then, that Physical Theology teaches three Divine Attributes, I may say, exclusively; and of these, most of Power, and least of Goodness.

And in the next place, what, on the contrary, are those special Attributes, which are the immediate correlatives of religious sentiment? Sanctity, omniscience, justice, mercy, faithfulness. What does Physical Theology, what does the

179

Argument from Design, what do fine disquisitions about final causes, teach us, except very indirectly, faintly, enigmatically, of these transcendently important, these essential portions of the idea of Religion? Religion is more than Theology; it is something relative to us; and it includes our relation towards the Object of it. What does Physical Theology tell us of duty and conscience? of a particular providence? and, coming at length to Christianity, what does it teach us even of the four last things, death, judgment, heaven, and hell, the mere elements of Christianity? It cannot tell us anything of Christianity at all.

Let me press this point upon your earnest attention. I say Physical Theology cannot, from the nature of the case, tell us one word about Christianity proper; it cannot be Christian, in any true sense, at all:—and from this plain reason, because it is derived from informations which existed just as they are now, before man was created, and Adam fell. How can that be a real substantive Theology, though it takes the name, which is but an abstraction, a particular aspect of the whole truth, and is dumb almost as regards the moral attributes of the Creator, and utterly so as regards the evangelical?

Nay, more than this; I do not hesitate to say that, taking men as they are, this so-called science tends, if it occupies the mind, to dispose it against Christianity. And for this plain reason, because it speaks only of laws; and cannot contemplate their suspension, that is, miracles, which are of the essence of the idea of a Revelation. Thus, the God of Physical Theology may very easily become a mere idol; for He comes to the inductive mind in the medium of fixed appointments, so excellent, so skillful, so beneficent, that when it has for a long time gazed upon them, it will think them too beautiful to be broken, and will at length so contract its notion of Him as to conclude that He never could have the heart (if I may dare use such a term) to undo or mar His own work; and this conclusion will be the first step towards its degrading its idea of God a second time, and identifying Him with His works. Indeed, a Being of Power, Wisdom, and Goodness, and nothing else, is not very different from the God of the Pantheist.

In thus speaking of the Theology of the modern Physical School, I have said but a few words on a large subject; yet, though few words, I trust they are clear enough not to hazard the risk of being taken in a sense which I do not intend. Graft the science, if it is so to be called, on Theology proper, and it will be in its right place, and will be a religious science. Then it will illustrate the awful, incomprehensible, adorable Fertility of the Divine Omnipotence; it will serve to prove the real miraculousness of the Revelation in its various parts, by impressing on the mind vividly what are the laws of nature, and how immutable they are in their own order; and it will in other ways subserve theological truth. Separate it from the supernatural teaching, and make it stand on its own base, and (though of course it is better for the individual philosopher himself), yet, as regards his influence on the world and the interests of Religion, I really doubt whether I should not prefer that he should be an atheist at once than such a naturalistic, pantheistic religionist. His profession of Theology deceives others, perhaps deceives himself.

Do not for an instant suppose that I would identify the great mind of Bacon with so serious a delusion: he has expressly warned us against it; but I cannot deny that many of his school have from time to time in this way turned physical research against Christianity.

Nothing is easier than to use the word "God," and mean

nothing by it. The heathens used to say, "God wills," when they meant "Fate"; "God provides," when they meant "Chance"; "God acts," when they meant "Instinct" or "Sense"; and "God is every where," when they meant "the Soul of Nature." The Almighty is something infinitely different from a principle, or a centre of action, or a quality, or a generalization of phenomena. If, then, by the word, you do but mean a Being who keeps the world in order, who acts in it, but only in the way of general Providence, who acts towards us but only through what are called [physical] laws of Nature, who is more certain not to act at all than to act independent of those laws, who is known and approached indeed, but only through the medium of those laws; such a God it is not difficult for any one to conceive, not difficult for any one to endure. If, I say, as you would revolutionize society, so you would revolutionize heaven, if you have changed the divine sovereignty into a sort of constitutional monarchy, in which the Throne has honour and ceremonial enough, but cannot issue the most ordinary command except through legal forms and precedents, and with the counter-signature of a minister, then belief in a God is no more than an acknowledgment of existing, sensible powers and phenomena, which none but an idiot can deny.

If [we must agree with Physical Theology that] the Supreme Being is powerful or skilful, just so far forth as the telescope shows power, and the microscope shows skill, if His moral law is to be ascertained simply by the physical processes of the animal frame, or His will gathered from the immediate issues of human affairs, if His Essence is just as high and deep and broad and long as the universe, and no more; if this be the fact, then will I confess that there is no specific science about God, that theology is but a name, and a protest in its behalf an hypocrisy. Then is He but coincident with the laws of the universe; then is He but a function, or correlative, or subjective reflection and mental impression, of each phenomenon of the material or moral world, as it flits before us. Then, pious as it is to think of Him, while the pageant of experiment or abstract reasoning passes by, still, such piety is nothing more than a poetry of thought or an ornament of language, and has not even an infinitesimal influence upon philosophy or science, of which it is rather the parasitical production.

I understand, in that case, why [Physical] Theology should require no specific teaching, for there is nothing to mistake about; why it is powerless against scientific anticipations, for it merely is one of them; why it is simply absurd in its denunciations of heresy, for heresy does not lie in the region of fact and experiment. I understand, in that case, how it is that the religious sense is but a "sentiment," and its exercise a "gratifying treat," for it is like the sense of the beautiful or the sublime. I understand how the contemplation of the universe "leads onwards to *divine* truth," for [on this view,] divine truth is not something separate from Nature, but it is Nature with a divine glow upon it. I understand the zeal expressed for Physical Theology, for this study is but a mode of looking at Physical Nature, a certain view taken of Nature, private and personal, which one man has, and another has not, which gifted minds strike out, which others see to be admirable and ingenious, and which all would be the better for adopting. It is but the theology of Nature, just as we talk of the *philosophy* or the *romance* of history, or the *poetry* of childhood, or the picturesque, or the sentimental, or the humorous, or any other abstract

183

quality, which the genius or the caprice of the individual, or the fashion of the day, or the consent of the world, recognizes in any set of objects which are subjected to its contemplation.

And this remark bears upon a fact which has sometimes perplexed Christians,—that those philosophers, ancient and modern, who have been eminent in physical science, have not infrequently shown a tendency to infidelity. The system of physical causes is so much more tangible and satisfying than that of final, that unless there be a pre-existent and independent interest in the inquirer's mind, leading him to dwell on the phenomena which betoken an Intelligent Creator, he will certainly follow out those which terminate in the hypothesis of a settled order of nature and self-sustained laws. It is indeed a great question whether Atheism is not as philosophically consistent with the phenomena of the physical world, taken by themselves[4], as the doctrine of a creative and governing Power. But, however this be, the practical safeguard against Atheism in the case of scientific inquirers is the inward need and desire, the inward experience of that Power, existing in the mind before and independently of their examination of His material world.

From religious investigations, as such, physics must be excluded, and from physical, as such, religion; and if we mix them, we shall spoil both. The theologian, speaking of Divine Omnipotence, for the time simply ignores the laws of nature as existing restraints upon its exercise; and the physical philosopher, on the other hand, in his experiments upon natural phenomena, is simply ascertaining those laws, putting aside the question of that Omnipotence. If the theologian, in tracing the ways of Providence, were stopped with objections grounded on the impossibility of physical

184

miracles, he would justly protest against the interruption; and were the philosopher, who was determining the motion of the heavenly bodies, to be questioned about their Final or their First Cause, he too would suffer an illogical interruption. The latter asks the cause of volcanoes, and is impatient at being told it is "the divine vengeance"; the former asks the cause of the overthrow of the guilty cities, and is preposterously referred to the volcanic action still visible in their neighbourhood. The inquiry into final causes for the moment passes over the existence of established laws; the inquiry into physical, passes over for the moment the existence of God. In other words, physical science is in a certain sense atheistic, for the very reason it is not theology.

In Physics is comprised that family of sciences which is concerned with the sensible world, with the phenomena which we see, hear, and handle, or, in other words, with matter. It is the philosophy of matter. Its basis of operations, what it starts from, what it falls back upon, is the phenomena which meet the senses. Those phenomena it ascertains, catalogues, compares, combines, arranges, and then uses for determining something beyond themselves, viz., the order to which they are subservient, or what we commonly call the laws of nature. It never travels beyond the examination of cause and effect. Its object is to resolve the complexity of phenomena into simple elements and principles; but when it has reached those first elements, principles, and laws, its mission is at an end; it keeps within that material system with which it began, and never ventures beyond the "flammantia moenia mundi." It may, indeed, if it chooses, feel a doubt of the completeness of its analysis hitherto, and for that reason endeavour to arrive at more simple laws and fewer principles. It may be dissatis-

185

fied with its own combinations, hypotheses, systems; and leave Ptolemy for Newton, the alchemists for Lavoisier and Davy;—that is, it may decide that it has not yet touched the bottom of its own subject; but still its aim will be to get to the bottom, and nothing more. With matter it began, with matter it will end; it will never trespass into the province of mind. The Hindoo notion is said to be that the earth stands upon a tortoise; but the physicist, as such, will never ask himself by what influence, external to the universe, the universe is sustained; simply because he is a physicist.

If indeed he be a religious man, he will of course have a very definite view of the subject; but that view of his is private, not professional,—the view, not of a physicist, but of a religious man; and this, not because physical science says any thing different, but simply because it says nothing at all on the subject, nor can do so by the very undertaking with which it set out. The question is simply *extra artem.* The physical philosopher has nothing whatever to do with final causes, and will get into inextricable confusion, if he introduces them into his investigations. He has to look in one definite direction, not in any other. It is said that in some countries, when a stranger asks his way, he is at once questioned in turn what place he came from: something like this would be the unseasonableness of a physicist, who inquired how the phenomena and laws of the material world primarily came to be, when his simple task is that of ascertaining what they are. Within the limits of those phenomena he may speculate and prove; he may trace the operation of the laws of matter through periods of time; he may penetrate into the past, and anticipate the future; he may recount the changes which they have effected upon matter, and the rise, growth, and decay of phenomena; and so in a certain sense he may write the history of the material world, as far as he can; still he will always advance from phenomena, and conclude upon the internal evidence which they supply. He will not come near the questions, what that ultimate element is, which we call matter, how it came to be, whether it can cease to be, whether it ever was not, whether it will ever come to nought, in what its laws really consist, whether they can cease to be, whether they can be suspended, what causation is, what time is, what the relations of time to cause and effect, and a hundred other questions of a similar character.

Such is Physical Science, and Theology, as is obvious, is just what such Science is not. Theology begins, as its name denotes, not with any sensible facts, phenomena, or results, not with nature at all, but with the Author of nature,—with the one invisible, unapproachable Cause and Source of all things, it begins at the other end of knowledge, and is occupied, not with the finite, but the Infinite. It unfolds and systematizes what He Himself has told us of Himself; of His nature, His attributes, His will, and His acts. As far as it approches towards Physics, it takes just the counterpart of the questions which occupy the Physical Philosopher. He contemplates facts before him; the Theologian gives the reasons of those facts. The Physicist treats of efficient causes; the Theologian of final. The Physicist tells us of laws; the Theologian of the Author, Maintainer, and Controller of them; of their scope, of their suspension, if so be; of their beginning and their end. This is how the two schools stand related to each other, at that point where they approach the nearest; but for the most part they are absolutely divergent. What Physical Science is engaged in I have already said; as to Theology, it contemplates the world, not of matter, but of mind; the Supreme Intelligence; souls and their destiny; conscience and duty; the past, present, and future dealings of the Creator with the creature.

CHAPTER XIII

BELIEF IN GOD AND THE DESIGN ARGUMENT[1]

April 13, 1870

My dear Brownlow,

It is very pleasant to me to hear what you say about my new book [*Grammar of Assent*], which has given me great anxiety. I *have* spoken of the argument for the being of a God from the visible Creation: "Order implies purpose" etc.[2] I have not insisted on the argument from *design,* because I am writing for the 19th Century, by which, as represented by its philosophers, design is not admitted as proved. And to tell the truth, though I should not wish to preach on the subject, for 40 years I have been unable to see the logical force of the argument myself. I believe in design because I believe in God; not in a God because I see design. You will say that the 19th Century does not believe in conscience either—true—but then it does not believe in a God at all. Something I must assume, and in assuming conscience I assume what is least to assume, and what most will admit. Half the world knows nothing of the argument from design—and, when you have got it, you do not prove by it the moral attributes of God—except very faintly. Design teaches me power, skill, and goodness, not sanctity, not mercy, not a future judgment, which three are of the essence of religion.

189

CHAPTER XIV

EXPERIENCE, MIND, AND REASONING[1]

I WANT TO make out what are the elementary and primary principles or conditions of thought; and I begin by granting that they are not innate in that sense in which sight or touch are congenital with us.

I grant or I assume, that the soul would not think without some external stimulus; that if it were cut off from all external communication from the external world, it would pass this life in a sort of torpor. But then, as soon as it is roused, it reflects upon itself, and thereby gains a number of ideas, quite independently of the external world, and with indefinitely more intimateness than the external world could convey them. In what I am going to say, I suppose the soul awake, without going into the question what are the conditions of its being so.

I suppose if we do not think, we should have nothing to show that we existed—even though we had the power of consciousness. According to the principle, Cogito ergo sum.

Again, it is scarcely possible to believe that we could think without the experience of the senses, which as it were awaken thought.

Next follows the question whether all our thoughts come

ultimately from the senses, or whether the (intelligent) thinking sentient principle, which is I, has any power of creation or origination.

To me it seems at first sight certain that it has—and for this reason, that the senses do not suggest any thing, when taken by themselves, beyond colour, flavour, feeling, pleasure and pain. Sight, e.g. does not combine, it cannot form a whole, it does not suggest personality. We can fancy a mind such as to look at a landscape as so many lights, shades, outlines, and motions—as it is said to the born blind who gain sight, or to infants; like a kaleidoscope. Such seems to be the sole information of mere sense to any one—and the first information.

We may be said to have not infrequent instances of this raw or pure effect of the senses, showing that the power of combination, the reference to centres, and the aggregating into unities is not the primary or natural state of the mind; (or in other words, the power of location) e.g.

1. I may be somewhat deaf, and hear a sound; I don't know whence it comes, I cannot refer it to a centre or subject—it may be in the street, in the air, in the house, in my ears,—I start and am troubled and alarmed.

2. Hence it is perhaps that horses shy, and dogs and other animals look with suspicion at strange objects. They are vague, unlocated, undistributed, uncombined, collections of forms and colour.

3. We have a sort of test or criterion of this in the difficulty we have sometimes in fixing the focus of our pupil. How different things seem, how unmeaning, if a wrong focus! We begin to squint, when we cannot fix the focus. Here we have an instance and proof of the exercise of mind, pure mind, as distinct from sense in seeing.

4. Hence some pains make us faint when first felt. Medical men say that it is the *novelty*. We have not learned to locate it. The story is well known of the man who laughed the second time he was racked. He said that the pain could not be repeated. I recollect having the nerve of a tooth cauterized. I never had such pain in my life. It was a single tooth (not a double tooth) and one application *or* act finished the operation. Soon after I had a double tooth submitted to the same operation. There was a vast number of nervous roots to be operated on, and I was forty minutes under the dentist's hands, drilling and then applying the needle. I did not suffer to compare what I had at the first operation. I recollect at the time attributing the difference, as far as my own testimony went, to the novelty and want of novelty.

5. Sometimes when people are near death, they suddenly cry out with terror, "Is this death?" A new set of feelings comes on them, which they never conceived before, which they cannot account for, which they cannot grasp so to say grasp or master, and fills them with an inexpressible awe. This last instance, however, is not so cogent, because the sensations are in themselves new.

The objects then presented by the senses are unmeaning till they are interpreted by the mind; and the mind interprets out of its own resources. It brings to their contemplation the idea of order, arrangement, whole and parts, which seem original. As the mind may be said, as I have argued above, to interpret the senses by its own ideas, so it cannot be denied that the information supplied by experience through the senses interprets the experience of the mind.

Here is a circle, but the way out of it is nothing to the present purpose. E.g. the feeling of conscience is one of a specific kind, but which we could not describe except from the example and analogy of sensible experience. We could but say, "It is peculiar, special; it is not like a taste, not like a feeling of propriety, of honor, of mathematical truth, etc. etc. It is one which he who feels knows and bears witness about to others who feel it, but it is indescribable." But *when* he has the experience of this world, he finds a key to his perplexity of *grasping* and defining. He says, "It is *like* the feelings I have in obeying or disobeying a dear *superior* or *father*." And then from this analogy a Personal Being is suggested as its object.

The question is, whether all our determinations, principles of arrangement, forms of thought do not in like manner come from visible, sensible experience, though our thoughts have a real *matter* of knowledge independent of the senses.

I am conscious that I am. As I have not faith in my existence, much less can it be said that I have faith in my consciousness, which is the faculty (which brutes perhaps have not) through which I know that I exist. And as it would be absurd to say that I have faith in my consciousness, so it is improper, and (strictly speaking) absurd, to say that I have faith in my sensation. I feel pain: I have not faith in the feeling, but the feeling is part of me, or bound up in my "I am." Consciousness indeed is not of simple being, but of action or passion, of which pain is one form. I am conscious that I am, because I am conscious I am thinking (cogito ergo sum) or feeling, or remembering or comparing or exercising *discourse*.

This view of the subject brings us a step further, as revealing an important principle. Sentio ergo sum. To call this an act of argumentation or deduction, and that it implies faith in that reasoning process which is denoted by the symbol of "ergo" seems to be a fallacy. I do not advance from one proposition to another, when I know my existence from being conscious of my feeling, but one and the same act of consciousness brings home to me that which afterwards at leisure I draw out into two propositions, denoting two out of many aspects of the one thing.

If this be so, it follows that, whereas all such acts, as of memory, sensation, reasoning etc. are bound up in the original object of consciousness, and are the mode in which my existence is known to me and inseparable from it, of these various acts, (of which I have not yet attempted a complete list) that which is commonly called reasoning is (after consciousness) the nearest of all. For, whereas the consciousness which I possess that I exist may be drawn out into "I am, *for* I feel," "I am, *for* I remember," "I am, *for* I think," "I am, *for* I reason," in all cases there is the "*for*," or the consciousness of the presence of that condition on which the coincidence of the initial and secondary object of consiousness depends. I am conscious I exist in that I feel; but this "in that" is what is commonly called a reason or the symbol of an act of reasoning.

Not only then is it improper to say I have faith in consciousness, sensation, memory, thought, reason, as to say I have faith in my existence, but of all of these improprieties, none is so great as to say I have faith in consciousness, and in reason or reasoning, for reasoning is the very breath of my existence, for by it I know that I exist.

What the whole list of these exercises is which are bound up in being such wise, that it is improper to say that we have faith in them as to say that I have faith in my existence, is a difficult task to determine. This only I say here, that consciousness and reasoning are those portions of the idea of being which are most essentially bound up with it. And, as there is no *faith* properly in these exercises of my being, so there is no scepticism about them properly—and it is as absurd to speak of being sceptical of consciousness, reasoning, memory, sensation, as to say that I am sceptical whether I am. I have not at the moment pretended to undertake the difficult task of saying what exercises of being are involved in my consciousness of being; but it is easier to say what are not.

I have a sensation of colours and forms—this is one thing. I have a persuasion that these colours and forms convey to me the presence etc. of external objects—this is a second thing. I have said that the sensation is not an object of faith—but of consciousness—but the second is an object of faith—its truth is not bound up in that act of consciousness by which I know I am. Though those colours and forms meant nothing beyond themselves, my consciousness of my existence would not be affected. I do not learn that I am, by answering the second point one way or the other but by the sensation.

Kant, whose philosophy I have just been reading in Chalybäus, would say as to consciousness: Yes, it bears witness to internal facts of the mind, but it is impossible to connect them, whatever they are, with anything external to it.[2] Well then, I say:—You can reduce me to a state of absolute scepticism about everything external to consciousness—but this is a reductio ad absurdum of all knowledge external to us whatever, of *senses* as well as (*I* should say *much more* than) supersensuous knowledge—but if you do not go to *this extreme length*, which makes it hopeless even to reason or investigate at all, you must allow *something*—

195

and all I ask you to allow is *this*—that it is *true* that I *am*—or that my consciousness that I am represents the fact external to my consciousness (viz.) of my existence. Now see what is involved in this one assumption: Viz. my consciousness that I am is not *immediate,* but indirect. "Sentio ergo sum." In this is involved therefore the presence of a faculty by which from what I have experience of, I argue the certainty of that of which I have not experience, viz. my existence, my existence being a fact external to consciousness.—But if one external unexperienced fact may be known by reasoning upon experience, perhaps another may. Therefore the idea is not absurd that as from "sentio" I infer the existence of myself, so from "conscientiam habeo" I infer the existence of God, and again from the phenomena of sense I have the existence of matter.

CHAPTER XV

INSTINCT, PERCEPTION AND
INDUCTIVE INFERENCE[1]

July 25, 1869

My dear Dr. Meynell,

I thank you very much for your criticisms, which will be very useful to me.

The only one which I feel a difficulty about is that about two straight lines inclosing a space.[2] I cannot for the life of me, and never have, put it [a proposition about straight lines] on a level with the Moral Law. Lines are our own creation, the Moral Law is in the Nature of God Himself. The only thing which is not *ours* in reasoning is that "if it is true that A is, it is not true that A is not." But this foundation being allowed, lines are our own creation. They do not exist in nature. Who ever saw a line? it is an abstraction.

However, the next sheet [of proofs for the *Grammar of Assent*] will be my great difficulty—and I should not wonder if it was decisive one way or the other. You will find I there consider that the dictate of conscience is particular— not general—and that from the multiplication of particulars I *infer* the general—so that the moral sense, as a knowledge *generally* of the moral law, is a deduction from particulars.

Next, that this dictate of conscience, which is natural and the voice of God, is a moral *instinct,* and its own evidence—as the *belief* in an external world is an *instinct* on the apprehension of sensible phenomena.

That to *deny* those instincts is an absurdity, *because* they are the voice of nature.

That it is a duty to trust, or rather to use our nature—and not to do so is absurdity.

That to recognize our nature is really to *recognize God.*

Hence those *instincts* come from *God*—and as the moral law is an inference or generalization from those instincts, the moral law is ultimately taught us from God, *whose* nature it is.

Now if this is a wasp-nest, tell me. If the Church has said otherwise, I give it all up—but somehow it is so mixed up with my whole book, that, if it is not safe, I shall not go on.

July 27, 1869

I am extremely obliged to you for the trouble you are taking with me, and I hope my shying, as I do, will not keep you from speaking out. Pray bring out always what you have to say. I am quite conscious that metaphysics is a subject on which one cannot hope to agree with those with whom in other matters one agrees most heartily, from the extreme subtlety—but I am also deeply conscious of my own ignorance on the whole matter, and it sometimes amazes me that I have ventured to write on a subject which is even accidentally connected with it. And this makes me so very fearful lest I should be saying anything temerarious or dangerous—the ultimate angles being so small from which lines diverge to truth and error.

Be sure I should never hastily give over what I am doing, because I should have trouble in correcting or thinking out again what I have said—but if I found some irreconcilable difference, running through my view, between its conditions and what the Church teaches or has sanctioned, of course I should have no hesitation of stopping at once.

So please to bear with me if I start or plunge.

August 17, 1869

I only hope I am not spoiling your holiday. You are doing me great service.

To bring matters to a point, I propose to send you my chapter on the apprehension and assent to the doctrine of a Supreme Being. If you find principles in that chapter, which cannot be allowed, *res finita est*. As to your remarks on the printed slips, let me trouble you with the following questions.

1. You mean that it is dangerous to hold that we believe in matter as a conclusion from our sensations—for our belief in matter is in consequence of our consciousness of resistance, which is not a sensation. Will it mend matters to observe that I don't use the word "sensations"—but experiences? and surely resistance is an experience—but if we infer matter from resistance, therefore we infer it from experience.[3]

2. By instinct I mean a realization of a *particular;* by intuition, of a *general* fact—in both cases without *assignable* or *recognizable* media of realization. Is there any word I could use instead of instinct to denote the realization of particulars? Still, I do not see how you solve my difficulty of instinct leading brutes to the realization of something external to themselves? Perhaps it ought not to be called instinct in brutes, but by some other name.

3. Am I right in thinking that you wish me to infer matter as a *cause* from phenomena as an *effect,* from *my own*

view of cause and effect. But in *my own view* cause is *Will;* how can matter be Will?

4. "*Hypothetical* realism," yes—if conclusions are necessarily conditional. But I consider Ratiocination far higher, more subtle, wider, more certain than logical Inference—and its principle of action is the "Illative Sense," which I treat of towards the end of the volume. If I say that Ratiocination leads to absolute truth, am I still an hypothetical realist?[4]

August 18, 1869

I send you by post the MSS. which I spoke of in my last.

On second thoughts I don't see how I can change the word "instinct"—and I have not indeed any where used it for the *perception of God* from our experiences, but in later chapters I speak of Catholic instincts, Mother Margaret's instincts, the instinct of calculating boys, in all cases using the word "instinct" to mean a spontaneous impulse, physical or intelligent, in the individual, leading to a result without assignable or recognisable intellectual media.

Would it do, if I kept the passage and put a note to this effect,—"I speak thus under correction, and withdraw it prospectively, if it is contrary to the teaching of the theological Schola"?

August 20, 1869

Pray forgive me if unknown to myself and unintentionally I have led you to think, quite contrary to *my* thoughts, that you wrote dogmatically. Just the contrary, and you are doing me a great service in letting me see *how* matters stand in the philosophical school.

Forgive too the treacherousness of my memory, though

by "composition" I meant the composition of my matter, the drawing out of my argument, etc.

Nothing can be clearer than your remarks. Now let me say I had no intention at all of saying that I know, e.g. that I have a sheet of paper before me, by an *argument* from the impression on my senses—"that impression *must* have a cause—" but it is a *perception* (that is, a kind of instinct). I have used the word "perception" again and again; that perception comes to me *through* my senses—therefore I cannot call it *immediate*. If it were not for my senses, nothing would excite me to perceive—but as soon as I see the white paper, I perceive by instinct (as I call it) without *argumentative* media, *through* my senses, but not logically *by* my senses, that there is a *thing*, of which the white paper is the outward token. Then, when I have this experience again and again, I go on from the one, two, three etc. accompanying perceptions of one, two, three etc. external objects, to make an induction "There is a vast external world." This induction leads to a conclusion much larger than the particular perceptions—because it includes in it that the earth has an inside, and that the moon has a farther side, though I don't see it.

Therefore I hold that we do not *prove* external individual objects, but *perceive* them—I cannot say that we *immediately* perceive them, because it is through the *experience* as an instrument that we are led to them—and though we do not prove the particular, we *do* prove *the general,* i.e. by induction from the particular. I am sanguine in thinking this is in substance what you say yourself.

August 21, 1869

Your intention to give up has shocked and dismayed me more than I can say—*shocked* me because I fear I must

201

have said something or other in writing which has scared you;—and *dismayed* me, for what am I to do?

I quite understand that you must feel it a *most* unpleasant responsibility (though of course I shall not tell anyone) and an endless work, for when will it be finished? It is enough to spoil your holiday, and to bother your Professorial work, and I really have not a word to say besides thanking you for what you have already done for me, and begging you to forgive me if like a camel, when they are loading it, I have uttered dismal cries.

Well, now I am in a most forlorn condition, and, like Adam, I feel "the world is all before me."—Whom am I to ask to do the work which you have so kindly begun? I shall not get anyone so patient as you, and, alas, alas, what is to come is, for what I know, more ticklish even than what you have seen.

I have availed myself of all your remarks in some way or other, though I have not always taken them pure and simple.

Thank you for saying you will say Mass for me. It is a great kindness.

P.S. I have not said, what I feel most sadly, your language about your own littleness. If you are little, I must be less, because you are really teaching me. I should be a fool if I did not avail myself most thankfully of your remarks.

You know, any how, you have promised me some remarks on the MS.

October 8, 1869

Thank you for your criticism about the Echo⁵. I certainly ought to have taken notice of it, and my only difficulty will be how to bring it in.—You are ten times more likely to be right on such a point than I am—however, at present I don't follow you, though I will think about it. My reason is this, that consciousness or reflection on one's acts is an act different in kind from those acts themselves. Its object is distinct. If I walk, my eyes may watch my walking. If I sing, my ears listen to my voice and tell me if I am in tune. These are acts of reflection on my walking and singing, are they not? but the original act is bodily, and the reflex act is mental. I assure you I most deeply feel that I may be out of my depth.

P.S. By no manner or means ever dream of giving yourself the trouble of writing one word by letter, when marks on the margin [of the proof sheets] will do. I am not sure, from what you said, whether you read the inclosed bits of theology. Please to cast your eye over them. I must have a theological eye upon them, and one of your eyes is theological, though the other is philosophical.

November 17, 1869

I quite agree with you that the deepest men say that we can never be certain of any thing—and it has been my object therefore in a good part of my volume to prove that there is such a thing as *unconditional* assent.

I have defined certitude, a conviction of what is *true*. When a conviction of what is not true is considered as if it was a conviction of what is true, I have called it a false certitude.

You will be sadly disappointed in my "illative sense"— which is a grand word for a common thing.

203

CHAPTER XVI

OUR KNOWLEDGE OF MATTER AND

BRUTE CONSCIOUSNESS[1]

November 17, 1875

My dear Blachford,

As to your paper [for the Metaphysical Society], let it be only a squib or a cracker, yet such small things may kindle a great fire, and this I meant when I said, I hoped you would have to write again. As to your being only half a metaphysician, I don't know who is a whole one, though some men have more confidence in themselves than others. The assumptions of Mill are for an able man incomprehensible. For myself I am very far from agreeing with many of your positions, e.g., that matter is "that which occupies space"; I am utterly ignorant what matter is objectively—phenomena prove that it exists, but not what it is. Therefore space is only the word for the *idea* of a break in the continuity of phenomena, and is doubly subjective, as depending on phenomena which are subjective and as being bowed out of actual existence by the actual continuity of phenomena. While we thus differ, is not metaphysical science in abeyance?

But this does not help Mr. [Thomas] Huxley in your quarrel with him. If he would be modest in his teaching, he would be tolerable, but from all I know of him, I must consider him intolerant and therefore intolerable. Your argument anyhow is good. You say first, we must from the analogy of self and of our experience of others, i.e., men, (whom we determine to have sensation and volition from external indications) determine from like indications that brute animals can feel and can will. How is this conclusion to be touched as regards brute animals, without our holding that our friend feels nothing when he is subjected to a surgical operation?

Your second position was that, tho' there was, or might be, such a phenomenon as unconscious cerebration, yet, because there was, sometimes in the case of man, it did not follow that to it was to be attributed *all* that seems like sensation and volition in brutes, or else we might similarly infer, that, because patients under the operation of chloroform utter cries when the knife touches them, but recollect nothing afterwards of having suffered pain, therefore none of us know what pain is, however we may show signs of it.

This is how I understand you—and I don't see how you are to be answered—and I rejoice that Professor Huxley is put on the defensive.

CHAPTER XVII

INTERROGATING OUR OWN HEARTS[1]

June 25, 1869

You MUST begin all thought about religion by mastering what is the fact, that anyhow the question has an inherent, ineradicable diffculty in it. As in tuning a piano, you may throw the fault here or there, but no theory can anyone take up without that difficulty remaining. It will come up in one shape or other. If we say, "Well, I will not believe any thing," there is a difficulty in believing nothing, an intellectual difficulty. There is a difficulty in doubting; a difficulty in determining there is no truth; in saying that there is a truth, but that no one can find it out; in saying that all religious opinions are true, or one is as good as another; a difficulty in saying there is no God; that there is a God but that He has not revealed Himself except in the way of nature; and there is doubtless a difficulty in Christianity. The question is, whether on the whole our reason does not tell us that it is a duty to accept the arguments commonly urged for its truth as sufficient, and a duty in consequence to believe heartily in Scripture and the Church.

Another thought which I wish to put before you is, whether our nature does not tell us that there is something which has more intimate relations with the question of religion than intellectual exercises have, and that is our conscience. We have the idea of duty—duty suggests something or someone to which it is to be referred, to which we are responsible. That something that has dues upon us is to us God. I will not assume it is a personal God, or that it is more than a law (though of course I hold that it is the Living Seeing God), but still the idea of duty, and the terrible anguish of conscience, and the irrepressible distress and confusion of face which the transgression of what we believe to be our duty, causes us, all this is an intimation, a clear evidence, that there is something nearer to religion than intellect; and that, if there is a way of finding religious truth, it lies, not in exercises of the intellect, but close on the side of duty, of conscience, in the observance of the moral law. Now all this may seem a truism, and many an intellectualist will say that he grants it freely. But I think, that, when dwelt upon, it leads to conclusions which would both surprise and annoy him.

Now I think it best to stop here for the present. You must not suppose that I am denying the intellect its real place in the discovery of truth,—but it must ever be borne in mind that its exercise mainly consists in reasoning,—that is, in comparing things, classifying them, and inferring. It ever needs points to start from, first principles, and these it does not provide—but it can no more move one step without these starting points, than a stick, which supports a man, can move without the man's action. In physical matters, it is the senses which give us the first start—and what the senses give is physical fact—and physical facts do not lie on the surface of things, but are gained with pains and by genius, through experiment. Thus Newton, or Davy, or

Franklin ascertained those physical facts which have made their names famous. After these primary facts are gained, intellect can act; it acts too of course in gaining them; but they must be gained; it is the senses which *enable* the intellect to act, by giving it something to act upon.

In like manner we have to ascertain the starting points for arriving at religious truth. The intellect will be useful in gaining them and after gaining them—but to attempt to *see* them by means of the intellect is like attempting by the intellect to see the physical facts which are the basis of physical exercises of the intellect, a method of proceeding which was the very mistake of the Aristotelians of the middle age, who, instead of what Bacon calls "interrogating nature" for facts, reasoned out everything by syllogisms. To gain religious starting points, we must in a parallel way, interrogate our hearts, and, (since it is a personal individual matter,) our *own* hearts,—interrogate our own consciences, interrogate, I will say, the God who dwells there.

I think you must ask the God of conscience to enable you to do your duty in this matter. I think you should, with prayer to Him for help, meditate upon the gospels, and on St. Paul's second epistle to the Corinthians, unless the translation of its disturbs you; and this with an earnest desire to know the truth and a sincere intention of following it.

CHAPTER XVIII

FROM CONSCIENCE TO GOD[1]

[WILLIAM GEORGE] Ward thinks I hold that moral obligation is, because there is a God. But I hold just the reverse, viz. there is a God, because there is a moral obligation. I have a certain feeling on my mind which I call conscience. When I analyse this, I feel it involves the idea of a Father and Judge—of one who sees my heart etc.

By conscience I mean the discrimination of acts as worthy of praise or blame. Now such praise or blame is a phenomenon of my existence, one of those phenomena, through which, as I have said, my existence is brought home to me. But the accuracy or truth of the praise or blame in the particular case, is a matter not of faith, but of judgement. Here then are two senses of the word conscience. It either stands for the act of moral judgement, or for the particular judgement formed. In the former case it is the foundation of religion, in the latter of ethics.

To explain this more fully. If I practise deceit, or am grossly intemperate, or commit some very selfish act, I have a double feeling—first that I am transgressing a law, secondly that the law says this or that. This latter conviction I may change, and yet the former notion will remain. If in any particular my conscience is false, and I come to see it, then I reverse my judgement in the *particular* case about what is right or wrong, but I do not thereby at all weaken my sense of a law and consequent obligation.

Now let me try to bring out more accurately the doctrine contained in these extracts.

I have said,—assumed, if you will, that this feeling of a *law*, whatever its dictates, and which I call conscience, is, not a law of the mind, but one of those phenomena which like thought or consciousness, are bound up with or convey to me the idea and the fact of my being *or* existence. Now I say that, as consciousness of thought is a reflex act implying existence, (I think, therefore I am), so this sensation of conscience is the recognition of an obligation involving the notion of an external being obliging. I say this, not from any abstract argument from the force of the terms (e.g., "A Law implies a Lawgiver"), but from the peculiarity of that feeling to which I give the name Conscience.

Now I can best explain what I mean by this peculiarity of feeling, by contrasting it with the rules of Taste. As we have a notion of right and wrong, so we have of beautiful and ugly; but this latter set of notions is attended by no *sanction:* No hope or fear, no misgiving of the future, no feeling of being hurt, no tender sorrow, no sunny self-satisfaction, no lightness of heart attends on the acting with beauty or deformity. It is these feelings, which *carry the mind out of itself and beyond itself*, which imply a tribunal in future, or reward and punishment, which are so special.

The notion of future judgement is thus involved in the feeling of conscience. And more than that—the feeling is one analogous or similar to that which we feel in human matters towards a person whom we have offended, there is a tenderness almost tearful in going wrong, and a grateful cheerfulness when we go right, which is just what we feel in displeasing a father or revered superior. So that contemplating and revolving on this feeling, the mind will reasonably conclude that it is an unseen father who is the object of this feeling.

Such is the argument for the being of God which I should wish, if it were possible, to maintain. It has been my own chosen proof of that fundamental doctrine [of theism] for thirty years past—as the extracts which I have made pretty well show.

I am led to it, not only by its truth, but by its great convenience and appositeness in this day. 1. It is a proof common to all, high and low, from earliest infancy. It is carried about in a compact form in every soul. It is ever available— it requires no learning—it is possessed by pagans as well as Christians. 2. And next it is intimately combined with practice. It is not some abstract truth wrought out by the pure intellect, or wrought out theoretically, as that from design. It goes to the root of the matter, and is the source of practical religion as well as speculative. 3. It explains and refutes the supposed philosophical sin, which according to it will be the conversion into a *mere taste* of that which is the voice of God directing or rewarding. 4. It forms a basis for belief in the senses. For if there be a God, and I am His creature with a mission, He *means* me to *use* the senses— and I accept what they convey as coming from Him, whatever be its intellectual and philosophical worth.

211

CHAPTER XIX

PROPOSED SUBSTITUTES FOR CONSCIENCE[1]

I OBSERVE THAT the guide of life, implanted in our nature, discriminating right from wrong, and investing right with authority and sway, is our Conscience, which Revelation does but enlighten, strengthen, and refine. Coming from one and the same Author, these internal and external monitors of course recognize and bear witness to each other; Nature warrants without anticipating the Supernatural, and the Supernatural completes without superseding Nature. Such is the divine order of things; but man,—not being divine, nor over partial to so stern a reprover within his breast, yet seeing too the necessity of some rule or other, some common standard of conduct, if Society is to be kept together, and the children of Adam to be saved from setting up each for himself with every one else his foe,—as soon as he has secured for himself some little cultivation of intellect, looks about him how he can manage to dispense with Conscience, and find some other principle to do its work. The most plausible and obvious and ordinary of these expedients, is the Law of the State, human law; the more plausible and ordinary, because it really comes to us with a divine sanction, and necessarily has a place in every society or community of men. Accordingly it is very widely used instead of Conscience, as but a little experience of life will show us; "the law says this"; "would you have me go against the law?" is considered an unanswerable argument in every case; and, when the two come into collision, it follows of course that Conscience is to give way, and the Law to prevail.

Another substitute for Conscience is the rule of Expediency. Conscience is pronounced superannuated and retires on a pension, whenever a people is so far advanced in illumination, as to perceive that right and wrong can to a certain extent be measured and determined by the useful on the one hand, and by the hurtful on the other; according to the maxim, which embodies this principle, that "honesty is the best policy."

Another substitute of a more refined character is, the principle of Beauty:—it is maintained that the Beautiful and the Virtuous mean the same thing, and are convertible terms. Accordingly Conscience is found out to be but slavish; and a fine taste, an exquisite sense of the decorous, the graceful, and the appropriate, this is to be our true guide for ordering our mind and our conduct, and bringing the whole man into shape. These are great sophisms, it is plain; for, true though it be, that virtue is always expedient, always fair, it does not therefore follow that every thing which is expedient, and every thing which is fair, is virtuous. A pestilence is an evil, yet may have its undeniable uses; and war, "glorious war," is an evil, yet an army is a very beautiful object to look upon; and what holds in these cases, may hold in others; so that it is not very safe or logical to say that Utility and Beauty are guarantees for Virtue.

However, there are these three principles of conduct,

213

which may be plausibly made use of in order to dispense with Conscience; viz., Law, Expedience, and Propriety. The Athenians chose the last of them, as became so exquisite a people, and professed to practise virtue on no inferior consideration, but simply because it was so praiseworthy, so noble, and so fair. Not that they discarded Law, not that they had not an eye to their interest; but they boasted that "grasshoppers" like them, old of race and pure of blood, could be influenced in their conduct by nothing short of a fine and delicate taste, a sense of honour, and an elevated, aspiring spirit. Their model man, like the pattern of chivalry, was a gentleman,[2] *kalokagathos;*—a word which has hardly its equivalent in the sterner language of Rome, where, on the contrary,

Vir bonus est quis?
Qui consulta patrum, qui leges juraque servat.

For the Romans deified Law, as the Athenians deified the Beautiful.

Conscience indeed is implanted in the breast by nature, but it inflicts upon us fear as well as shame; when the mind is simply angry with itself and nothing more, surely the true import of the voice of nature and the depth of its intimations have been forgotten, and a false philosophy has misinterpreted emotions which ought to lead to God. Fear implies the transgression of a law, and a law implies a lawgiver and judge; but the tendency of intellectual culture is to swallow up the fear in the self-reproach, and self-reproach is directed and limited to our mere sense of what is fitting and becoming. Fear carries us out of ourselves, whereas shame may act upon us only within the round of

214

our own thoughts. Such, I say, is the danger which awaits a civilized age; such is its besetting sin (not inevitable, God forbid! or we must abandon the use of God's own gifts), but still the ordinary sin of the Intellect; conscience tends to become what is called a moral sense; the command of duty is a sort of taste; sin is not an offence against God, but against human nature.

The less amiable specimens of this spurious religion are those which we meet not unfrequently in my own country. I can use with all my heart the poet's words,

England, with all thy faults, I love thee still;

but to those faults no Catholic can be blind. We find there men possessed of many virtues, but proud, bashful, fastidious, and reserved. Why is this? it is because they think and act as if there were really nothing objective in their religion; it is because conscience to them is not the word of a law-giver, as it ought to be, but the dictate of their own minds and nothing more; it is because they do not look out of themselves, because they do not look through and beyond their own minds to their Maker, but are engrossed in notions of what is due to themselves, to their own dignity and their own consistency. Their conscience has become a mere self-respect. Instead of doing one thing and then another, as each is called for, in faith and obedience, careless of what may be called the *keeping* of deed with deed, and leaving Him who gives the command to blend the portions of their conduct into a whole, their one object, however unconscious to themselves, is to paint a smooth and perfect surface, and to be able to say to themselves that they have done their duty.

When they do wrong, they feel, not contrition, of which God is the object, but remorse, and a sense of degradation.

215

They call themselves fools, not sinners; they are angry and impatient, not humble. They shut themselves up in themselves; it is misery to them to think or to speak of their own feelings; it is misery to suppose that others see them, and their shyness and sensitiveness often become morbid. As to confession, which is so natural to the Catholic, to them it is impossible; unless indeed, in cases where they have been guilty, an apology is due to their own character, is expected of them, and will be satisfactory to look back upon. They are victims of an intense self-contemplation.

And hence again, conscience, which intimates a Law-giver, being superseded by a moral taste or sentiment, which has no sanction beyond the constitution of our nature, it follows that our great rule is to contemplate ourselves, if we would gain a standard of life and morals. Thus [Lord Shaftesbury] has entitled one of his Treatises a "Soliloquy," with the motto, "Nec te quaesiveris extra"; and he observes, "The chief interest of ambition, avarice, corruption, and every sly insinuating vice, is to prevent this interview and familiarity of discourse, which is consequent upon close retirement and inward recess. 'Tis the grand artifice of villainy and lewdness, *as well as of superstition and bigotry,* to put us upon terms of greater distance and formality with ourselves, and evade our *proving* method of soliloquy. . . . A passionate lover, whatever solitude he may affect, can never be truly by himself. . . . 'Tis the same reason which keeps the imaginary saint or mystic from being capable of this entertainment. Instead of looking narrowly into his own nature and mind, that he may be no longer a mystery to himself, he is taken up with *the contemplation of other mysterious natures,* which he never can explain or comprehend."[3]

216

Taking [this passage as a specimen] of what I call the Religion of Philosophy, it is obvious to observe that there is no doctrine contained in it which is not in a certain sense true; yet, on the other hand, that almost every statement is perverted and made false, because it is not the whole truth. They are exhibitions of truth under one aspect, and therefore insufficient; conscience is most certainly a moral sense, but it is more; vice again, is a deformity, but it is worse. Lord Shaftesbury may insist, if he will, that simple and solitary fear cannot effect a moral conversion, and we are not concerned to answer him; but he will have a difficulty in proving that any real conversion follows from a doctrine which makes virtue a mere point of good taste, and vice vulgar and ungentlemanlike.

Such a doctrine is essentially superficial, and such will be its effects. It has no better measure of right and wrong than that of visible beauty and tangible fitness. Conscience indeed inflicts an acute pang, but that pang, forsooth, is irrational, and to reverence it is an illiberal superstition. But, if we will make light of what is deepest within us, nothing is left but to pay homage to what is more upon the surface. To *seem* becomes to *be;* what looks fair will be good, what causes offence will be evil; virtue will be what pleases, vice what pains. As well may we measure virtue by utility as by such a rule.

CHAPTER XX

OUR MORAL IMAGE OF THE PERSONAL GOD[1]

As INTELLECT IS common to all men as well as imagination, every religious man is to a certain extent a theologian, and no theology can start or thrive without the initiative and abiding presence of religion. As in matters of this world, sense, sensation, instinct, intuition, supply us with facts, and the intellect uses them; so, as regards our relations with the Supreme Being, we get our facts from the witness, first of nature, then of revelation, and our doctrines, in which they issue, through the exercise of abstraction and inference. This is obvious; but it does not interfere with holding that there is a theological habit of mind, and a religious, each distinct from each, religion using theology, and theology using religion. This being understood, I propose to consider the dogmas of the Being of a God, and of the Divine Trinity in Unity[2], in their relation to assent, both notional and real, and principally to real assent;—however, I have not yet finished all I have to say by way of introduction.

Now first, my subject is assent, and not inference. I am not proposing to set forth the arguments which issue in the belief of these doctrines, but to investigate what it is to believe in them, what the mind does, what it contemplates, when it makes an act of faith. It is true that the same elementary facts which create an object for an assent, also furnish matter for an inference: and in showing what we believe, I shall unavoidably be in a measure showing why we believe; but this is the very reason that makes it necessary for me at the outset to insist on the real distinction between these two concurring and coincident courses of thought, and to premise by way of caution, lest I should be misunderstood, that I am not considering the question that there is a God, but rather what God is.

And secondly, I mean by belief, not precisely faith, because faith, in its theological sense, includes a belief, not only in the thing believed, but also in the ground of believing; that is, not only belief in certain doctrines, but belief in them expressly because God has revealed them; but here I am engaged only with what is called the material object of faith, with the thing believed, not with the formal. I shall consider "He is One," not as a revealed truth, but as, what it is also, a natural truth, the foundation of all religion. And with it I begin.

There is one God, such and such in Nature and Attributes. I say "such and such," for, unless I explain what I mean by "one God," I use words which may mean any thing or nothing. I may mean a mere *anima mundi;* or an initial principle which once was in action and now is not; or collective humanity. I speak then of the God of the Theist and of the Christian: a God who is numerically One, who is Personal; the Author, Sustainer, and Finisher of all things, the Life of Law and Order, the Moral Governor; One who is Supreme and Sole; like Himself, unlike all things besides Himself, which all are but His creatures; distinct from, independent of them all; One who is self-existing, absolutely infinite, who has ever been and ever will be, to whom nothing is past or future; who is all perfection, and the fulness and archetype of every possible excellence, the Truth Itself, Wisdom, Love, Justice, Holiness; One who is All-powerful, All-knowing, Omnipresent, Incomprehensible. These are some of the distinctive prerogatives which I ascribe unconditionally and unreservedly to the great Being whom I call God.

This being what Theists mean when they speak of God, their assent to this truth admits without difficulty of being what I have called a notional assent. It is an assent following upon acts of inference, and other purely intellectual exercises; and it is an assent to a large development of predicates, correlative to each other, or at least intimately connected together, drawn out as if on paper, as we might map a country which we had never seen, or construct mathematical tables, or master the methods of discovery of Newton or Davy, without being geographers, mathematicians, or chemists ourselves.

So far is clear; but the question follows, Can I attain to any more vivid assent to the Being of a God, than that which is given merely to notions of the intellect? Can I enter with a personal knowledge into the circle of truths which make up that great thought? Can I rise to what I have called an imaginative apprehension of it? Can I believe as if I saw? Since such a high assent requires a present experience or memory of the fact, at first sight it would seem as if the answer must be in the negative; for how can I assent as if I saw, unless I have seen? but no one in this life can see God. Yet I conceive a real assent is possible, and I proceed to show how.

When it is said that we cannot see God, this is unde-

220

niable; but still in what sense have we a discernment of His creatures, of the individual beings which surround us? The evidence which we have of their presence lies in the phenomena which address our senses, and our warrant for taking these for evidence is our instinctive certitude that they are evidence. By the law of our nature we associate those sensible phenomena or impressions with certain units, individuals, substances, whatever they are to be called, which are outside and out of the reach of sense, and we picture them to ourselves in those phenomena. The phenomena are as if pictures; but at the same time they give us no exact measure or character of the unknown things beyond them; —for who will say there is any uniformity between the impressions which two of us would respectively have of some third thing, supposing one of us had only the sense of touch, and the other only the sense of hearing? Therefore, when we speak of our having a picture of the things which are perceived through the senses, we mean a certain representation, true as far as it goes, but not adequate.

And so of those intellectual and moral objects which are brought home to us through our senses:—that they exist, we know by instinct; that they are such and such, we apprehend from the impressions which they leave upon our minds. Thus the life and writings of Cicero or Dr. Johnson, of St. Jerome or St. Chrysostom, leave upon us certain impressions of the intellectual and moral character of each of them, *sui generis*, and unmistakable.[3] We take up a passage of Chrysostom or a passage of Jerome; there is no possibility of confusing the one with the other; in each case we see the man in his language. And so of any great man whom we may have known: that he is not a mere impression on our senses, but a real being, we know by instinct; that he is

221

such and such, we know by the matter or quality of that impression.

Now certainly the thought of God, as Theists entertain it, is not gained by an instinctive association of His presence with any sensible phenomena; but the office which the senses directly fulfil as regards creation, that devolves indirectly on certain of our mental phenomena as regards the Creator. Those phenomena are found in the sense of moral obligation. As from a multitude of instinctive perceptions, acting in particular instances, of something beyond the senses, we generalize the notion of an external world, and then picture that world in and according to those particular phenomena from which we started, so from the perceptive power which identifies the intimations of conscience with the reverberations or echoes (so to say) of an external admonition, we proceed on to the notion of a Supreme Ruler and Judge, and then again we image Him and His attributes in those recurring intimations, out of which, as mental phenomena, our recognition of His existence was originally gained. And, if the impressions which His creatures make on us through our senses oblige us to regard those creatures as *sui generis* respectively, it is not wonderful that the notices which He indirectly gives us, through our conscience, of His own nature are such as to make us understand that He is like Himself and like nothing else.

I have already said I am not proposing here to prove the Being of a God; yet I have found it impossible to avoid saying where I look for the proof of it. For I am looking for that proof in the same quarter as that from which I would commence a proof of His attributes and character,—by the same means as those which I show how we apprehend Him, not merely as a notion, but as a reality. The last indeed of these three investigations alone concerns me here, but I cannot altogether exclude the two former from my consideration. However, I repeat, what I am directly aiming at, is to explain how we gain an image of God and give a real assent to the proposition that He exists. And next, in order to do this, of course I must start from some first principle;—and that first principle, which I assume and shall not attempt to prove, is that which I should also use as a foundation in those other two inquiries, viz. that we have by nature a conscience.

I assume, then, that Conscience has a legitimate place among our mental acts; as really so, as the action of memory, of reasoning, of imagination, or as the sense of the beautiful; that, as there are objects which, when presented to the mind, cause it to feel grief, regret, joy, or desire, so there are things which excite in us approbation or blame, and which we in consequence call right or wrong; and which, experienced in ourselves, kindle in us that specific sense of pleasure or pain, which goes by the name of a good or bad conscience. This being taken for granted, I shall attempt to show that in this special feeling, which follows on the commission of what we call right or wrong, lie the materials for the real apprehension of a Divine Sovereign and Judge.

The feeling of conscience being, I repeat, a certain keen sensibility, pleasant or painful,—self-approval and hope, or compunction and fear,—attendant on certain of our actions, which in consequence we call right or wrong, is two-fold:—it is a moral sense, and a sense of duty; a judgment of the reason and a magisterial dictate. Of course its act is indivisible; still it has these two aspects, distinct from each other, and admitting of a separate consideration. Though I lost my sense of the obligation which I lie under to abstain from acts of dishonesty, I should not in consequence lose my sense that such actions were an outrage offered to my moral nature. Again; though I lost my sense of their moral deformity, I should not therefore lose my sense that they were forbidden to me. Thus conscience has both a critical and a judicial office, and though its promptings, in the breasts of the millions of human beings to whom it is given, are not in all cases correct, that does not necessarily interfere with the force of its testimony and of its sanction: its testimony that there is a right and a wrong, and its sanction to that testimony conveyed in the feelings which attend on right or wrong conduct. Here I have to speak of conscience in the latter point of view, not as supplying us, by means of its various acts, with the elements of morals, such as may be developed by the intellect into an ethical code, but simply as the dictate of an authoritative monitor bearing upon the details of conduct as they come before us, and complete in its several acts, one by one.

Let us then thus consider conscience, not as a rule of right conduct, but as a sanction of right conduct. This is its primary and most authoritative aspect; it is the ordinary sense of the word. Half the world would be puzzled to know what was meant by the moral sense; but every one knows what is meant by a good or bad conscience. Conscience is ever forcing on us by threats and by promises that we must follow the right and avoid the wrong; so far it is one and the same in the mind of every one, whatever be its particular errors in particular minds as to the acts which it orders to be done or to be avoided; and in this respect it corresponds to our perception of the beautiful and deformed. As we have naturally a sense of the beautiful and graceful in nature and art, though tastes proverbially differ, so we have a sense of duty and obligation, whether we all associate it with the same certain actions in particular or not.

Here, however, Taste and Conscience part company: for the sense of beautifulness, as indeed the Moral Sense, has no special relations to persons, but contemplates objects in themselves; conscience, on the other hand, is concerned with persons primarily, and with actions mainly as viewed in their doers, or rather with self alone and one's own actions, and with others only indirectly and as if in association with self. And further, taste is its own evidence, appealing to nothing beyond its own sense of the beautiful or the ugly, and enjoying the specimens of the beautiful simply for their own sake; but conscience does not repose on itself, but vaguely reaches forward to something beyond self, and dimly discerns a sanction higher than self for its decisions, as is evidenced in that keen sense of obligation and responsibility which informs them. And hence it is that we are accustomed to speak of conscience as a voice,—a term which we should never think of applying to the sense of the beautiful; and moreover a voice, or the echo of a voice, imperative and constraining, like no other dictate in the whole of our experience.

And again, in consequence of this prerogative of dictating and commanding, which is of its essence, Conscience has an intimate bearing on our affections and emotions, leading us to reverence and awe, hope and fear, especially fear, a feeling which is foreign for the most part, not only to Taste, but even to the Moral Sense, except in consequence of accidental associations. No fear is felt by any one who recognizes that his conduct has not been beautiful, though he may be mortified at himself, if perhaps he has thereby forfeited some advantage; but, if he has been be-

225

trayed into any kind of immorality, he has a lively sense of responsibility and guilt, though the act be no offence against society,—of distress and apprehension, even though it may be of present service to him,—of compunction and regret, though in itself it be most pleasurable,—of confusion of face, though it may have no witnesses.[4] These various perturbations of mind, which are characteristic of a bad conscience, and may be very considerable,—self-reproach, poignant shame, haunting remorse, chill dismay at the prospect of the future,—and their contraries, when the conscience is good, as real though less forcible, self-approval, inward peace, lightness of heart, and the like,—these emotions constitute a specific difference between conscience and our other intellectual senses,—common sense, good sense, sense of expedience, taste, sense of honour, and the like,—as indeed they would also constitute between conscience and the moral sense, supposing these two were not aspects of one and the same feeling, exercised upon one and the same subject-matter.

So much for the characteristic phenomena, which conscience presents, nor is it difficult to determine what they imply. I refer once more to our sense of the beautiful. This sense is attended by an intellectual enjoyment, and is free from whatever is of the nature of emotion, except in one case, viz. when it is excited by personal objects; then it is that the tranquil feeling of admiration is exchanged for the excitement of affection and passion. Conscience too, considered as a moral sense, an intellectual sentiment, is a sense of admiration and disgust, of approbation and blame: but it is something more than a moral sense, it is always, what the sense of the beautiful is only in certain cases; it is always emotional. No wonder then that it always implies what that sense only sometimes implies; that it always involves the recognition of a living object, towards which it is directed. Inanimate things cannot stir our affections; these are correlative with persons. If, as is the case, we feel responsibility, are ashamed, are frightened, at transgressing the voice of conscience, this implies that there is One to whom we are responsible, before whom we are ashamed, whose claims upon us we fear. If, on doing wrong, we feel the same tearful, broken-hearted sorrow which overwhelms us on hurting a mother; if, on doing right, we enjoy the same sunny serenity of mind, the same soothing, satisfactory delight which follows on our receiving praise from a father, we certainly have within us the image of some person, to whom our love and veneration look, in whose smile we find our happiness, for whom we yearn, towards whom we direct our pleadings, in whose anger we are troubled and waste away.

These feelings in us are such as require for their exciting cause an intelligent being: we are not affectionate towards a stone, nor do we feel shame before a horse or a dog; we have no remorse or compunction on breaking mere human law: yet, so it is, conscience excites all these painful emotions, confusion, foreboding, self-condemnation; and on the other hand it sheds upon us a deep peace, a sense of security, a resignation, and a hope, which there is no sensible, no earthly object to elicit. "The wicked flees, when no one pursueth"; then why does he flee? whence his terror? Who is it that he sees in solitude, in darkness, in the hidden chambers of his heart? If the cause of these emotions does not belong to this visible world, the Object to which his perception is directed must be Supernatural and Divine; and thus the phenomena of Conscience, as a dictate, avail to impress the imagination with the picture of a Supreme Governor, a Judge, holy, just, powerful, all-seeing, retributive, and is the creative principle of religion, as the Moral Sense is the principle of ethics.

And let me here refer again to the fact, to which I have already drawn attention, that this instinct of the mind recognizing an external Master in the dictate of conscience, and imaging the thought of Him in the definite impressions which conscience creates, is parallel to that other law of, not only human, but of brute nature, by which the presence of unseen individual beings is discerned under the shifting shapes and colours of the visible world. Is it by sense, or by reason, that brutes understand the real unities, material and spiritual, which are signified by the lights and shadows, the brilliant ever-changing kaleidoscope, as it may be called, which plays upon their *retina*? Not by reason, for they have not reason; not by sense, because they are transcending sense; therefore it is an instinct.

This faculty on the part of brutes, unless we were used to it, would strike us as a great mystery. It is one peculiarity of animal natures to be susceptible of phenomena through the channels of sense; it is another to have in those sensible phenomena a perception of the individuals to which this or that group of them belongs. This perception of individual things amid the maze of shapes and colours which meets their sight, is given to brutes in large measures, and that, apparently from the moment of their birth. It is by no mere physical instinct, such as that which leads him to his mother for milk, that the new-dropped lamb recognizes each of his fellow lambkins as a whole, consisting of many parts bound up in one, and, before he is an hour old, makes experience of his and their rival individualities. And much more distinctly do the horse and dog recognize even the personality of their masters. How are we to explain this apprehension of things, which are one and individual, in the midst of a world of pluralities and transmutations, whether in the instance of brutes or again of children? But until we account for the knowledge which an infant has of his mother or his nurse, what reason have we to take exception at the doctrine, as strange and difficult, that in the dictate of conscience, without previous experiences or analogical reasoning, he is able gradually to perceive the voice, or the echoes of the voice, of a Master, living, personal, and sovereign?

I grant, of course, that we cannot assign a date, ever so early, before which he had learned nothing at all, and formed no mental associations, from the words and conduct of those who have the care of him. But still, if a child of five or six years old, when reason is at length fully awake, has already mastered and appropriated thoughts and beliefs, in consequence of their teaching, in such sort as to be able to handle and apply them familiarly, according to the occasion, as principles of intellectual action, those beliefs at the very least must be singularly congenial to his mind, if not connatural with its initial action. And that such a spontaneous reception of religious truths is common with children, I shall take for granted, till I am convinced that I am wrong in so doing. The child keenly understands that there is a difference between right and wrong; and when he has done what he believes to be wrong, he is conscious that he is offending One to whom he is amenable, whom he does not see, who sees him. His mind reaches forward with a strong presentiment to the thought of a Moral Governor, sovereign over him, mindful, and just. It comes to him like an impulse of nature to entertain it.

229

It is my wish to take an ordinary child, but still one who is safe from influences destructive of his religious instincts. Supposing he has offended his parents, he will all alone and without effort, as if it were the most natural of acts, place himself in the presence of God, and beg of Him to set him right with them. Let us consider how much is contained in this simple act. First, it involves the impression on his mind of an unseen Being with whom he is in immediate relation, and that relation so familiar that he can address Him whenever he himself chooses; next, of One whose goodwill towards him he is assured of, and can take for granted—nay, who loves him better, and is nearer to him, than his parents; further, of One who can hear him, wherever he happens to be, and who can read his thoughts, for his prayer need not be vocal; lastly, of One who can effect a critical change in the state of feeling of others towards him. That is, we shall not be wrong in holding that this child has in his mind the image of an Invisible Being, who exercises a particular providence among us, who is present every where, who is heart-reading, heart-changing, ever-accessible, open to impetation. What a strong and intimate vision of God must he have already attained, if, as I have supposed, an ordinary trouble of mind has the spontaneous effect of leading him for consolation and aid to an Invisible Personal Power!

Moreover, this image brought before his mental vision is the image of One who by implicit threat and promise commands certain things which he, the same child, coincidently, by the same act of his mind, approves; which receive the adhesion of his moral sense and judgment, as right and good. It is the image of One who is good, inasmuch as enjoining and enforcing what is right and good, and who, in consequence, not only excites in the child hope and fear,—nay (it may be added), gratitude towards Him, as giving a law and maintaining it by reward and punishment,—but kindles in him love towards Him, as giving him a good law, and therefore as being good Himself, for it is the property of goodness to kindle love, or rather the very object of love is goodness; and all those distinct elements of the moral law, which the typical child, whom I am supposing, more or less consciously loves and approves,— truth, purity, justice, kindness, and the like,—are but shapes and aspects of goodness. And having in his degree a sensibility towards them all, for the sake of them all he is moved to love the Lawgiver, who enjoins them upon him. And, as he can contemplate these qualities and their manifestations under the common name of goodness, he is prepared to think of them as indivisible, correlative, supplementary of each other in one and the same Personality, so that there is no aspect of goodness which God is not; and that the more, because the notion of a perfection embracing all possible excellences, both moral and intellectual, is especially congenial to the mind, and there are in fact intellectual attributes, as well as moral, included in the child's image of God, as above represented.

Such is the apprehension which even a child may have of his Sovereign, Lawgiver, and Judge; which is possible in the case of children, because, at least, some children possess it, whether others possess it or no; and which, when it is found in children, is found to act promptly and keenly, by reason of the paucity of their ideas. It is an image of the good God, good in Himself, good relatively to the child, with whatever incompleteness; an image before it has been reflected on, and before it is recognized by him as a notion. Though he

231

cannot explain or define the word "God," when told to use it, his acts show that to him it is far more than a word. He listens, indeed, with wonder and interest to fables or tales; he has a dim, shadowy sense of what he hears about persons and matters of this world; but he has that within him which actually vibrates, responds, and gives a deep meaning to the lessons of his first teachers about the will and providence of God.

How far this initial religious knowledge comes from without, and how far from within, how much is natural, how much implies a special divine aid which is above nature, we have no means of determining, nor is it necessary for my present purpose to determine. I am not engaged in tracing the image of God in the mind of a child or a man to its first origins, but showing that he can become possessed of such an image, over and above all mere notions of God, and in what that image consists. Whether its elements, latent in the mind, would ever be elicited without extrinsic help is very doubtful; but whatever be the actual history of the first formation of the divine image within us, so far at least is certain, that, by informations external to ourselves, as time goes on, it admits of being strengthened and improved. It is certain too, that, whether it grows brighter and stronger, or, on the other hand, is dimmed, distorted, or obliterated, depends on each of us individually, and on his circumstances.

It is more than probable that, in the event, from neglect, from the temptations of life, from bad companions, or from the urgency of secular occupations, the light of the soul will fade away and die out. Men transgress their sense of duty, and gradually lose those sentiments of shame and fear, the natural supplements of transgression, which, as

I have said, are the witnesses of the Unseen Judge. And, even were it deemed impossible that those who had in their first youth a genuine apprehension of Him, could ever utterly lose it, yet that apprehension may become almost undistinguishable from an inferential acceptance of the great truth, or may dwindle into a mere notion of their intellect. On the contrary, the image of God, if duly cherished, may expand, deepen, and be completed, with the growth of their powers and in the course of life, under the varied lessons, within and without them, which are brought home to them concerning that same God, One and Personal, by means of education, social intercourse, experience, and literature.

To a mind thus carefully formed upon the basis of its natural conscience, the world, both of nature and of man, does but give back a reflection of those truths about the One Living God, which have been familiar to it from childhood. Good and evil meet us daily as we pass through life, and there are those who think it philosophical to act towards the manifestations of each with some sort of impartiality, as if evil had as much right to be there as good, or even a better, as having more striking triumphs and a broader jurisdiction. And because the course of things is determined by fixed laws, they consider that those laws preclude the present agency of the Creator in the carrying out of particular issues. It is otherwise with the theology of a religious imagination. It has a living hold on truths which are really to be found in the world, though they are not upon the surface. It is able to pronounce by anticipation, what it takes a long argument to prove—that good is the rule, and evil the exception. It is able to assume that, uniform as are the laws of nature, they are consistent with a

233

particular Providence. It interprets what it sees around it by this previous inward teaching, as the true key of that maze of vast complicated disorder; and thus it gains a more and more consistent and luminous vision of God from the most unpromising materials.

Thus conscience is a connecting principle between the creature and his Creator; and the firmest hold of theological truths is gained by habits of personal religion. When men begin all their works with the thought of God, acting for His sake and to fulfil His will, when they ask His blessing on themselves and their life, pray to Him for the objects they desire, and see Him in the event, whether it be according to their prayers or not, they will find everything that happens tend to confirm them in the truths about Him which live in their imagination, varied and unearthly as those truths may be. Then they are brought into His presence as that of a Living Person, and are able to hold converse with Him, and that with a directness and simplicity, with a confidence and intimacy, *mutatis mutandis*, which we use towards an earthly superior; so that it is doubtful whether we realize the company of our fellow-men with greater keenness than these favoured minds are able to contemplate and adore the Unseen, Incomprehensible Creator.

RELIGION AND

SOCIAL DEVELOPMENT

RELIGION AND SOCIAL DEVELOPMENT

IN PART THREE, we find some of Newman's contributions to the philosophy of human social institutions. His interest is drawn particularly toward the fact of development and integration in the case of socially powerful ideas and toward the possibility of finding some general criteria indicating a constructive and historically important type of development. The broad notion of evolution was in the air during the decades preceding Darwin's *Origin of Species*. Romantic poets and historians, idealistic philosophers, eirenical theologians, theorizing geologists, and probing biologists—all sorts of ingenious minds were engaged in elaborating theories of development applicable to various spheres of our experience. Apart from helping to sustain a common atmosphere, however, these thinkers did not converge for the sake of framing some grand argument about the modes of development. Each of the major researchers went along his own path and elaborated the conception in his own way. This is certainly the case with Newman, who is driven to think along developmental lines in order to answer a problem raised in his own professional domain of theology. His views on development are framed as aids in forming a hypothesis about how the Christian Church can remain faithful to its original deposit of revelation and yet continue to grow and meet fresh challenges. That these views on development have a still wider import than the theological one is brought home, however, by Newman's analysis of the growth of three other influential and socially embodied principles: the idea of the university, the idea of civilization, and that of the political constitution.

Selection (21) performs the double service of identifying the kind of idea in question and explaining why it must undergo development. Newman is not concerned chiefly with ideas formed in the individual perceiver and which are amenable to a genetic analysis of the sort furnished by classical British empiricism or empirical psychology. Nor does he come to the life of ideas with an idealistic postulate about their being modes in the self-development of the absolute. His approach is more socially orientated than the former viewpoint and more descriptively realistic than the latter. The ideas which attract his interest are socially influential beliefs or types, rather than purely individual conceptions, and their development is a thoroughly human affair which sometimes symbolizes the divine presence without ever being the means for the latter's own actualization. Developmental ideas cannot be condensed into a mathematical formula or confined to a well plotted evolution on paper, since they have their being in our living human interpretative activities and practical decisions. Newman calls them real and living ideas, since they refer to meanings expressible in concrete imagery (and which can thus evoke the process of realization), and do so in respect to a complex and continuous interpretation of their

238

significance (thus generating a living response in society and history). His working axiom is that growth is the only evidence of life, when we come to test the claims for real and living ideas.

To show why such principles must evolve, Newman also refers to them as leading ideas. This is meant in the double sense that they propose a thematic view of some important aspect of human reality, and that they tend to organize around themselves some effective institutional forms of social realization. A temporal development is needed because the object intended by such ideas can only be grasped through the cooperative judgments and evaluations of many minds operating over many ages, because the complex leading principles have many aspects or features which can only be brought to maturity through a historical growth, and because their objective fulfillment looks toward some visible institutional incarnation, such as the Church, the university, and the constitutional state. Newman's theory can be compared profitably with what the phenomenologists say about the profile approaches and the gradual weaving of a thematic idea, as well as with the findings in the sociology of knowledge on the growth and warfare of organizing ideals.

The seven criteria proposed by Newman for determining a healthy growth of an ideal are given in Selection (22). He draws his illustrations from a rich and varied field. Newman does not pretend to make a simple abstraction or induction of the pattern of development from the particular cases, but shows the fruitfulness of his hypothesis and suggests its use in many areas. A vital development should combine fidelity to traditional sources with openness to new situa-

239

tions. This suits our human way of existing: "In a higher world it is otherwise, but here below to live is to change, and to be perfect is to have changed often."[1]

Newman's conception of development in the philosophical sphere is found in Selection (23), a section from a memorandum which he drew up in 1868 in consequence of some private theological discussions about the relation between his theory of development and the then burning question of papal infallibility. In explaining his meaning for doctrinal development, he used the example of how the later Aristotelians were faithful to Aristotle and yet were men of their own intellectual age. Philosophical development within a school is a communal and historical achievement, involving some real advances in the degree that later minds work out some implicit meanings, develop some new interrelations among doctrines, and judge properly in regard to new problems and evidences. Newman locates the life of the Aristotelian philosophical tradition in the living intellectual habits and actual judgments of the philosophers, not in the schemas and definitions which get solidified in the philosophy manuals, although even the latter have a subsidiary value. When Pope Leo XIII issued his 1879 encyclical *Aeterni Patris,* on the restoration of Christian philosophy, Cardinal Newman drafted a letter of congratulation and agreement. Selection (24) expresses his conviction that sound philosophical development among Christian thinkers must be the outcome of familiarity with the intellectual tradition of the past as well as awareness of modern problems and the philosophies coming in their wake.

The next group of readings, Selections (25) to (27), helps us to view Newman's lectures on the *Idea of a Uni-*

240

versity in the light of his fundamental views on knowledge and God, the sciences and the patterns of social development. One of those "original forms of thinking or formative ideas" animating Western culture is that of the university, an ideal which Newman recognizes as becoming more and more the pivot for our modern intellectual tendencies and their practical consequences. Even though the university outlook may appear to be permanently established among us, however, the work of clarifying and enriching it is still going on. The Selections are so arranged that we can follow Newman's treatment of what C. P. Snow has called the grand bifurcation of the two cultures: the scientific and the humanistic. Newman thinks that this problem is creatively aggravated by the fact that the religious view of existence forms a third party to the cultural tension. The intellectual crisis centering around the meaning of the university involves a three-cornered relationship between the sciences, the humanities, and religion. The university should take account of this further complexity of the situation and, for their part, the Christian intellectual leaders should use their philosophical and theological resources for seeking a new unification of the knowledges of mankind precisely within the university community itself. Newman's point is that the university will either include an openness to the religious interpretation or firmly exclude it from the actual concerns of higher education, depending upon the quality of participation of Christian thinkers in the ongoing discussion of the issue.

In Selection (25), Newman begins where the modern scientific attitude also took its beginning: with the case of Galileo. He does not try to soften the circumstances but only to draw a positive lesson for the Christian intelligence from the proceedings. Whatever the fine points involved, the official action of condemnation did betray a dangerous condition of intellectual unpreparedness concerning the nature of the modern physical method and the relation of its propositions to those of theology. When properly reflected upon, the case of Galileo has a liberating effect upon the mind of the Christian believer, as well as upon the scientist's mind. It brings out the slow, cooperative manner of our search for natural truths. And it etches deeply into our awareness the distinction in principle between the intent of the inspired writings of the Judaeo-Christian revelation and the intent of modern physical research. Once we realize in a lively way this difference of purpose and the consequence that Scripture should not be misused to settle issues which have been formulated within the context of the scientific methods, we can give our effective support to the freedom of scientific research and teaching, as well as to the free presentation of the religious message within the university situation.

That Newman does not equate such intellectual freedom with a policy of separatism is the burden of Selection (26). There, he explores the disastrous results of trying to isolate from each other the scientific, literary, and religious reports on the universe and man. Special attention is paid to the effect of an isolated approach upon our concrete intelligence or imagination, our intimate way of reaching a unified interpretation of the meaning of human existence in this world. When the university is organized around an exclusively scientific reading of the universe or an exclusively literary-humanistic approach to man, the student whose imagination is being molded finds it very difficult to keep alive his belief in God or make it relevant to his educational growth. The Christian mind then feels tempted either to dilute the university ideal or to withdraw entirely from the university effort. Yet the whole meaning of Christian interpretation at the intellectual level is to work toward the ordering and intercommunication of knowledges, rather than toward a fragmentation or suppression of the components in the university enterprise.

Newman, indeed, is fiercely insistent upon the responsibility of university teachers of literature and history to give as complete and honest a report of our actual human condition as the physical scientist does on the physical universe. The man of faith today cannot avoid the challenge of either respecting the integrity of the university ideal of a full presentation of the findings in the sciences and humanities or else of withdrawing entirely from university work, and thus abandoning the core principle of development in modern intellectual and practical life. Newman argues that acceptance of the former path involves acceptance of his own theme of furnishing the "antecedent probability," i.e., the living matrix of religious belief, intellectual interpretation, and moral conviction in the university world which will dispose the inquiring mind to keep the scientific and literary approaches open to the further meanings provided by a theistic philosophy and Christian revelation. It will do no good to give theology a formal place in the curriculum, unless the individual minds of the teachers and students comprising the university community help to keep alive the theistic and religious context for interpreting our existence.

The theme of liberal knowledge as the goal of university education is set forth in Selection (27). Newman is sometimes misunderstood as fatuously advocating that the university make an easy encyclopedic summary of the several disciplines and label this digest a philosophy. He explicitly criticizes the "viewiness" behind vague and grandiose syntheses. It is true that he uses the term "philosophy" very broadly and diversely, in a range of meanings reaching from a technical discipline to a faith-shaped outlook, and that he does not fully realize the role of the modern university in sponsoring research as well as reporting its results. But in point of fact, Newman does defend the distinctness of every discipline and the right of scholars to develop their research projects in full freedom and depth. His chief interest concerns how the university is to discharge its primary office of teaching under these conditions. It can do so only by trying to develop a critical, philosophical temper of mind which recognizes that specialized work occurs within an abstractive framework and a limitation of method, and which is also alert to finding ways of correlating and unifying the several specialized approaches. This is a distinctive responsibility without which the unity of the idea of a university fails to become realized and enriched in our age.

The liberal ideal in education is to remain perpetually dissatisfied with the partial reports and the given instances of synthesis, and to seek more effective ways of achieving the common reference of all the arts and sciences to our humanly experienced world. When Newman calls this integrative habit of mind "philosophy," he does not mean some particular system or some supersynthesis of the departments of learning, but rather a persistent attitude of finding a common ground and base of communication and vision for the several disciplines. Working within his own field of competence, the additional contribution of the Christian teacher is to keep the entire process open to the religious significance of life. If he be a theologian or a philosopher in the professional sense, he will try to analyze and distinguish the various methods and modes of knowing which together constitute the living idea of the university.

The remaining Selections in this Part furnish some materials from Newman's social and political thought, which is a prolongation of his general theme concerning the operation of living ideas in human history. Selection (28) is fundamental for understanding his position, since it presents some of his basic social generalizations. There is a characteristic blending of some notions which have been traditional in Christian social theory since St. Augustine with other elements taken from the British philosophers. Newman regards the social condition as natural, in the sense of being dynamically perfective of our human tendencies. Hence he does not interpret the state of nature in an atomistic, Hobbesian fashion, but rather as the barbarous mode of social existence itself in which moral conscience, reason, and the emotions are active in an undisciplined, imperfectly unified way. A real continuity exists between the barbarous and the civilized condition of human society, because they are expressions of human self-development and involve the acceptance of some common social ideal. We find Newman here transposing the Augustinian theme of the bond of social love into that of a commonly possessed social ideal as constitutive of the very being of a society. And we also find him reworking the conviction of the French and British Enlightenment about man as being the principle of progress, of social self-development which is limitless within our modern scientific and technological horizon. The distinction between social objects proposed to a ruder society by the imagination and those which

245

appeal to the sense or rational self-interest of modern civilization enables Newman both to retain the social unity in human history and to take into account the new factors of disciplined inquiry and social organization.

One consequence of this distinction is brought out in Selection (29), which deals with the relation between Christianity and civilization. Among the scholars whom Newman had invited to staff his proposed university in Dublin was Thomas William Allies, himself a convert and a keen student of Church history. He was to have taught modern history and especially the philosophy of history at the Irish university. When that project fell through, he continued his work for English Catholic education and wrote his masterwork, *The Formation of Christendom,* completed in eight volumes in 1895. Already in 1860, he submitted to Newman some sections dealing with the Church and medieval society. Newman had grown more and more critical of the Romantic conception of history, its claims for a philosophy of history, and its rosy view of the Christian Middle Ages. These letters record his firm protest against idealizing the medieval period, compromising the transcendence of Christianity in respect to any moment of civilization, and suspending for the medieval period the opposition between the Church and that Biblical meaning of "the world" which signifies an evil counter-principle to God and revelation. Although Newman would not agree with Kierkegaard that Christendom is an unholy contradiction, he would concur with the Danish critic's verdict that it encourages a dangerous confusion of distinct principles and social categories.

Newman's own view of the relation between Christianity and the historical forms of human civilization is complex

246

and delicately balanced. The civilizing function is a naturally good tendency of man, the open and progressing social being. Christianity embodies the ideal of civilization, insofar as it encourages our efforts at human realization, control over nature, and social unification, as well as provides us with supernatural motives and aids in performing our social and cultural duties. But the relation between Christianity and the civilizing process is intimate without ever becoming an identity of the two, and without ever overlooking the fact that this same process is capable of being detached from Christian influences and even oriented against the values of theism and Christianity. In his correspondence with Allies, Newman observes that the use of the resources of civilization against Christianity is constantly active in history, and that the medieval civilization is no exception to this tension and its consequent tendency to subordinate or eliminate the distinctive aims of the Church.

Applying his distinction between societies dominated by imagination and by sense, he explains the special secular role of the Church in the feudal system with its need for imaginative views of social power and ideals. But the historically conditioned position of the Church in medieval society does not give to that arrangement an everlasting sanction and does not warrant our seeking to impose a medieval settlement upon modern society. The Gospel is for all times, not in some empty sense of applying in the same way in every age, but as addressing men in the different modes suitable to historically different ages. The relationship of Christianity with modern civilization cannot overlook the fact that we have moved into an age dominated by notional assent, i.e., by reflective methods of inquiry, social organization, and appraisal of human temporal goods.

247

Under our concrete circumstances, the Church will find it most in accord with its own responsibility toward its religious aim and its civilizing activity to work constructively with modern states on the basis of religious toleration, rather than on that of the civil establishment of a particular religion.

Newman was careful to distinguish between liberalism in religion and liberalism in politics, even though he never fully disentangled his social and political thought from the ambiguities surrounding the terms "liberal" and "conservative." He was a lifelong opponent of religious liberalism, which he described as the anti-dogmatic principle depreciating the place of dogma in religious belief and accepting doctrines only in the conditional degree of their justification by our reason. He took the occasion of his elevation to the cardinalate to underline his permanent criticism of indifferentism in religious belief. In his remarkable *biglietto* speech in Rome, Selection (30), he also noted that religious liberalism can have the political consequences of neutralizing the social influence of religion and substituting for it a purely naturalistic program of education and ethical formation. To the extent that political liberalism meant precisely this substitutional attitude toward religion, Newman was also its opponent. But he did not hold that all the measures advocated by liberal politicians in his day were indissolubly bound up with this substitutional form of political liberalism. Newman remained a critical and independent sort of conservative. The heart of the matter for him was that the civilizing process has been detached from its religious context by many leading scientific and literary minds, and that the Christian intelligence must invent fresh ways of incorporating our civilizing tendencies within a religious interpretation of existence, without turning backwards to the feudal system or the established Church.

Along with the idea of the university and that of civilization, Newman paid special attention to the idea of the free constitutional state as a creative principle in modern political life. Selection (31) shows how he accepted the theory of the limited state, which is distinct from the people or nation and which results from the social agreement made by the people for their well-being and convenience, peace and freedom. The political arrangement of society does not issue solely from the rational will of the people or solely from their sentiments and traditions, but combines both these factors in various concrete ways, as Locke and Burke had suggested. Newman was also careful to keep a distinction, within the state, between the government as the settled way of using political power and the constitution. The latter is closely related with the living traditions and aspirations of the people, serving as the expression of these ideals and the safeguard of social freedom. In his books, private correspondence, and even a current affairs column (contributed for a few months in 1859 to the *Rambler*), Newman proved himself to be a fairly shrewd observer of political events. He applied his political theory to the Crimean War in order to explain why Great Britain was so successful in internal affairs and so inept in foreign adventures at this part of the century.

In a wider perspective, however, Newman's political analysis helps to articulate his general theories of development and real assent. He emphasizes the constitutional side of political order, because it is here that one can see the operations of a leading principle or developmental ideal.

249

Furthermore, a state is to be understood and evaluated by reference to the object desired by the people, by the common possession in which they participate through a real social assent. In place of the somewhat artificial contract theory, Newman substitutes that of the real social assent or social love which a people concretely exhibits in its common pursuits and its way of becoming civilized. Newman uses here his previous distinction between an imaginative apprehension of a social ideal and a sensible-reflective apprehension of it. He himself is committed to the constitutional state as the way in which a people living in a sensible-reflective age can seek its temporal welfare and also secure human liberty and the reign of law. The social object or common possession animating British political life, as Newman describes it, is a reverence for law joined with a high sense of human liberty. He also notices that in America the people or nation is vigorous enough to sustain a broad sphere of nonpolitical functions, including religious worship and education. The aim of the religious mind is not to change this political arrangement but to permeate the civilizing activities and social assent of the people with a new awareness of God's presence and providential ordering in nature, human history, and the free person.

CHAPTER XXI

WHY REAL AND LIVING IDEAS
MUST DEVELOP[1]

1

IT IS THE characteristic of our minds to be ever engaged in passing judgment on the things which come before us. No sooner do we apprehend than we judge: we allow nothing to stand by itself: we compare, contrast, abstract, generalize, connect, adjust, classify: and we view all our knowledge in the associations with which these processes have invested it.[2]

Of the judgments thus made, which become aspects in our minds of the things which meet us, some are mere opinions which come and go, or which remain with us only till an accident displaces them, whatever be the influence which they exercise meanwhile. Others are firmly fixed in our minds, with or without good reason, and have a hold upon us, whether they relate to matters of fact, or to principles of conduct, or are views of life and the world, or are prejudices, imaginations, or convictions. Many of them attach to one and the same object, which is thus variously viewed, not only by various minds, but by the same. They sometimes lie in such near relation, that each implies the

RELIGION AND SOCIAL DEVELOPMENT

others; some are only not inconsistent with each other, in that they have a common origin: some, as being actually incompatible with each other, are, one or other, falsely associated in our minds with their object, and in any case they may be nothing more than ideas, which we mistake for things.

Thus Judaism is an idea which once was objective, and Gnosticism is an idea which was never so. Both of them have various aspects: those of Judaism were such as monotheism, a certain ethical discipline, a ministration of divine vengeance, a preparation for Christianity: those of the Gnostic idea are such as the doctrine of two principles, that of emanation, the intrinsic malignity of matter, the inculpability of sensual indulgence, or the guilt of every pleasure of sense, of which last two one or other must be in the Gnostic a false aspect and subjective only.

2

The idea which represents an object or supposed object is commensurate with the sum total of its possible aspects, however they may vary in the separate consciousness of individuals; and in proportion to the variety of aspects under which it presents itself to various minds is its force and depth, and the argument for its reality. Ordinarily an idea is not brought home to the intellect as objective except through this variety; like bodily substances, which are not apprehended except under the clothing of their properties and results, and which admit of being walked round, and surveyed on opposite sides, and in different perspectives, and in contrary lights, in evidence of their reality. And, as views of a material object may be taken from points so remote or so opposed, that they seem at first sight incompatible, and especially as their shadows will be disproportionate, or even monstrous, and yet all these anomalies will disappear and all these contrarieties be adjusted, on ascertaining the point of vision or the surface of projection in each case; so also all the aspects of an idea are capable of coalition, and of a resolution into the object to which it belongs; and the *prima facie* dissimilitude of its aspects becomes, when explained, an argument for its substantiveness and integrity, and their multiplicity for its originality and power.

3

There is no one aspect deep enough to exhaust the contents of a real idea, no one term or proposition which will serve to define it; though of course one representation of it is more just and exact than another, and though when an idea is very complex, it is allowable, for the sake of convenience, to consider its distinct aspects as if separate ideas. Thus, with all our intimate knowledge of animal life and of the structure of particular animals, we have not arrived at a true definition of any one of them, but are forced to enumerate properties and accidents by way of description. Nor can we inclose in a formula that intellectual fact, or system of thought, which we call the Platonic philosophy, or that historical phenomenon of doctrine and conduct, which we call the heresy of Montanus or of Manes. Again, if Protestantism were said to lie in its theory of private judgment, and Lutheranism in its doctrine of justification, this indeed would be an approximation of the truth; but it is plain that to argue or to act as if the one or the other aspect were a sufficient account of those forms of religion severally, would be a serious mistake.

Sometimes an attempt is made to determine the "leading idea," as it has been called, of Christianity, an ambitious essay as employed on a supernatural work, when, even as regards the visible creation and the inventions of man, such a task is beyond us. Thus its one idea has been said by some to be the restoration of our fallen race, by others philanthropy, by others the tidings of immortality, or the spirituality of true religious service, or the salvation of the elect, or mental liberty, or the union of the soul with God. If, indeed, it is only thereby meant to use one or other of these as a central idea for convenience, in order to group others around it, no fault can be found with such a proceeding: and in this sense I should myself call the Incarnation the central aspect of Christianity, out of which the three main aspects of its teaching take their rise, the sacramental, the hierarchical, and the ascetic. But one aspect of Revelation must not be allowed to exclude or to obscure another; and Christianity is dogmatical, devotional, practical all at once; it is esoteric and exoteric; it is indulgent and strict; it is light and dark; it is love, and it is fear.

4

When an idea, whether real or not, is of a nature to arrest and possess the mind, it may be said to have life, that is, to live in the mind which is its recipient. Thus mathematical ideas, real as they are, can hardly properly be called living, at least ordinarily. But, when some great enunciation, whether true or false, about human nature, or present good, or government, or duty, or religion, is carried forward into the public throng of men and draws attention, then it is not merely received passively in this or that form into many minds, but it becomes an active principle within them, leading them to an ever-new contemplation of itself, to an application of it in various directions, and a propagation of it on every side. Such is the doctrine of the divine right of kings, or of the rights of man, or of the anti-social bearings of a priesthood, or utilitarianism, or free trade, or the duty of benevolent enterprises, or the philosophy of Zeno or Epicurus, doctrines which are of a nature to attract and influence, and have so far a *prima facie* reality, that they may be looked at on many sides and strike various minds very variously.

Let one such idea get possession of the popular mind, or the mind of any portion of the community, and it is not difficult to understand what will be the result. At first men will not fully realize what it is that moves them, and will express and explain themselves inadequately. There will be a general agitation of thought, and an action of mind upon mind. There will be a time of confusion, when conceptions and misconceptions are in conflict, and it is uncertain whether anything is to come of the idea at all, or which view of it is to get the start of the others. New lights will be brought to bear upon the original statements of the doctrine put forward; judgments and aspects will accumulate. After a while some definite teaching emerges; and, as time proceeds, one view will be modified or expanded by another, and then combined with a third; till the idea to which these various aspects belong, will be to each mind separately what at first it was only to all together.

It will be surveyed too in its relation to other doctrines or facts, to other natural laws or established customs, to the

255

varying circumstances of times and places, to other religions, polities, philosophies, as the case may be. How it stands affected towards other systems, how it affects them, how far it may be made to combine with them, how far it tolerates them, when it interferes with them, will be gradually wrought out. It will be interrogated and criticized by enemies, and defended by well-wishers. The multitude of opinions formed concerning it in these respects and many others will be collected, compared, sorted, sifted, selected, rejected, gradually attached to it, separated from it, in the minds of individuals and of the community. It will, in proportion to its native vigour and subtlety, introduce itself into the framework and details of social life, changing public opinion, and strengthening or undermining the foundations of established order. Thus in time it will have grown into an ethical code, or into a system of government, or into a theology, or into a ritual, according to its capabilities: and this body of thought, thus laboriously gained, will after all be little more than the proper representative of one idea, being in substance what that idea meant from the first, its complete image as seen in a combination of diversified aspects, with the suggestions and corrections of many minds, and the illustration of many experiences.

5

This process, whether it be longer or shorter in point of time, by which the aspects of an idea are brought into consistency and form, I call its *development*, being the germination and maturation of some truth or apparent truth on a large mental field. On the other hand this process will not be a development, unless the assemblage of aspects which constitute its ultimate shape, really belongs to the idea from which they start. A republic, for instance, is not a development from a pure monarchy, though it may follow upon it; whereas the Greek "tyrant" may be considered as included in the idea of a democracy. Moreover a development will have this characteristic, that, its action being in the busy scene of human life, it cannot progress at all without cutting across, and thereby destroying or modifying and incorporating with itself existing modes of thinking and operating.

The development then of an idea is not like an investigation worked out on paper, in which each successive advance is a pure evolution from a foregoing, but it is carried on through and by means of communities of men and their leaders and guides; and it employs their minds as its instruments, and depends upon them, while it uses them. And so, as regards existing opinions, principles, measures, and institutions of the community which it has invaded; it develops by establishing relations between itself and them; it employs itself, in giving them a new meaning and direction, in creating what may be called a jurisdiction over them, in throwing off whatever in them it cannot assimilate. It grows when it incorporates, and its identity is found, not in isolation, but in continuity and sovereignty. This it is that imparts to the history both of states and of religion, its specially turbulent and polemical character. Such is the explanation of the wranglings, whether of schools or of parliaments. It is the warfare of ideas under their various aspects striving for the mastery, each of them enterprising, engrossing, imperious, more or less incompatible with the

257

rest, and rallying followers or rousing foes, according as it acts upon the faith, the prejudices, or the interest of parties or classes.

6

Moreover, an idea not only modifies, but is modified, or at least influenced, by the state of things in which it is carried out, and is dependent in various ways on the circumstances which surround it. Its development proceeds quickly or slowly, as it may be; the order of succession in its separate stages is variable; it shows differently in a small sphere of action and in an extended; it may be interrupted, retarded, mutilated, distorted, by external violence; it may be enfeebled by the effort of ridding itself of domestic foes; it may be impeded and swayed or even absorbed by counter energetic ideas; it may be coloured by the received tone of thought into which it comes, or depraved by the intrusion of foreign principles, or at length shattered by the development of some original fault within it.

7

But whatever be the risk of corruption from intercourse with the world around, such a risk must be encountered if a great idea is duly to be understood, and much more if it is to be fully exhibited. It is elicited and expanded by trial, and battles into perfection and supremacy. Nor does it escape the collision of opinion even in its earlier years, nor does it remain truer to itself, and with a better claim to be considered one and the same, though externally protected from vicissitude and change.

It is indeed sometimes said that the stream is clearest near the spring. Whatever use may fairly be made of this image, it does not apply to the history of a philosophy or belief, which on the contrary is more equable, and purer, and stronger, when its bed has become deep, and broad, and full. It necessarily rises out of an existing state of things, and for a time savours of the soil. Its vital element needs disengaging from what is foreign and temporary, and is employed in efforts after freedom which become more vigorous and hopeful as its years increase. Its beginnings are no measure of its capabilities, nor of its scope. At first no one knows what it is worth. It remains perhaps for a time quiescent; it tries, as it were, its limbs, and proves the ground under it, and feels its way. From time to time it makes essays which fail, and are in consequence abandoned. It seems in suspense which way to go; it wavers, and at length strikes out in one definite direction. In time it enters upon strange territory; points of controversy alter their bearing; parties rise and fall around it; dangers and hopes appear in new relations; and old principles reappear under new forms. It changes with them in order to remain the same. In a higher world it is otherwise, but here below to live is to change, and to be perfect is to have changed often.

CHAPTER XXII

TESTS FOR A GENUINE DEVELOPMENT[1]

I VENTURE TO set down seven Notes of varying cogency, independence and applicability, to discriminate healthy developments of an idea from its state of corruption and decay, as follows:—There is no corruption if it retains one and the same type, the same principle, the same organization; if its beginnings anticipate its subsequent phases, and its later phenomena protect and subserve its earlier; if it has a power of assimilation and revival, and a vigorous action from first to last. On these tests I shall now enlarge, nearly in the order in which I have enumerated them.

First Note of A Genuine Development: Preservation of Type

This is readily suggested by the analogy of physical growth, which is such that the parts and proportions of the developed form, however altered, correspond to those which belong to its rudiments. The adult animal has the same make, as it had on its birth; young birds do not grow into fishes, nor does the child degenerate into the brute, wild or domestic, of which he is by inheritance lord. Vincentius of Lerins adopts this illustration in distinct reference to Christian doctrine. "Let the soul's religion," he says, "imitate the law of the body, which, as years go on, develops indeed and opens out its due proportions, and yet remains identically what it was. Small are a baby's limbs, a youth's are larger, yet they are the same."[2]

In like manner every calling or office has its own type, which those who fill it are bound to maintain; and to deviate from the type in any material point is to relinquish the calling. Thus both Chaucer and Goldsmith have drawn pictures of a true parish priest; these differ in details, but on the whole they agree together, and are one in such sense, that sensuality, or ambition, must be considered a forfeiture of that high title. Those magistrates, again, are called "corrupt," who are guided in their judgments by love of lucre or respect of persons, for the administration of justice is their essential function. Thus collegiate or monastic bodies lose their claim to their endowments or their buildings, as being relaxed and degenerate, if they neglect their statutes or their Rule. Thus, too, in political history, a mayor of the palace, such as he became in the person of Pepin, was no faithful development of the office he filled, as originally intended and established.

An idea then does not always bear about it the same external image; this circumstance, however, has no force to weaken the argument for its substantial identity, as drawn from its external sameness, when such sameness remains. On the contrary, for that very reason, *unity of type* becomes so much the surer guarantee of the healthiness and soundness of developments, when it is persistently preserved in spite of their number or importance.

261

Second Note: Continuity of Principles

As in mathematical creations figures are formed on distinct formulae, which are the laws under which they are developed, so it is in ethical and political subjects. Doctrines expand variously according to the mind, individual or social, into which they are received; and the peculiarities of the recipient are the regulating power, the law, the organization, or, as it may be called, the form of the development. The life of doctrines may be said to consist in the law or principle which they embody.

Principles are abstract and general, doctrines relate to facts; doctrines develope, and principles at first sight do not; doctrines grow and are enlarged, principles are permanent; doctrines are intellectual, and principles are more immediately ethical and practical. Systems live in principles and represent doctrines. Personal responsibility is a principle, the Being of a God is a doctrine; from that doctrine all theology has come in due course, whereas that principle is not clearer under the Gospel than in paradise, and depends, not on belief in an Almighty Governor, but on conscience.

Yet the difference between the two sometimes merely exists in our mode of viewing them; and what is a doctrine in one philosophy is a principle in another. Personal responsibility may be made a doctrinal basis, and develope into Arminianism or Pelagianism. Again, it may be discussed whether infallibility is a principle or a doctrine of the Church of Rome, and dogmatism a principle or doctrine of Christianity. Again, consideration for the poor is a doctrine of the Church considered as a religious body, and a principle when she is viewed as a political power.

Doctrines stand to principles, as the definitions to the axioms and postulates of mathematics. Thus the 15th and 17th propositions of Euclid's book I, are developments, not of the three first axioms, which are required in the proof, but of the definition of a right angle. Perhaps the perplexity, which arises in the mind of a beginner, on learning the early propositions of the second book, arises from these being more prominently exemplifications of axioms than developments of definitions. He looks for developments from the definition of the rectangle, and finds but various particular cases of the general truth, that "the whole is equal to its parts."

The science of grammar affords another instance of the existence of special laws in the formation of systems. Some languages have more elasticity than others, and greater capabilities; and the difficulty of explaining the fact cannot lead us to doubt it. There are languages, for instance, which have a capacity for compound words, which, we cannot tell why, is in matter of fact denied to others. We feel the presence of a certain character of genius in each, which determines its path and its range; and to discover and enter into it is one part of refined scholarship. And when particular writers, in consequence perhaps of some theory, tax a language beyond its powers, the failure is conspicuous. Very subtle, too, and difficult to draw out, are the principles on which depends the formation of proper names in a particular people. In works of fiction, names of titles, significant or ludicrous, must be invented for the characters introduced; and some authors excel in their fabrication, while others are equally unfortunate. Foreign novels, perhaps, attempt to frame English surnames, and signally fail; yet what every one feels to be the case, no one can analyze:

that is, our surnames are constructed on a law which is only exhibited in particular instances, and which rules their formation on certain, though subtle, determinations.

And so in philosophy, the systems of physics or morals, which go by celebrated names, proceed upon the assumption of certain conditions which are necessary for every stage of their development. The Newtonian theory of gravitation is based on certain axioms; for instance, that the fewest causes assignable for phenomena are the true ones: and the application of science to practical purposes depends upon the hypothesis that what happens to-day will happen to-morrow.

And so in military matters, the discovery of gunpowder developed the science of attack and defence in a new instrumentality. Again, it is said that when Napoleon began his career of victories, the enemy's generals pronounced that his battles were fought against rule, and that he ought not to be victorious.

So states have their respective policies, on which they move forward, and which are the conditions of their well-being. Thus it is sometimes said that the true policy of the American Union, or the law of its prosperity, is not the enlargement of its territory, but the cultivation of its internal resources. Thus Russia is said to be weak in attack, strong in defence, and to grow, not by the sword, but by diplomacy. Thus Islamism is said to be the form or life of the Ottoman, and Protestantism of the British Empire, and the admission of European ideas into the one, or of Catholic ideas into the other, to be the destruction of the respective conditions of their power. Thus Augustus and Tiberius governed by dissimulation; thus Pericles in his "Funeral Oration" draws out the principles of the Athenian commonwealth, viz., that it is carried on, not by formal and severe enactments, but by the ethical character and spontaneous energy of the people.

The political principles of Christianity, if it be right to use such words of a divine polity, are laid down for us in the Sermon on the Mount. Contrariwise to other empires, Christians conquer by yielding; they gain influence by shrinking from it; they possess the earth by renouncing it. Gibbon speaks of "the vices of the clergy" as being "to a philosophic eye far less dangerous than their virtues."[3]

Again, as to Judaism, it may be asked on what law it developed; that is, whether Mahometanism may not be considered as a sort of Judaism, as formed by the presence of a different class of influences. In this contrast between them, perhaps it may be said that the expectation of a Messiah was the principle or law which expanded the elements, almost common to Judaism with Mahometanism, into their respective characteristic shapes.

One of the points of discipline to which Wesley attached most importance was that of preaching early in the morning. This was his principle. In Georgia, he began preaching at five o'clock every day, winter and summer. "Early preaching," he said, "is the glory of the Methodists; whenever this is dropt, they will dwindle away into nothing, they have lost their first love, they are a fallen people."

Now, these instances show, as has been incidentally observed of some of them, that the destruction of the special laws or principles of a development is its corruption. Thus, as to nations, when we talk of the spirit of a people being lost, we do not mean that this or that act has been committed, or measure carried, but that certain lines of thought or conduct by which it has grown great are abandoned.

265

Thus the Roman Poets consider their State in course of ruin because its *prisci mores* and *pietas* were failing. And so we speak of countries or persons as being in a false position, inconsistent with their natural interests or real character. Judaism, again, was rejected when it rejected the Messiah.

Thus the *continuity or the alteration of the principles* on which an idea has developed is a second mark or discrimination between a true development and a corruption.

Third Note: Power of Assimilation

In the physical world, whatever has life is characterized by growth, so that in no respect to grow is to cease to live. It grows by taking into its own substance external materials; and this absorption or assimilation is completed when the materials appropriated come to belong to it or enter into its unity. Two things cannot become one, except there be a power of assimilation in one or the other. Sometimes assimilation is effected only with an effort; it is possible to die of repletion, and there are animals who lie torpid for a time under the contest between the foreign substance and the assimilating power. And different food is proper for different recipients.

This analogy may be taken to illustrate certain peculiarities in the growth or development in ideas. It is otherwise with mathematical and other abstract creations, which, like the soul itself, are solitary and self-dependent; but doctrines and views which relate to man are not placed in a void, but in the crowded world, and make way for themselves by interpenetration, and develope by absorption. Facts and opinions, which have hitherto been regarded in other relations and grouped round other centres, henceforth are gradually attracted to a new influence and subjected to a new sovereign. They are modified, laid down afresh, thrust aside, as the case may be. A new element of order and composition has come among them; and its life is proved by this capacity of expansion, without disarrangement or dissolution. An eclectic, conservative, assimilating, healing, moulding process, a unitive power, is of the essence, and a third test, of a faithful development.

Thus, a power of development is a proof of life, not only in its essay, but especially in its success; for a mere formula either does not expand or is shattered in expanding. A living idea becomes many, yet remains one.

The attempt at development shows the presence of a principle, and its success the presence of an idea. Principles stimulate thought, and an idea concentrates it.

The idea never was that throve and lasted, yet, like mathematical truth, incorporated nothing from external sources. So far from the fact of such incorporation implying corruption, as is sometimes supposed, development is a process of incorporation. Mahometanism may be in external developments scarcely more than a compound of other theologies, yet no one would deny that there has been a living idea somewhere in a religion, which has been so strong, so wide, so lasting a bond of union in the history of the world. Why it has not continued to develope after its first preaching, if this be the case, as it seems to be, cannot be determined without a greater knowledge of that religion, and how far it is merely political, how far theological, than we commonly possess.

In Christianity, opinion, while a raw material, is called philosophy or scholasticism; when a rejected refuse, it is called heresy.

Ideas are more open to an external bias in their commencement than afterwards; hence the great majority of writers who consider the Medieval Church corrupt, trace its corruption to the first four centuries, not to what are called the dark ages.

That an idea more readily coalesces with these ideas than with those does not show that it has been unduly influenced, that is, corrupted by them, but that it has an antecedent affinity to them. At least it shall be assumed here that, when the Gospels speak of virtue going out of our Lord, and of His healing with the clay which His lips had moistened, they afford instances, not of a perversion of Christianity, but of affinity to notions which were external to it; and that St. Paul was not biassed by Orientalism, though he said, after the manner of some Eastern sects, that it was "excellent not to touch a woman."

Thus in politics, too, ideas are sometimes proposed, discussed, rejected, or adopted, as it may happen, and sometimes they are shown to be unmeaning and impossible; sometimes they are true, but partially so, or in subordination to other ideas, with which, in consequence, they are as wholes or in part incorporated, as far as these have affinities to them, the power to incorporate being thus recognized as a property of life. Mr. Bentham's system was an attempt to make the circle of legal and moral truths developments of certain principles of his own;—those principles of his may, if it so happen, prove unequal to the weight of truths which are eternal, and the system founded on them may break into pieces; or again, a State may absorb certain of them, for which it has affinity, that is, it may develope in Benthamism, yet remain in substance what it was before. In the history of the French Revolution we read of many middle parties, who attempted to form theories of constitutions short of those which they would call extreme, and successively failed from the want of power or reality in their characteristic ideas. The Semi-arians attempted a middle way between orthodoxy and heresy, but could not stand their ground; at length part fell into Macedonianism, and part joined the Church.

The stronger and more living is an idea, that is, the more powerful hold it exercises on the minds of men, the more able is it to dispense with safeguards, and trust to itself against the danger of corruption. As strong frames exult in their agility, and healthy constitutions throw off ailments, so parties or schools that live can afford to be rash, and will sometimes be betrayed into extravagances, yet are brought right by their inherent vigour. On the other hand, unreal systems are commonly decent externally. Forms, subscriptions, or Articles of religion are indispensable when the principle of life is weakly. Thus Presbyterianism has maintained its original theology in Scotland where legal subscriptions are enforced, while it has run into Arianism or Unitarianism where that protection is away. We have yet to see whether the Free Kirk can keep its present theological ground. The Church of Rome can consult expedience more freely than other bodies, as trusting to her living tradition, and is sometimes thought to disregard principle and scruple, when she is but dispensing with forms. Thus Saints are often characterized by acts which are no pattern for others; and the most gifted men are, by reason of their very gifts, sometimes led into fatal inadvertences. Hence vows are the wise defence of unstable virtue, and general rules the refuge of feeble authority.

And so much may suffice on the *unitive power* of faith-

ful developments, which constitutes their third characteristic.

Fourth Note: Logical Sequence

Logic is the organization of thought, and, as being such,
is a security for the faithfulness of intellectual developments; and the necessity of using it is undeniable as far as
this, that its rules must not be transgressed. That it is not
brought into exercise in every instance of doctrinal development is owing to the varieties of mental constitution,
whether in communities or in individuals, with whom
great truths or seeming truths are lodged. The question
indeed may be asked whether a development can be other
in any case than a logical operation; but, if by this is meant
a conscious reasoning from premisses to conclusion, of
course the answer must be in the negative. An idea under
one or other of its aspects grows in the mind by remaining
there; it becomes familiar and distinct, and is viewed in its
relations; it leads to other aspects, and these again to others,
subtle, recondite, original, according to the character, intellectual and moral, of the recipient; and thus a body of
thought is gradually formed without his recognizing what
is going on within him. And all this while, or at least from
time to time, external circumstances elicit into formal statement the thoughts which are coming into being in the
depths of his mind; and soon he has to begin to defend
them; and then again a further process must take place, of
analyzing his statements and ascertaining their dependence
one on another. And thus he is led to regard as consequences, and to trace to principles, what hitherto he has
discerned by a moral perception, and adopted on sym-

pathy; and logic is brought in to arrange and inculcate what no science was employed in gaining.

And so in the same way, such intellectual processes, as are carried on silently and spontaneously in the mind of a party or school, of necessity come to light at a later date, and are recognized, and their issues are scientifically arranged. And then logic has the further function of propagation; analogy, the nature of the case, antecedent probability, application of principles, congruity, expedience, being some of the methods of proof by which the development is continued from mind to mind and established in the faith of the community.

Yet even then the analysis is not made on a principle, or with any view to its whole course and finished results. Each argument is brought for an immediate purpose; minds develope step by step, without looking behind them or anticipating their goal, and without either intention or promise of forming a system. Afterwards, however, this logical character which the whole wears becomes a test that the process has been a true development, not a perversion or corruption, from its evident naturalness; and in some cases from the gravity, distinctness, precision, and majesty of its advance, and the harmony of its proportions, like the tall growth, and graceful branching, and rich foliage, of some vegetable production.

The process of development, thus capable of a logical expression, has sometimes been invidiously spoken of as rationalism and contrasted with faith. But, though a particular doctrine or opinion which is subjected to development may happen to be rationalistic, and, as is the original, such are its results: and though we may develope erroneously, that is, reason incorrectly, yet the developing itself

271

as little deserves that imputation in any case, as an inquiry into an historical fact, which we do not thereby make but ascertain,—for instance, whether or not St. Mark wrote his Gospel with St. Matthew before him, or whether Solomon brought his merchandise from Tartessus or some Indian port. Rationalism is the exercise of reason instead of faith in matters of faith; but one does not see how it can be faith to adopt the premisses, and unbelief to accept the conclusion.

At the same time it may be granted that the spontaneous process which goes on within the mind itself is higher and choicer than that which is logical; for the latter, being scientific, is common property, and can be taken and made use of by minds who are personally strangers, in any true sense, both to the ideas in question and to their development.

Thus, the holy Apostles would without words know all the truths concerning the high doctrines of theology, which controversialists after them have piously and charitably reduced to formulae, and developed through argument. Thus, St. Justin or St. Irenaeus might be without any digested idea of Purgatory or Original Sin, yet have an intense feeling, which they had not defined or located, both of the fault of our first nature and the responsibilities of our nature regenerate. Thus St. Anthony said to the philosophers who came to mock him, "He whose mind is in health does not need letters"; and St. Ignatius Loyola, while yet an unlearned neophyte, was favoured with transcendent perceptions of the Holy Trinity during his penance at Manresa. Thus St. Anthanasius himself is more powerful in statement and exposition than in proof; while in Bellarmine we find the whole series of doctrines carefully drawn out, duly adjusted with one another, and exactly analyzed one by one.

There is a certain continuous advance and determinate path which belong to the history of a doctrine, policy, or institution, and which impress upon the common sense of mankind, that what it ultimately becomes is the issue of what it was at first. This sentiment is expressed in the proverb, not limited to Latin, *Exitus acta probat;* and is sanctioned by Divine wisdom, when, warning us against false prophets, it says, "Ye shall know them by their fruits."

A doctrine, then, professed in its mature years by a philosophy or religion, is likely to be a true development, not a corruption, in proportion as it seems to be the *logical issue* of its original teaching.

Fifth Note: Anticipation of Its Future

Since, when an idea is living, that is, influential and effective, it is sure to develope according to its own nature, and the tendencies, which are carried out on the long run, may under favourable circumstances show themselves early as well as late, and logic is the same in all ages, instances of a development which is to come, though vague and isolated, may occur from the very first, though a lapse of time be necessary to bring them to perfection. And since developments are in great measure only aspects of the idea from which they proceed, and all of them are natural consequences of it, it is often a matter of accident in what order they are carried out in individual minds; and it is in no wise strange that here and there definite specimens of advanced teaching should very early occur, which in the historical course are not found till a late date. The fact, then, of such early or recurring intimations of tendencies which afterwards are fully realized, is a sort of evidence that those later and more systematic fulfilments are only in accordance with the original idea.

Nothing is more common, for instance, than accounts or legends of the anticipations, which great men have given in boyhood of the bent of their minds, as afterwards displayed in their history; so much so that the popular expectation has sometimes led to the invention of them. The child Cyrus mimics a despot's power, and St. Athanasius is elected Bishop by his playfellows.

It is noticeable that in the eleventh century, when the Russians were but pirates upon the Black Sea, Constantinople was their aim; and that a prophesy was in circulation in that city that they should one day gain possession of it.

In the reign of James the First, we have an observable anticipation of the system of influence in the management of political parties, which was developed by Sir R. Walpole a century afterwards. This attempt is traced by a living writer to the ingenuity of Lord Bacon. "He submitted to the King that there were expedients for more judiciously managing a House of Commons; . . . that much might be done by fore-thought towards filling the House with well-affected persons, winning or blinding the lawyers . . . and drawing the chief constituent bodies of the assembly, the country gentlemen, the merchants, the courtiers, to act for the King's advantage; that it would be expedient to tender voluntarily certain graces and modifications of the King's prerogative," etc.[4] The writer adds, "This circumstance, like several others in the present reign, is curious, as it shows the rise of a systematic parliamentary influence, which was one day to become the mainspring of government."

Arcesilas and Carneades, the founders of the later Academy, are known to have innovated on the Platonic doctrine by inculcating a universal scepticism; and they did this, as if on the authority of Socrates, who had adopted the method of *ironia* against the Sophists, on their profession to know everything. This, of course, was an insufficient plea. However, could it be shown that Socrates did on one or two occasions evidence deliberate doubts on the great principles of theism or morals, would any one deny that the innovation in question had grounds for being considered a true development, not a corruption?

Another evidence, then, of the faithfulness of an ultimate development is its *definite anticipation* at an early period in the history of the idea to which it belongs.

Sixth Note: Conservative Action upon Its Past

As developments which are preceded by definite indications have a fair presumption in their favour, so those which do but contradict and reverse the course of doctrine which has been developed before them, and out of which they spring, are certainly corrupt; for a corruption is a development in that very stage in which it ceases to illustrate, and begins to disturb, the acquisitions gained in its previous history.

It is the rule of creation, or rather of the phenomena which it presents, that life passes on to its termination by a gradual, imperceptible course of change. There is ever a maximum in earthly excellence, and the operation of the same causes which made things great makes them small again. Weakness is but the resulting product of power.

Events move in cycles; all things come round, "the sun ariseth and goeth down, and hasteth to his place where he arose." Flowers first bloom, and then fade; fruit ripens and decays. The fermenting process, unless stopped at the due point, corrupts the liquor which it has created. The grace of spring, the richness of autumn are but for a moment, and worldly moralists bid us *Carpe diem*, for we shall have no second opportunity. Virtue seems to lie in a mean, between vice and vice; and as it grew out of imperfection, so to grow into enormity. There is a limit to human knowledge, and both sacred and profane writers witness that overwisdom is folly. And in the political world states rise and fall, the instruments of their aggrandizement becoming the weapons of their destruction. And hence the frequent ethical maxims, such as, "*Ne quid nimis,*" "*Medio tutissimus,*" "Vaulting ambition," which seem to imply that too much of what is good is evil.

So great a paradox of course cannot be maintained as that truth literally leads to falsehood, or that there can be an excess of virtue; but the appearance of things and the popular language about them will at least serve us in obtaining an additional test for the discrimination of a *bona fide* development of an idea from its corruption.

A true development, then, may be described as one which is conservative of the course of antecedent developments being really those antecedents and something besides them: it is an addition which illustrates, not obscures, corroborates, not corrects, the body of thought from which it proceeds; and this is its characteristic as contrasted with a corruption.

For instance, a gradual conversion from a false to a true

religion, plainly, has much of the character of a continuous process, or a development, in the mind itself, even when the two religions, which are the limits of its course, are antagonists. Now let it be observed, that such a change consists in addition and increase chiefly, not in destruction. "True religion is the summit and perfection of false religions; it combines in one whatever there is of good and true separately remaining in each. And in like manner the Catholic Creed is for the most part the combination of separate truths, which heretics have divided among themselves, and err in dividing. So that, in matter of fact, if a religious mind were educated in and sincerely attached to some form of heathenism or heresy, and then were brought under the light of truth, it would be drawn off from error into the truth, not by losing what it had, but by gaining what it had not, not by being unclothed, but by being 'clothed upon,' 'that mortality may be swallowed up of life.' That same principle of faith which attaches it at first to the wrong doctrine would attach it to the truth; and that portion of its original doctrine, which was to be cast off as absolutely false, would not be directly rejected, but indirectly, *in* the reception of the truth which is its opposite. True conversion is ever of a positive, not a negative character."[5]

Such too is the theory of the Fathers as regards the doctrines fixed by Councils, as is instanced in the language of St. Leo. "To be seeking for what has been disclosed, to reconsider what has been finished, to tear up what has been laid down, what is this but to be unthankful for what is gained?"[6] Vincentius of Lerins, in like manner, speaks of the development of Christian doctrine, as *profectus fidei, non permutatio.*[7] And so as regards the Jewish Law, our

Lord said that He came "not to destroy, but to fulfil."

And thus a sixth test of a true development is that it is of a *tendency conservative* of what has gone before it.

Seventh Note: Chronic Vigour

Since the corruption of an idea, as far as the appearance goes, is a sort of accident or affection of its development, being the end of a course, and a transition-state leading to a crisis, it is, as has been observed above, a brief and rapid process. While ideas live in men's minds, they are ever enlarging into fuller development: they will not be stationary in their corruption any more than before it; and dissolution is that further state to which corruption tends. Corruption cannot, therefore, be of long standing; and thus *duration* is another test of a faithful development.

Si gravis, brevis; si longus, levis; is the Stoical topic of consolation under pain; and of a number of disorders it can even be said, The worse, the shorter.

Sober men are indisposed to change in civil matters, and fear reforms and innovations, lest, if they go a little too far, they should at once run on to some great calamities before a remedy can be applied. The chance of a slow corruption does not strike them. Revolutions are generally violent and swift; now, in fact, they are the course of a corruption.

The course of heresies is always short; it is an intermediate state between life and death, or what is like death; or, if it does not result in death, it is resolved into some new, perhaps opposite, course of error, which lays no claim to be connected with it. And in this way indeed, but in this way only, an heretical principle will continue in life many years, first running one way, then another.

The abounding of iniquity is the token of the end approaching; the faithful in consequence cry out, How long? as if delay opposed reason as well as patience. Three years and a half are to complete the reign of Anti-christ.

Nor is it any real objection that the world is ever corrupt, and yet, in spite of this, evil does not fill up its measure and overflow; for this arises from the external counteractions of truth and virtue, which bear it back; let the Church be removed, and the world will soon come to its end.

And so again, if the chosen people age after age became worse and worse, till there was no recovery, still their course of evil was continually broken by reformations, and was thrown back upon a less advanced stage of declension.

It is true that decay, which is one form of corruption, is slow; but decay is a state in which there is no violent or vigorous action at all, whether of a conservative or a destructive character, the hostile influence being powerful enough to enfeeble the functions of life, but not to quicken its own process. And thus we see opinions, usages, and systems, which are of venerable and imposing aspect, but which have no soundness within them, and keep together from a habit of consistence, or from dependence on political institutions; or they become almost peculiarities of a country, or the habits of a race, or the fashions of society. And then, at length, perhaps, they go off suddenly and die out under the first rough influence from without. Such are the superstitions which pervade a population, like some ingrained dye or inveterate odour, and which at length come to an end, because nothing lasts for ever, but which run no course, and have no history; such was the established paganism of classical times, which was the fit subject of persecution, for its first breath made it crumble and disappear.

Such apparently is the state of the Nestorian and Mono-physite communions; such might have been the condition of Christianity had it been absorbed by the feudalism of the middle ages; such too is that Protestantism, or (as it sometimes calls itself) attachment to the Establishment, which is not unfrequently the boast of the respectable and wealthy among ourselves.

Whether Mahometanism external to Christendom, and the Greek Church within it, fall under this description is yet to be seen. Circumstances can be imagined which would even now rouse the fanaticism of the Moslem; and the Russian despotism does not meddle with the usages, though it may domineer over the priesthood, of the national religion.

Thus, while a corruption is distinguished from decay by its energetic action, it is distinguished from a development by its *transitory character*.

Such are seven out of various Notes, which may be assigned, of fidelity in the development of an idea. The point to be ascertained is the unity and identity of the idea with itself through all stages of its development from first to last, and these are seven tokens that it may rightly be accounted one and the same all along. To guarantee its own substantial unity, it must be seen to be one in type, one in its system of principles, one in its unitive power towards externals, one in its logical consecutiveness, one in the witness of its early phases to its later, one in the protection which its later extend to its earlier, and one in its union of vigour with continuance, that is, in its tenacity.

CHAPTER XXIII

HOW ARISTOTELIAN PHILOSOPHY DEVELOPS₁

WHAT DO WE mean by a man's being *master* of any subject, say science? What is meant by *knowing* the Aristotelic philosophy? Does it mean that he has before his mind always every doctrinal statement, every sentiment, opinion, intellectual and moral tendency of Aristotle? This is impossible. Not Aristotle himself, no human mind, can have a host of thoughts present to it at once. The philosophy, as a system, is stored in the *memory*, deeply rooted there if you will, but still in the memory, and is brought out according to the occasion. A learned Aristotelian is one who can answer any whatever philosophical questions in the way that Aristotle would have answered them. If they are questions which could not occur in Aristotle's age, he still answers them; and by two means, by the instinct which a thorough Aristotelic intellect, the habit set up in his mind, possesses; next, by never-swerving processes of ratiocination. And as a thoroughly grounded anatomist knows whether the smallest bone or bit of bone shown him is human or not, so the perfect Aristotelian will know whether this or that opinion, sentiment, conjecture, generalization, negation, is Aristotelic or not.

In one respect he knows more than Aristotle; because, in new emergencies after the time of Aristotle, he *can* and *does*

answer what Aristotle would have answered, but for want
of the opportunity did not. There is another point of view
in which he seems to have the advantage of Aristotle,
though it is no real superiority, viz. that, from the neces-
sities of the interval between Aristotle and himself, there
has been the growth of a technology, a scientific vocabulary, which makes the philosophy easier to remember, easier
to communicate and to defend—nay, which enables him to
view it as a whole, *per modum unius*, with a grasp of mind
which would be superior to the view taken of it by any
equal intellect, or in other words, *caeteribus paribus*, and,
if not more vigorous than Aristotle's grasp, because of the
superiority of Aristotle's vigorous creative intellect.

Such a technology with its explanations bears up his intellect, as corks a swimmer, as a pole a rope dancer, as a belt
a runner, and keeps him from accidental mistakes, momentary slips, from which Aristotle's more vigorous perspica-
cious intellect was the safeguard. It keeps his learning well
about him, and at command at any moment, as being a sort
of *memoria technica*, both as embodying elementary principles, and as condensing the tradition of a thousand questions and answers, of controversies and resolutions of them,
which have taken place between Aristotle's time and his.
Such a scientific apparatus has its evils. For common minds,
instead of throwing themselves into the genius and animus
of the philosophy, will make the technology the beginning
and end of their study; and will be formalists, pedants,
bigots, and will be as little made philosophers by their
verbal knowledge, as boys can swim because they have
corks or run because they have belts. I am not concerned
with an inconvenience which is accidental and indirect, and
no fault of technology itself:—its advantage is obvious.

CHAPTER XXIV

THE CATHOLIC TRADITION IN PHILOSOPHY[1]

I HOPE IT will not seem to your Holiness an intrusion upon your time if I address to you a few lines to thank you for the very seasonable and important encyclical [*Aeterni Patris*] which you bestowed upon us. All good Catholics must feel it a first necessity that the intellectual exercises, without which the Church cannot fulfil her supernatural mission duly, should be founded upon broad as well as true principles, that the mental creations of her theologians, and of her controversialists and pastors should be grafted on the Catholic tradition of philosophy, and should not start from a novel and simply original tradition, but should be substantially one with the teaching of St. Athanasius, St. Augustine, St. Anselm, and St. Thomas, as those great doctors in turn are one with each other.

At a time when there is so much cultivation of mind, so much intellectual excitement, so many new views, true and false, and so much temptation to overstep the old truth, we need just what your Holiness has supplied us with in your recent pastoral, and I hope my own personal gratitude for your wise and seasonable act may be taken by your Holiness as my apology, if I seem to outstep the limits of modesty and propriety in addressing this letter to your Holiness. [This letter was drafted but not sent to Pope Leo XIII.]

CHAPTER XXV

GALILEO, REVELATION, AND THE
EDUCATED MAN[1]

ONE OF THE characteristics of the day is the renewal of that
collision between men of science and believers in Revelation, and of that uneasiness in the public mind as to its
results, which are found in the history of the 17th century.
Then Galileo raised the jealousy of Catholics in Italy; and
now in England the religious portion of the community,
Catholic or not, is startled at the discoveries or speculations
of geologists, natural historians [i.e., biologists] and lin-
guists. Of course I am speaking, as regards both dates, of
the educated classes, of those whose minds have been sufficiently opened to understand the nature of proof, who have
a right to ask questions and to weigh the answers given to
them. It was of such, we must reasonably suppose, that
Father Commissary [of the Holy Office] was tender in
1637, and to such he alluded in his conversation with
Galileo, as he took him in his carriage of the Holy Office.
"As we went along," says Galileo, "he put many questions
to me, and showed an earnestness that I should repair *the
scandal, which I had given to the whole of Italy,* by maintaining the opinion of the motion of the earth; and for all
the solid and mathematical reasons which I presented to

him, he did but reply to me: 'Terra autem in aeternum stabit,' because 'Terra autem in aeternum stat,' as Scripture says."

There could not be a greater shock to religious minds of that day than Galileo's doctrine, whether they at once rejected it as contrary to the faith, or listened to the arguments by which he enforced it. The feeling was strong enough to effect Galileo's compulsory recantation, though a Pope was then on the throne who was personally friendly to him. Two Sacred Congregations represented the popular voice and passed decrees against the philosophers, which were in force down to the years 1822 and 1837 [when Galileo was taken off the Index].

Such an alarm never can occur again, for the very reason that it has occurred once. At least, for myself, I can say that, had I been brought up in the belief of the immobility of the earth as though a dogma of Revelation, and had associated it in my mind with the incommunicable dignity of man among created beings, with the destinies of the human race, with the locality of purgatory and hell, and other Christian doctrines, and then for the first time had heard of Galileo's thesis, and, moreover, had the prospect held out to me that perhaps there were myriads of globes like our own, all filled with rational creatures as worthy of the Creator's regard as we are, I should have been at once indignant at its presumption and frightened at its speciousness, as I never can be, at any parallel novelties in other human sciences bearing on religion; no, not though I found probable reasons for thinking that the first chapters of Genesis were not of an economical character, that there was a pre-Adamite race of rational animals, or that we are now 20,000 years from Noe. For that past controversy and its issue have taught me beyond all mistake, that men of the greatest theological knowledge may firmly believe that scientific conclusions are contrary to the Word of God, when they are not so, and pronounce that to be heresy which is truth. It has taught me, that Scripture is not inspired to convey mere secular knowledge, whether about the heaven, or the earth, or the race of man; and that I need not fear for Revelation whatever truths may be brought to light by means of observation and experience out of the world of phenomena which environ us.

And I seem to myself here to be speaking under the protection and sanction of the Sacred Congregation of the Index itself, which has since the time of Galileo prescribed to itself a line of action, indication of its fearlessness of any results which may happen to religion from physical sciences. Many books have since that time been placed upon its prohibited catalogue, the works of (humanly speaking) distinguished men, the works of Morkof (?), Puffendorf, Brucker, Ranke, Hallam, Macaulay and Mill; but I find no one (?) of physical celebrity, unless such writers as Dr. Erasmus Darwin, Bonucci, Klee and Burdach are so to be accounted.[2] One great lesson surely, if no other, is taught by the history of theological controversy since the 16th century: moderation to the assailant, equanimity to the assailed, and that as regards geological and ethnological conclusions as well as astronomical.

But there is more than this to give us confidence in this matter. Consider then the case before us: Galileo on his knees abjured the heresy that the earth moved; but the course of human thought, of observation, investigation and induction, could not be stayed; it went on and had its way. It penetrated and ran through the Catholic world as well as through the nations external to it. And then at length, in our own day, the doctrine, which was the subject of it, was found to be so harmless in a religious point of view, that the books advocating it were taken off the Index, and the prohibition to print and publish the like was withdrawn.

But the course of investigation has gone further, and done or is now even doing some positive service to the cause which it was accused of opposing. It is in the way to restore to the earth that prerogative and pre-eminence in the creation which it was thought to compromise. Thus investigation, which Catholics would have suppressed as dangerous, when, in spite of them, it has had its course, results in conclusions favourable to their cause. How little then need we fear from the free exercise of reason! How injurious is the suspicion entertained of it by religious men! How true it is that *nature* and *revelation* are nothing but two separate communications from the same infinite Truth!

Nor is this all. Much has been said of late years of the dangerous tendency of geological speculations or researches.[3] Well, what harm they have done to the Christian cause, others must say who are more qualified than I am to determine; but on one point, that is the point before us [of whether other planets are inhabited by rational beings], I observe it is acting on the side of Christian belief. In answer to the supposed improbability of there being planets with rational inhabitants, considering that our globe has such, geology teaches us that, in fact, whatever our religion may accidentally teach us to hope or fear about other worlds, in this world at least, long ages past, we had either no inhabitants at all, or none but those rude and vast brutal forms, which could perform no intelligent homage and service to their Creator. Thus one order of spiritual researches

287

bears upon another, and that in the interest or service of Christianity; and supposing, as some persons seem to believe in their hearts, that these researches are all in the hands of the enemy of God, we have the observable phenomenon of Satan casting out Satan and restoring the balance of physical arguments in favour of Revelation.

Now let us suppose that the influences which were in the ascendant throughout Italy in 1637 had succeeded in repressing any free investigation on the question of the motion of the earth. The mind of the educated class would have not the less felt that it *was* a question, and would have been haunted, and would have been poisoned, by the misgiving that there was some real danger to Revelation in the investigation; for otherwise the ecclesiastical authorities would not have forbidden it. There would have been in the Catholic community a mass of irritated, ill-tempered, feverish and festering suspicion, engendering general scepticism and hatred of the priesthood, and relieving itself in a sort of tacit freemasonry, of which secret societies are the development, and then in sudden outbreaks perhaps of violence and blasphemy. Protestantism is a dismal evil; but in this respect Providence has overruled it for good. It has, by allowing free inquiry in science, destroyed a bugbear, and thereby saved Catholics themselves so far from the misery of hollow profession and secret infidelity.

I think, then, I must say distinctly that I have no sympathy at all in that policy, which will not look difficulties or apparent difficulties in the face, and puts off the evil day of considering them as long as it can. It is the way of politicians who live from hand to mouth, only careful that the existing state of things should last their time. If I find that scientific inquiries are running counter against certain theological opinions, it is not expedient to refuse to examine whether those opinions are well founded, merely because those inquiries have not yet reached their issue or attained a triumphant success.

The history of Galileo is the proof of it. Are we not at a disadvantage as regards that history? and why? Why, except because our theologians, instead of cautiously examining what Scripture, that is the Written Word of God, really said, thought it better to put down with a high hand the astronomical views which were opposed to its popular interpretation? The contrary course was pursued in our own day; but what is not against the faith now, was not against the faith three centuries ago; yet Galileo was forced to pronounce his opinion a heresy. It might not indeed have been prudent to have done in 1637 what was done in 1822; but, though in the former date it might have been unjustifiable to allow the free publication of his treatises with the sanction of the Church, that does not show that it was justifiable to pronounce that they were against the faith and to enforce their abjuration.

I am not certain that I might not go further and advocate the full liberty to teach the motion of the earth, as a philosophical truth, not only now, but even three centuries ago. The Father Commissary said, it was a scandal to the whole of Italy; that is, I suppose, an offence, a shock, a perplexity. This might be, but there was a class, whose claims to consideration are too little regarded now, and were passed over then. I mean the educated class; to them the prohibition would be a real scandal in the true meaning of the world, an occasion of their falling.

289

Men who have sharpened their intellects by exercise and study anticipate the conclusions of the many by some centuries. If the tone of public opinion in 1822 called for a withdrawal of the prohibition at Trent of the earth's motion, the condition of the able and educated called for it in Galileo's age; and it is as clear to me that their spiritual state ought to be consulted for, as it is difficult to say why in fact it so often is not. They are to be tenderly regarded for their own sake; they are to be respected and conciliated for the sake of their influence upon other classes.[4] I cannot help feeling that, in high circles, the Church is sometimes looked upon as made up of the hierarchy and the poor, and that the educated portion, men and women, are viewed as a difficulty, as incumbrance, as the seat and source of heresy, as almost aliens to the Catholic body, whom it would be a great gain, if possible, to annihilate.

For all those reasons, I cannot agree with those who would have us stand by what is probably or possible erroneous, as if it were dogma, till it is acknowledged on all hands, by the force of demonstrations, to be actually such. If she [the Catholic Church] affirms, as I do not think she will affirm, that every thing was made and finished in a moment, though Scripture seems to say otherwise, and though science seems to prove otherwise, I affirm it too, and with an inward and sincere assent. And, as Her word is to believed, so Her command is to be obeyed. I am as willing then to be silenced on doctrinal matters which are not of faith as to be taught in matters which are. It would be nothing else than a great gain to be rid of the anxiety which haunts a person circumstanced as I am, lest, by keeping silence on points as that on which I have begun to speak, I should perchance be hiding my talent in a napkin. I should welcome the authority which by its decision allowed me to turn my mind to subjects more congenial to it. On the other hand, it is legitimate authority alone which I have any warrant to recognize; as to the *ipse dixit* of individual divines, I have long essayed to divest myself of what spiritual writers call "human respect." I am indeed too old to be frightened, and my past has set loose my future.

CHAPTER XXVI

THE ISOLATION OF SCIENCE, LITERATURE, AND RELIGION[1]

[NATURALISTIC EDUCATORS] trust to the influence of the modern sciences on what may be called the Imagination. When any thing, which comes before us, is very unlike what we commonly experience, we consider it on that account untrue; not because it really shocks our reason as improbable, but because it startles our imagination as strange. Now, Revelation presents to us a perfectly different aspect of the universe from that presented by the Sciences. The two informations are like the distinct subjects represented by the lines of the same drawing, which, accordingly as they are read on their concave or convex side, exhibit to us now a group of trees with branches and leaves, and now human faces hid amid the leaves, or some majestic figures standing out from the branches. Thus is faith opposed to sight: it is parallel to the contrast afforded by plane astronomy and physical; plane, in accordance with our senses, discourses of the sun's rising and setting, while physical, in accordance with our reason, asserts, on the contrary, that the sun is all but stationary, and that it is the earth that moves. This is what is meant by saying that truth lies in a well; phenomena are no measure of fact; *prima facie* representations, which we receive from without, do not reach to the real state of things, or put them before us simply as they are.

While, then, Reason and Revelation are consistent in fact, they often are inconsistent in appearance; and this seeming discordance acts most keenly and alarmingly on the Imagination, and may suddenly expose a man to the temptation, and even hurry him on to the commission, of definite acts of unbelief, in which reason itself really does not come into exercise at all. I mean, let a person devote himself to the studies of the day; let him be taught by the astronomer that our sun is but one of a million central luminaries, and our earth but one of ten million globes moving in space; let him learn from the geologist that on that globe of ours enormous revolutions have been in progress through innumerable ages; let him be told by the comparative anatomist of the minutely arranged system of organized nature; by the chemist and physicist, of the peremptory yet intricate laws to which nature, organized and inorganic, is subjected; by the ethnologist, of the originals, and ramifications, and varieties, and fortunes of nations; by the antiquarian [v.g., archeologist and anthropologist], of old cities disinterred, and primitive countries laid bare, with the specific forms of human society once existing; by the linguist, of the slow formation and development of languages; by the psychologist, the physiologist, and the economist, of the subtle, complicated structure of the breathing, energetic, restless world of men; I say, let him take in and master the vastness of the view thus afforded him of Nature, its infinite complexity, its awful comprehensiveness, and its diversified yet harmonious colouring; and then, when he has for years drunk in and fed upon this vision, let him turn round to peruse the inspired records, or listen to the authoritative teaching of Revelation, the book of Genesis, or the warnings and prophecies of the Gospels, or the Symbolum *Quicumque,* or the Life of St. Antony or St. Hilarion, and he may certainly experience a most distressing revulsion of feeling,— not that his reason really deduces any thing from his much loved studies contrary to the faith, but that his imagination is bewildered, and swims with the sense of the ineffable distance of that faith from the view of things which is familiar to him, with its strangeness, and then again its rude simplicity, as he considers it, and its apparent poverty contrasted with the exuberant life and reality of his own world.[2]

In matter of fact, as Science is the reflection of Nature, so is Literature also—the one, of Nature physical, the other, of Nature moral and social. Circumstances, such as locality, period, language, seem to make little or no difference in the character of Literature, as such; on the whole, all Literatures are one; they are the voices of the natural man.

I wish this were all that had to be said to the disadvantage of Literature; but while Nature physical remains fixed in its laws, Nature moral and social has a will of its own, is self-governed, and never remains any long while in that state from which it started into action. Man will never continue in a mere state of innocence; he is sure to sin, and his literature will be the expression of his sin, and this whether he be heathen or Christian. Christianity has thrown gleams of light on him and his literature; but as it has not converted him, but only certain choice specimens of him, so it has not changed the characters of his mind or of his history; his literature is either what it was, or worse than what it was, in proportion as there has been an abuse of knowledge granted and a rejection of truth. On the whole, then, I think it will be found, and ever found, as a matter of course, that Literature, as such, no matter of what nation, is the science or history, partly and at best of the natural man, partly of man in rebellion.

Here then, I say, you are involved in a difficulty greater than that which besets the cultivation of Science; for, if Physical Science be dangerous, as I have said, it is dangerous, because it necessarily ignores the idea of moral evil; but Literature is open to the more grievous imputation of recognizing and understanding it too well. Some one will say to me perhaps: "Our youth shall not be corrupted. We will dispense with all general or national Literature whatever, if it be so exceptionable; we will have a Christian Literature of our own, as pure, as true, as the Jewish." You cannot have it:—I do not say you cannot form a select literature for the young, nay, even for the middle or lower classes; this is another matter altogether: I am speaking of University Education, which implies an extended range of reading, which has to deal with standard works of genius, or what are called the *classics* of a language: and I say, from the nature of the case, if Literature is to be made a study of human nature, you cannot have a Christian Literature. It is a contradiction in terms to attempt a sinless Literature of sinful man. You may gather together something very great and high, something higher than any Literature ever was; and when you have done so, you will find that it is not Literature at all. You will have simply left the delineation of man, as such, and have substituted for it, as far as you have had any thing to substitute, that of man, as he is or might be, under certain special advantages.

Give up the study of man, as such, if so it must be; but say you do so. Do not say you are studying him, his history, his mind and his heart, when you are studying something else. Man is a being of genius, passion, intellect, conscience, power. He exercises these various gifts in various ways, in great deeds, in great thoughts, in heroic acts, in hateful crimes. He founds states, he fights battles, he builds cities, he ploughs the forest, he subdues the elements, he rules his kind. He creates vast ideas, and influences many generations. He takes a thousand shapes, and undergoes a thousand fortunes. Literature records them all to the life,

> Quicquid agunt homines, votum, timor, ira, voluptas.
> Gaudia, discursus.

He pours out his fervid soul in poetry; he sways to and fro, he soars, he dives, in his restless speculations; his lips drop eloquence; he touches the canvas, and it glows with beauty; he sweeps the strings, and they thrill with an ecstatic meaning. He looks back into himself, and he reads his own thoughts, and notes them down; he looks out into the universe, and tells over and celebrates the elements and principles of which it is the product.

Such is man: put him aside, keep him before you; but, whatever you do, do not take him for what he is not, for something more divine and sacred, for man regenerate. Nay, beware of showing God's grace and its work at such disadvantage as to make the few whom it has thoroughly influenced compete in intellect with the vast multitude who either have it not, or use it ill. The elect are few to choose out of, and the world is inexhaustible. From the first, Jabel and Tubalcain, Nimrod "the stout hunter," the learning of the Pharaohs, and the wisdom of the East country, are of the world. Every now and then they are rivalled by a Solomon or a Beseleel, but the *habitat* of natural gifts is the natural man. The Church may use them, she cannot at her will originate them. Not till the whole human race is made new will its literature be pure and true. Possible of course it is in idea, for nature, inspired by heavenly grace, to exhibit itself on a large scale, in an originality of thought or action, even far beyond what the world's literature has recorded or exemplified; but, if you would in fact have a literature of saints, first of all have a nation of them.

What is a clearer proof of the truth of all this than the structure of the Inspired Word itself? It is undeniably *not* the reflection or picture of the many, but of the few; it is no picture of life, but an anticipation of death and judgment. Human literature is about all things, grave or gay, painful or pleasant; but the Inspired Word views them only in one aspect, and as they tend to one scope. It gives us little insight into the fertile developments of mind; it has no terms in its vocabulary to express with exactness the intellect and its separate faculties: it knows nothing of genius, fancy, wit, invention, presence of mind, resource. It does not discourse of empire, commerce, enterprise, learning, philosophy, or the fine arts. Slightly too does it touch on the more simple and innocent courses of nature and their reward. Little does it say of those temporal blessings which rest upon our worldly occupations, and make them easy; of the blessings which we derive from the sunshine day and the serene night, from the succession of the seasons, and the produce of the earth. Little about our recreations and our daily domestic comforts; little about the ordinary occasions of festivity and mirth, which sweeten human life; and nothing at all about various pursuits or amusements, which it would be going too much into detail to mention. We read indeed of the feast when Isaac was weaned, and of Jacob's courtship,

297

and of the religious merry-makings of holy Job; but exceptions, such as these, do but remind us what might be in Scripture, and is not. If then by Literature is meant the manifestation of human nature in human language, you will seek for it in vain except in the world. Put up with it, as it is, or do not pretend to cultivate it; take things as they are, not as you could wish them.

Nay, I am obliged to go further still; even if we could, still we should be shrinking from our plain duty, did we leave out Literature from Education. For why do we educate, except to prepare for the world? Why do we cultivate the intellect of the many beyond the first elements of knowledge, except for this world? Will it be much matter in the world to come whether our bodily health or whether our intellectual strength was more or less, except of course as this world is in all its circumstances a trial for the next? If then a University is a direct preparation for this world, let it be what it professes. It is not a Convent, it is not a Seminary; it is a place to fit men of the world for the world. We cannot possibly keep them from plunging into the world, with all its ways and principles and maxims, when their time comes; but we can prepare them against what is inevitable; and it is not the way to learn to swim in troubled waters, never to have gone into them.

Proscribe (I do not merely say particular authors, particular works, particular passages) but Secular Literature as such; cut out from your class books all broad manifestations of the natural man; and those manifestations are waiting for your pupil's benefit at the very doors of your lecture room in living and breathing substance. They will meet him there in all the charm of novelty, and all the fascination of genius or of amiableness. To-day a pupil, to-morrow a mem-

298

ber of the great world: to-day confined to the Lives of the Saints, to-morrow thrown upon Babel;—thrown on Babel, without the honest indulgence of wit and humour and imagination having ever been permitted to him, without any fastidiousness of taste wrought into him, without any rule given him for discriminating "the precious from the vile," beauty from sin, the truth from the sophistry of na-ture, what is innocent from what is poison. You have refused him the masters of human thought, who would in some sense have educated him, because of their incidental cor-ruption: you have shut up from him those whose thoughts strike home to our hearts, whose words are proverbs, whose names are indigenous to all the world, who are the standard of their mother tongue, and the pride and boast of their countrymen, Homer, Ariosto, Cervantes, Shakespeare, be-cause the old Adam smelt rank in them; and for what have you reserved him? You have given him "a liberty unto" the multitudinous blasphemy of his day; you have made him free of its newspapers, its reviews, its magazines, its novels, its controversial pamphlets, of its Parliamentary debates, its law proceedings, its platform speeches, its songs, its drama, its theatre, of its enveloping, stifling atmosphere of death. You have succeeded but in this,—in making the world his University.

Difficult then as the question may be, and much as it may try the judgments and even divide the opinions of zealous and religious Catholics, I cannot feel any doubt myself that the Church's true policy is not to aim at the exclusion of Literature from Secular Schools, but at her own admission into them. Let her do for Literature in one way what she does for Science in another; each has its imper-fection, and she has her remedy for each. She fears no knowledge, but she purifies all; she represses no element of our nature, but cultivates the whole. Science is grave, methodical, logical; with Science then she argues, and opposes reason to reason. Literature does not argue, but declaims and insinuates; it is multiform and versatile: it persuades instead of convincing, it seduces, it carries captive; it appeals to the sense of honour, or to the imagination, to to the stimulus of curiosity; it makes its way by means of gaiety, satire, romance, the beautiful, the pleasurable. Is it wonderful that with an agent like this the Church should claim to deal with a vigour corresponding to its restlessness, to interfere in its proceedings with a higher hand, and to wield an authority in the choice of its studies and of its books which would be tyrannical, if reason and fact were the only instruments of its conclusions? But, any how, her principle is one and the same throughout: not to prohibit truth of any kind, but to see that no doctrines pass under the name of Truth but those which claim it rightfully.

CHAPTER XXVII

THE PHILOSOPHICAL INTEGRATION OF KNOWLEDGE IN THE UNIVERSITY[1]

TRUTH IS THE object of Knowledge of whatever kind; and when we inquire what is meant by Truth, I suppose it is right to answer that Truth means facts and their relations, which stand towards each other pretty much as subjects and predicates in logic. All that exists, as contemplated by the human mind, forms one large system or complex fact, and this of course resolves itself into an indefinite number of particular facts, which, as being portions of a whole, have countless relations of every kind, one towards another. Knowledge is the apprehension of these facts, whether in themselves, or in their mutual positions and bearings. And, as all taken together form one integral subject for contemplation, so there are no natural or real limits between part and part; one is ever running into another; all, as viewed by the mind, are combined together, and possess a correlative character one with another, from the internal mysteries of the Divine Essence down to our own sensations and consciousness, from the most solemn appointments of the Lord of all down to what may be called the accident of the hour, from the most glorious seraph down to the vilest and most noxious of reptiles.

Now, it is not wonderful that, with all its capabilities, the human mind cannot take in this whole vast fact at a single glance, or gain possession of it at once. Like a short-sighted reader, its eye pores closely, and travels slowly, over the awful volume which lies open for its inspection. Or again, as we deal with some huge structure of many parts and sides, the mind goes round about it, noting down, first one thing, then another, as it best may, and viewing it under different aspects, by way of making progress towards mastering the whole. So by degrees and by circuitous advances does it rise aloft and subject to itself a knowledge of that universe into which it has been born.

These various partial views or abstractions, by means of which the mind looks out upon its object, are called sciences, and embrace respectively larger or smaller portions of the field of knowledge; sometimes extending far and wide, but superficially, sometimes with exactness over particular departments, sometimes occupied together on one and the same portion, sometimes holding one part in common, and then ranging on this side or that in absolute divergence one from the other. Thus Optics has for its subject the whole visible creation, so far forth as it is simply visible; Mental Philosophy has a narrower province, but a richer one. Astronomy, plane and physical, each has the same subject-matter, but views it or treats it differently; lastly, Geology and Comparative Anatomy have subject-matters partly the same, partly distinct.

Now these views or sciences, as being abstractions, have far more to do with the relations of things than with things themselves. They tell us what things are, only or principally by telling us their relations, or assigning predicates to subjects; and therefore they never tell us all that can be said

302

about a thing, even when they tell something, nor do they bring it before us, as the senses do. They arrange and classify facts; they reduce separate phenomena under a common law; they trace effects to a cause. Thus they serve to transfer our knowledge from the custody of memory to the surer and more abiding protection of philosophy, thereby providing both for its spread and its advance;—for, inasmuch as sciences are forms of knowledge, they enable the intellect to master and increase it; and, inasmuch as they are instruments, to communicate it readily to others. Still after all, they proceed on the principle of a division of labour, even though that division is an abstraction, not a literal separation into parts; and, as the maker of a bridle or an epaulet has not, on that account, any idea of the science of tactics or strategy, so in a parallel way, it is not every science which equally, nor any one which fully, enlightens the mind in the knowledge of things, as they are, or brings home to it the external object on which it wishes to gaze. Thus they differ in importance; and according to their importance will be their influence, not only on the mass of knowledge to which they all converge and contribute, but on each other.

Since then sciences are the results of mental processes about one and the same subject-matter, viewed under its various aspects, and are true results, as far as they go, yet at the same time separate and partial, it follows that on the one hand they need external assistance, one by one, by reason of their incompleteness, and on the other that they are able to afford it to each other, by reason, first, of their independence in themselves, and then of their connexion in their subject-matter. Viewed altogether, they approximate to a representation or subjective reflection of the objective truth, as nearly as is possible to the human mind, which advances towards the accurate apprehension of that object, in proportion to the number of sciences which it has mastered; and which, when certain sciences are away, in such a case has but a defective apprehension, in proportion to the value of the sciences which are thus wanting, and the importance of the field on which they are employed.

Let us take, for instance, man himself as our object of contemplation; then at once we shall find we can view him in a variety of relations; and according to those relations are the sciences of which he is the subject-matter, and according to our acquaintance with them is our possession of a true knowledge of him. We may view him in relation to the material elements of his body, or to his mental constitution, or to his household and family, or to the community in which he lives, or to the Being who made him; and in consequence we treat of him respectively as physiologists, or as moral philosophers, or as writers of economics, or of politics, or as theologians. When we think of him in all these relations together, or as the subject at once of all the sciences I have named, then we may be said to reach unto and rest in the idea of man as an object or external fact, similar to that which the eye takes of his outward form. On the other hand, according as we are only physiologists, or only politicians, or only moralists, so is our idea of man more or less unreal; we do not take in the whole of him, and the defect is greater or less, in proportion as the relation is, or is not, important, which is omitted, whether his relation to God, or to his king, or to his children, or to his own component parts. And if there be one relation, about which we know nothing at all except that it exists, then is our knowledge of him, confessedly and to our own consciousness, deficient and partial, and that, I repeat, in proportion to the importance of the relation.

That therefore is true of sciences in general which we are apt to think applies only to pure mathematics, though to pure mathematics it applies especially viz., that they cannot be considered as simple representations or informants of things as they are. We are accustomed to say, and say truly, that the conclusions of pure mathematics are applied, corrected, and adapted, by mixed [or applied mathematics]; but so too the conclusions of Anatomy, Chemistry, Dynamics, and other sciences, are revised and completed by each other. Those several conclusions do not represent whole and substantive things, but views, true, so far as they go; and in order to ascertain how far they do go, that is, how far they correspond to the object to which they belong, we must compare them with the views taken out of that object by other sciences. Did we proceed upon the abstract theory of forces, we should assign a much more ample range to a projectile than in fact the resistance of the air allows it to accomplish. Let, however, that resistance be made the subject of scientific analysis, and then we shall have a new science, assisting, and to a certain point completing, for the benefit of questions of fact, the science of projection. On the other hand, the science of projection itself, considered as belonging to the forces it contemplates, is not more perfect, as such, by this supplementary investigation.

And in like manner, as regards the whole circle of sciences, one corrects another for purposes of fact, and one without the other cannot dogmatize, except hypothetically and upon its own abstract principles. For instance, the Newtonian philosophy requires the admission of certain metaphysical postulates, if it is to be more than a theory or an hypothesis; as, for instance, that what happened yesterday will happen to-morrow; that there is such a thing as matter, that our senses are trustworthy, that there is a logic of induction, and so on. Now to Newton metaphysicians grant all that he asks; but, if so be, they may not prove equally accommodating to another who asks something else, and then all his most logical conclusions in the science of physics would remain hopelessly on the stocks, though finished, and never could be launched into the sphere of fact.

Again, did I know nothing about the movement of bodies, except what the theory of gravitation supplies, were I simply absorbed in that theory so as to make it measure all motion on earth and in the sky, I should indeed come to many right conclusions, I should hit off many important facts, ascertain many existing relations, and correct many popular errors: I should scout and ridicule with great success the old notion, that light bodies flew up and heavy bodies fell down; but I should go on with equal confidence to deny the phenomenon of capillary attraction. Here I should be wrong, but only because I carried out my science irrespectively of other sciences. In like manner, did I simply give myself to the investigation of the external action of body upon body, I might scoff at the very idea of chemical affinities and combinations, and reject it as simply unintelligible. Were I a mere chemist, I should deny the influence of mind upon bodily health; and so on, as regards the devotees of any science, or family of sciences, to the exclusion of others; they necessarily become bigots and quacks, scorning all principles and reported facts which do not belong to their own pursuit, and thinking to effect everything without aid

306

from any other quarter. Thus, before now, chemistry has been substituted for medicine; and again, political economy, or intellectual enlightenment, or the reading of the Scriptures, has been cried up as a panacea against vice, malevolence, and misery.

Summing up, all knowledge forms one whole, because its subject-matter is one; for the universe in its length and breadth is so intimately knit together, that we cannot separate off portion from portion, and operation from operation, except by a mental abstraction; and then again, as to its Creator, though He of course in His own Being is infinitely separate from it, and Theology has its departments towards which human knowledge has no relations, yet He has so implicated Himself with it, and taken it into His very bosom, by His presence in it, His providence over it, His impressions upon it, and His influences through it, that we cannot truly or fully contemplate it without in some main aspects contemplating Him. Next, sciences are the results of that mental abstraction, which I have spoken of, being the logical record of this or that aspect of the whole subject-matter of knowledge. As they all belong to one and the same circle of objects, they are one and all connected together; as they are but aspects of things, they are severally incomplete in their relation to the things themselves, though complete in their own idea and for their own respective purposes; on both accounts they at once need and subserve each other. And further, the comprehension of the bearings of one science on another, and the use of each to each, and the location and limitation and adjustment and due appreciation of them all, one with another, this belongs, I conceive, to a sort of science distinct from all of them, and in some sense a science of sciences, which is my own conception of what is meant by Philosophy, in the true sense of the word, and of a philosophical habit of mind.

I am asked what is the end of University Education, and of the Liberal or Philosophical Knowledge which I conceive it to impart: I answer, that what I have already said has been sufficient to show that it has a very tangible, real, and sufficient end, though the end cannot be divided from that knowledge itself. Knowledge is capable of being its own end. Such is the constitution of the human mind, that any kind of knowledge, if it be really such, is its own reward. And if this is true of all knowledge, it is true also of that special Philosophy, which I have made to consist in a comprehensive view of truth in all its branches, of the relations of science to science, of their mutual bearings, and their respective values. What the worth of such an acquirement is, compared with other objects which we seek,—wealth or power or honour or the conveniences and comforts of life, I do not profess here to discuss; but I would maintain, and mean to show, that it is an object, in its own nature so really and undeniably good, as to be the compensation of a great deal of thought in the compassing, and a great deal of trouble in the attaining.

All that I have been now saying is summed up in a few characteristic words of the great Philosopher [Aristotle]. "Of possessions," he says, "those rather are useful, which bear fruit; those *liberal, which tend to enjoyment*. By fruitful, I mean, which yield revenue; by enjoyable, where *nothing accrues of consequence beyond the using*."[2]

Do not suppose, that in thus appealing to the ancients, I am throwing back the world two thousand years, and fettering Philosophy with the reasonings of paganism. While the world lasts, will Aristotle's doctrine on these matters

308

last, for he is the oracle of nature and of truth. While we are men, we cannot help, to a great extent, being Aristotelians, for the great Master does but analyze the thoughts, feelings, views, and opinions of human kind. He has told us the meaning of our own words and ideas, before we were born. In many subject-matters, to think correctly, is to think like Aristotle; and we are his disciples whether we will or no, though we may not know it. Now, as to the particular instance before us, the word "liberal" as applied to Knowledge and Education, expresses a specific idea, which ever has been, and ever will be, while the nature of man is the same, just as the idea of the Beautiful is specific, or of the Sublime, or of the Ridiculous, or of the Sordid. It is in the world now, it was in the world then; and, as in the case of the dogmas of faith, it is illustrated by a continuous historical tradition, and never was out of the world, from the time it came into it. There have indeed been differences of opinion from time to time, as to what pursuits and what arts came under that idea, but such differences are but an additional evidence of its reality.

That idea must have a substance in it, which has maintained its ground amid these conflicts and changes, which has ever served as a standard to measure things withal, which has passed from mind to mind unchanged, when there was so much to colour, so much to influence any notion or thought whatever, which was not founded in our very nature. Were it a mere generalization, it would have varied with the subjects from which it was generalized; but though its subjects vary with the age, it varies not itself. The palaestra may seem a liberal exercise to Lycurgus, and illiberal to Seneca; coach-driving and prize-fighting may be recognized in Elis, and be condemned in England; music may be despicable in the eyes of certain moderns, and be in the highest place with Aristotle and Plato,—(and the case is the same in the particular application of the idea of Beauty, or of Goodness, or of Moral Virtue, there is a difference of tastes, a difference of judgments)—still these variations imply, instead of discrediting, the archetypal idea, which is but a previous hypothesis or condition, by means of which issue is joined between contending opinions, and without which there would be nothing to dispute about.

I consider, then, that I am chargeable with no paradox, when I speak of a Knowledge which is its own end, when I call it liberal knowledge, or a gentleman's knowledge, when I educate for it, and make it the scope of a University. And still less am I incurring such a charge, when I make this acquisition consist, not in Knowledge in a vague and ordinary sense, but in that Knowledge which I have especially called Philosophy or, in an extended sense of the word, Science; for whatever claims Knowledge has to be considered as a good, these it has in a higher degree when it is viewed not vaguely, not popularly, but precisely and transcendently as Philosophy.[3] Knowledge, I say, is then especially liberal, or sufficient for itself, apart from every external and ulterior object, when and so far as it is philosophical, and this I proceed to show.

Now bear with me, if what I am about to say, has at first sight a fanciful appearance. Philosophy, then, or Science, is related to Knowledge in this way:—Knowledge is called by the name of Science or Philosophy, when it is acted upon, informed, or if I may use a strong figure, impregnated by Reason. Reason is the principle of that intrinsic fecundity of Knowledge, which, to those who possess it, is its especial value, and which dispenses with the necessity of their looking abroad for any end to rest upon external to itself. Knowledge, indeed, when thus exalted into a scientific form, is also power; not only is it excellent in itself, but whatever such excellence may be, it is something more, it has a result beyond itself. Doubtless; but that is a further consideration, with which I am not concerned. I only say that, prior to its being a power, it is a good; that it is, not only an instrument, but an end. I know well it may resolve itself into an art, and terminate in a mechanical process, and in tangible fruit; but it also may fall back upon that Reason which informs it, and resolve itself into Philosophy. In one case it is called Useful Knowledge, in the other Liberal. The same person may cultivate it in both ways at once; but this again is a matter foreign to my subject; here I do but say that there are two ways of using Knowledge, and in matter of fact those who use it in one way are not likely to use it in the other, or at least in a very limited measure.

You see, then, here are two methods of Education; the end of the one is to be philosophical, of the other to be mechanical; the one rises towards general ideas, the other is exhausted upon what is particular and external. Let me not be thought to deny the necessity, or to decry the benefit, of such attention to what is particular and practical, as belongs to the useful or mechanical arts; life could not go on without them; we owe our daily welfare to them; their exercise is the duty of the many, and we owe to the many a debt of gratitude for fulfilling that duty. I only say that Knowledge, in proportion as it tends more and more to be particular, ceases to be Knowledge. It is a question whether Knowledge can in any proper sense be predicated of the brute creation; without pretending to metaphysical exactness of phraseology, which would be unsuitable to an occasion like this, I say, it seems to me improper to call that passive sensation, or perception of things, which brutes seem to possess, by the name of Knowledge. When I speak of Knowledge, I mean something intellectual, something which grasps what it perceives through the senses; something which takes a view of things; which sees more than the senses convey; which reasons upon what it sees, and while it sees; which invests it with an idea. It expresses itself, not in a mere enunciation, but by an enthymeme; it is of the nature of science from the first, and in this consists its dignity. The principle of real dignity in Knowledge, its worth, its desirableness, considered irrespectively of its results, is this germ within it of a scientific or a philosophical process. This is how it comes to be an end in itself; this is why it admits of being called Liberal. Not to know the relative disposition of things is the state of slaves or children; to have mapped out the Universe is the boast, or at least the ambition, of Philosophy.

Moreover, such knowledge is not a mere extrinsic or accidental advantage, which is ours to-day and anothers' to-morrow, which may be got up from a book, and easily forgotten again, which we can command or communicate at our pleasure, which we can borrow for the occasion, carry about in our hand, and take into the market; it is an aquired illumination, it is a habit, a personal possession, and an inward endowment. And this is the reason, why it is more correct, as well as more usual, to speak of a University as a place of education, than of instruction, though, when knowledge is concerned, instruction would at first sight have seemed the more appropriate word. We are instructed, for instance, in manual exercises, in the fine and useful arts, in trades, and in ways of business; for these are methods, which have little or no effect upon the mind itself, are contained in rules committed to memory, to tradition, or to use, and bear upon an end external to themselves. But eduation is a higher word; it implies an action upon our mental nature, and the formation of a character; it is something individual and permanent, and is commonly spoken of in connexion with religion and virtue. When, then, we speak of the communication of Knowledge as being Education, we thereby really imply that that Knowledge is a state or condition of mind; and since cultivation of mind is surely worth seeking for its own sake, we are thus brought once more to the conclusion, which the word "Liberal" and the word "Philosophy" have already suggested, that there is a Knowledge, which is desirable, though nothing come of it, as being of itself a treasure, and a sufficient remuneration of years of labour.

General culture of mind is [nevertheless] the best aid to professional and scientific study, and educated men can do what illiterate cannot; and the man who has learned to think and to reason and to compare and to discriminate and to analyze, who has refined his taste, and formed his judgment, and sharpened his mental vision, will not indeed at once be a lawyer, or a pleader, or an orator, or a statesman, or a physician, or a good landlord, or a man of business, or a soldier, or an engineer, or a chemist, or a geologist, or an antiquarian, but he will be placed in that state of intellect in which he can take up any one of the sciences or callings I have referred to, or any other for which he has a taste or special talent, with an ease, a grace, a versatility, and a success, to which another is a stranger. In this sense then, and as yet I have said but a very few words on a large subject, mental culture is emphatically *useful*.

313

If then I am arguing, and shall argue, against Professional or [specialized] Scientific knowledge as the sufficient end of a University Education, let me not be supposed to be disrespectful towards particular studies, or arts, or vocations, and those who are engaged in them. In saying that Law or Medicine is not the end of a University course, I do not mean to imply that the University does not teach Law or Medicine. What indeed can it teach at all, if it does not teach something particular? It teaches *all* knowledge by teaching all *branches* of knowledge, and in no other way. I do but say that there will be this distinction as regards a Professor of Law, or of Medicine, or of Geology, or of Political Economy, in a University and out of it, that out of a University he is in danger of being absorbed and narrowed by his pursuit, and of giving Lectures which are the Lectures of nothing more than a lawyer, physician, geologist, or political economist; whereas in a University he will just know where he and his science stand, he has come to it, as it were, from a height, he has taken a survey of all knowledge, he is kept from extravagance by the very rivalry of other studies, he has gained from them a special illumination and largeness of mind and freedom of self-possession, and he treats his own in consequence with a philosophy and a resource, which belongs not to the study itself, but to his liberal education.

This then is how I should solve the fallacy, for so I must call it, by which Locke and his disciples would frighten us from cultivating the intellect, under the notion that no education is useful which does not teach us some temporal calling, or some mechanical art, or some physical secret.[4] I say that a cultivated intellect, because it is a good in itself, brings with it a power and a grace to every work and occupation which it undertakes, and enables us to be more useful, and to a greater number. There is a duty we owe to human society as such, to the state to which we belong, to the sphere in which we move, to the individuals toward whom we are variously related, and whom we successively encounter in life; and that philosophical or liberal education, as I have called it, which is the proper function of a University, if it refuses the foremost place to professional interests, does but postpone them to the formation of the citizen, and, while it subserves the larger interests of philanthropy, prepares also for the successful prosecution of those merely personal objects, which at first sight it seems to disparage.

CHAPTER XXVIII

THE IDEA OF CIVILIZATION[1]

A STATE IS in its very idea a society, and a society is a collection of many individuals made one by their participation in some common possession, and to the extent of that common possession, the presence of that possession held in common constitutes the life, and the loss of it constitutes the dissolution, of a state. In like manner, whatever avails or tends to withdraw that common possession, is either fatal or prejudicial to the social union.

Now, states may be broadly divided into *barbarous* and *civilized;* their common possession, or life, is some object either of *sense* or of *imagination;* and their bane and destruction is either *external* or *internal.* And, to speak in general terms, without allowing for exceptions or limitations (for I am treating the subject scientifically only so far as is requisite for my particular inquiry), we may pronounce that *barbarous* states live in a common *imagination,* and are destroyed *from without;* whereas *civilized* states live in some common object of *sense,* and are destroyed from *within.*

By *external* enemies I mean foreign wars, foreign influence, insurrection of slaves or of subject races, famine,

316

accidental enormities of individuals in power, and other instruments analogous to what, in the case of an individual, is called a violent death; by *internal* I mean civil contention, excessive changes, revolution, decay of public spirit, which may be considered analogous to natural death.

Again, by objects of *imagination,* I mean such as religion, true or false (for there are not only false imaginations but true), divine mission of a sovereign or of a dynasty, and historical fame; and by objects of *sense,* such as secular interests, country, home, protection of person and property.

I do not allude to the conservative power of habit when I speak of the social bond, because habit is rather the necessary result of possessing a common object, and protects all states equally, barbarous and civilized. Nor do I include moral degeneracy among the instruments of their destruction, because this too attaches to all states, civilized and barbarous, and is rather a disposition exposing them to the influence of what is their bane, than a direct cause of their ruin in itself.

But what is meant by the words *barbarous* and *civilized,* as applied to political bodies? this is a question which it will take more time to answer, even if I succeed in satisfying it at all. By "barbarism," then, I suppose, in itself is meant a state of nature; and by "civilization," a state of mental cultivation and discipline. In a state of nature man has reason, conscience, affections, and passions, and he uses these severally, or rather is influenced by them, according to circumstances; and whereas they do not one and all necessarily move in the same direction, he takes no great pains to make them agree together, but lets them severally take their course, and, if I may so speak, jostle into a sort of union, and get on together, as best they can. He does not

317

improve his talents; he does not simplify and fix his motives; he does not put his impulses under the control of principle, or form his mind upon a rule. He grows up pretty much what he was when a child; capricious, wayward, unstable, idle, irritable, excitable; with not much more of habituation than that which experience of living unconsciously forces even on the brutes. Brutes act upon instinct, not on reason; they are ferocious when they are hungry; they fiercely indulge their appetite; they gorge themselves; they fall into torpor and inactivity. In a like, but a more human way, the savage is drawn by the object held up to him, as if he could not help following it; an excitement rushes on him, and he yields to it without a struggle; he acts according to the moment, without regard to consequences; he is energetic or slothful, tempestuous or calm, as the winds blow or the sun shines. He is one being to-day, another to-morrow, as if he were simply the sport of influences or circumstances. If he is raised somewhat above this extreme state of barbarism, just one idea or feeling occupies the narrow range of his thoughts, to the exclusion of others.

Moreover, brutes differ from men in this; that they cannot invent, cannot progress. They remain in the use of those faculties and methods, which nature gave them at their birth. They are endowed by the law of their being with certain weapons of defence, and they do not improve on them. They have food, raiment, and dwelling, ready at their command. They need no arrow or noose to catch their prey, nor kitchens to dress it; no garment to wrap round them, nor roof to shelter them. Their claws, their teeth, their viscera, are their butcher and their cook; and their fur is their wardrobe. The cave or the jungle is their home; or if it is their nature to exercise some architectural craft, they

318

have not to learn it. But man comes into the world with the capabilities, rather than the means and appliances, of life. He begins with a small capital, but one which admits of indefinite improvement. He is, in his very idea, a creature of progress. He starts, the inferior of the brute animals, but he surpasses them in the long run; he subjects them to himself, and he goes forward on a career, which at least hitherto has not found its limit.

Even the savage of course in some measure exemplifies this law of human nature, and is lord of the brutes; and what he is and man is generally, compared with the inferior animals, such is man civilized compared with the barbarian. Civilization is that state to which man's nature points and tends; it is the systematic use, improvement, and combination of those faculties which are his characteristic; and, viewed in its idea, it is the perfection, the happiness of our mortal state. It is the development of art out of nature, and of self-government out of passion, and of certainty out of opinion, and of faith out of reason. It is the due disposition of the various powers of the soul, each in its place, the subordination or subjection of the inferior, and the union of all into one whole. Aims, rules, views, habits, projects; prudence, foresight, observation, inquiry, invention, resource, resolution, perseverance, are its characteristics. Justice, benevolence, expedience, propriety, religion, are its recognized, its motive principles. Supernatural truth is its sovereign law.

Such is it in its true idea, synonymous with Christianity; and, not only in idea, but in matters of fact also, is Christianity ever civilization, as far as its influence prevails; but, unhappily, in matter of fact, civilization is not necessarily Christianity. If we would view things as they really are, we

319

must bear in mind that, true as it is, that only a supernatural grace can raise man towards the perfection of his nature, yet it is possible,—without the cultivation of its spiritual part, which contemplates objects subtle, distant, delicate of apprehension, and slow of operation, nay, even with an actual contempt of faith and devotion, in comparison of objects tangible and present,—possible it is, I say, to combine in some sort the other faculties of man into one, and to progress forward, with the substitution of natural religion for faith, and a refined expediency or propriety for true morality, just as with practice a man might manage to run without an arm or without sight, and as the defect of one organ is sometimes supplied to a certain extent by the preternatural action of another.

And this is, in fact, what is commonly understood by civilization, and it is the sense in which the word must be used here; not that perfection which nature aims at, and requires, and cannot of itself reach; but a second-rate perfection of nature, being what it is, and remaining what it is, without any supernatural principle, only with its powers of ratiocination, judgment, sagacity, and imagination fully exercised, and the affections and passions under sufficient control. Such was it, in its higher excellences, in heathen Greece and Rome, where the perception of moral principles, possessed by the cultivated and accomplished intellect, by the mind of Plato or Isocrates, of Cleanthes, Seneca, Epictetus, or Antoninus, rivalled in outward pretensions the inspired teaching of the Apostle of the Gentiles. Such is it at the present day, not only in its reception of the elements of religion and morals (when Christianity is in the midst of it as an inexhaustible storehouse for natural reason to borrow from), but especially in a province peculiar to these times, viz., in science and art, in physics, in politics, in economics, and mechanics. And great as are its attainments at present, still, as I have said, we are far from being able to discern, even in the distance, the limit of its advancement and of its perfectibility.

It is evident from what has been said, that barbarism is a principle, not of society, but of isolation; he who will not submit even to himself, is not likely to volunteer a subjection to others; and this is more or less the price which, from the nature of the case, the members of society pay individually for the security of that which they hold in common. It follows, that no polity can be simply barbarous; barbarians may indeed combine in small bodies, as they have done in Gaul, Scythia, and America, from the gregariousness of our nature, from fellowship of blood, from accidental neighbourhood, or for self-preservation; but such societies are not bodies or polities; they are but the chance result of an occasion, and are destitute of a common life. Barbarism has no individuality, it has no history; quarrels between neighbouring tribes, grudges, blood-shedding, exhaustion, raids, success, defeat, the same thing over and over again, this is not the action of society, nor the subject-matter of narrative; it neither interests the curiosity, nor leaves any impression on the memory. *"Labitur et labetur"*; it forms and breaks again, like the billows of the sea, and is but a mockery of unity. When I speak of barbarian states, I mean such as consist of members not simply barbarous, but just so far removed from the extreme of savageness that they admit of having certain principles in common, and are able to submit themselves individually to the system which rises out of those principles; that they do recognize the ideas of government, property, and law, however imper-

321

fectly; though they still differ from civilized polities in those main points, which I have set down as analogous to the difference between brutes and the human species.

As instinct is perfect after its kind at first, and never advances, whereas the range of the intellect is ever growing, so barbarous states are pretty much the same from first to last, and this is their characteristic; and civilized states, on the other hand, though they have had a barbarian era, are ever advancing further and further from it, and thus their distinguishing badge is progress. So far my line of thought leads me to concur in the elaborate remarks on the subject put forth by the celebrated M. Guizot, in his "Lectures on European Civilization." Civilized states are ever developing into a more perfect organization, and a more exact and more various operation; they are ever increasing their stock of thoughts and of knowledge; ever creating, comparing, disposing, and improving.

Hence, while bodily strength is the token of barbarian power, mental ability is the honourable badge of civilized states. The one is like Ajax, the other like Ulysses; civilized nations are constructive, barbarous are destructive. Civilization spreads by the ways of peace, by moral suasion, by means of literature, the arts, commerce, diplomacy, institutions; and, though material power never can be superseded, it is subordinate to the influence of mind. Barbarians can provide themselves with swift and hardy horses, can sweep over a country, rush on with a shout, use the steel and firebrand, and frighten and overwhelm the weak or cowardly; but in the wars of civilized countries, even the implements of carnage are scientifically constructed, and are calculated to lessen or supersede it; and a campaign becomes coordinately a tour of *savants,* or a colonizing expedition, or a political demonstration. When Sesostris marched through Asia to the Euxine, he left upon his road monuments of himself, which have not utterly disappeared even at this day; and the memorials of the rule of the Pharoahs are still engraved on the rocks of Libya and Arabia. Alexander, again, in a later age, crossed from Macedonia to Asia with the disciples of Aristotle in his train. His march was the diffusion of the arts and commerce, and the acquisition of scientific knowledge; the countries he passed through were accurately described, as he proceeded, and the intervals between halt and halt regularly measured. His naval armaments explored nearly the whole distance from Attock on the Upper Indus to the Isthmus of Suez: his philosophers noted down the various productions and beasts of the unknown East; and his courtiers were the first to report to the western world the singular institutions of Hindostan.

Again, while Attila boasted that his horse's hoof withered the grass it trod on, and Zingis could gallop over the site of the cities he had destroyed, Seleucus, or Ptolemy, or Trajan, covered the range of his conquests with broad capitals, marts of commerce, noble roads, and spacious harbours. Lucullus collected a magnificent library in the East, and Caesar converted his northern expeditions into an antiquarian and historical research.

Ratiocination and its kindred processes, which are the necessary instruments of political progress, are, taking things as we find them, hostile to imagination and auxiliary to sense. It is true that a St. Thomas can draw out a whole system of theology from principles impalpable and invisible, and fix upon the mind by pure reason a vast multitude of facts and truths which have no pretence to a bodily form.

323

But, taking man as he is, we shall commonly find him dissatisfied with a demonstrative process from an undemonstrated premiss, and, when he has once begun to reason, he will seek to prove the point from which his reasoning starts, as well as that at which it arrives. Thus he will be forced back from immediate first principles to others more remote, nor will he be satisfied till he ultimately reaches those which are as much within his own handling and mastery as the reasoning apparatus itself. Hence it is that civilized states ever tend to substitute objects of sense for objects of imagination, as the basis of their existence. The Pope's political power was greater when Europe was semi-barbarous; and the divine right of the successors of the English St. Edward received a death-blow in the philosophy of Bacon and Locke. At present, I suppose, our own political life, as a nation, lies in the supremacy of the law; and that again is resolvable into the internal peace, and protection of life and property, and freedom of the individual, which are its result; and these I call objects of sense.

CHAPTER XXIX

RELIGION AND MEDIEVAL SOCIETY[1]

Nov. 22, 1860

I HAVE BEEN finishing some work which has thrown my letters greatly in arrears, and besides, your letter is an important one. Your book [*The Formation of Christendom*], as sketched in it, will be full of interest and instruction, and I certainly desire you to proceed with it.

At the same time, I hesitate in accepting your theory, though I don't think it necessary to your book. In so difficult a subject, obviously, all that I shall say will be unfeignedly meant as questions, not objections.

I do not see my way to hold that "Catholic civilisation," as you describe it, is *in fact* (I do not say in the abstract), but in fact, has been, or shall be, or can be, a good, or *per se* desirable. And in thus saying, I daresay I have not expressed myself with that exactness which precludes criticism upon me, but, I repeat, you must consider me, as I am, investigatory.

You say "Catholic civilisation . . . was the ideal which the Church aimed at in the Middle Ages, and which she worked into the laws, manners, institutions, public policy, or public opinion of Europe."

Now that it is the tendency of Christianity to impress

325

itself on the face of society, I grant: but so, in like manner, it is the tendency of devotion to increase Church lands and property, and to multiply religious houses; but as the state of the recipient (i.e. a given population *hic et nunc*) may hinder the latter tendency from working well (e.g. may lead to secularity and corruption in the clergy), so may certain peculiarities in this or that age or place interfere with the beneficial effect of the former, that is, it is not necessarily a good.

1. St. John says, *Mundus totus in maligno positus est* [*The whole world lies in the power of evil*]; is this the declaration of an ever-enduring fact? I think it is. If so, the world, though stamped with Christian civilisation, still *in maligno positus est*. While, then, I fully acknowledge the homage thus paid to Christianity, why should I think much of what is the kind of homage, and little more, which Achab, when he put on sackcloth, paid to the prophet?

2. Again, the world is one of our three deadly enemies. Did it cease to be so in the Middle Age? If so, I grant that the mediaeval type of society is in fact preferable to the previous and the later. Else, I do not see that that state was more than the shadow of Christianity visible from the accidental character of a certain stage of human affairs.

3. Again, during the Middle Ages Rome is spoken of, not only as the world, but even as Babylon. How strong is St. Thomas of Canterbury upon it! How the saints are used to look upon the Pontifical Court as in fact almost a road to perdition! Consider St. Philip's title of the Apostle of Rome, and that the correlation to Apostle is a state of heathenism. St. Bernard, I think, speaks as if a man could scarcely be saved who did not enter the cloister. Surely Christian society was the world, and nothing short of it.

4. Again, the noblest aspect of man is not the social, but the intellectual. In the Middle Ages Christianity has impressed its image on the social framework. It never has been able to do so on literature and science. As to the *Middle Ages*, the *prima facie* judgment passed on a philosopher was that he was in league with the evil powers. And no one doubts that both in primitive and in modern times the intellect of the world has been untamed. If, then, Christianity has not compelled the *intellect* of the world, viewed in the mass, to confess Christ, why insist as a great gain on its having compelled the *social* framework of the world to confess Him? If it was part of a Divine scheme that Christianity should subdue, first the individual, then the family, then the framework of society, etc. etc., why was the subjection of Literature and Science omitted in the progressive series of triumphs?

5. Lastly, since the object of Christianity is to save souls, I ask, Have we any reason to suppose that more souls were saved (relatively to the number of Christians) under the Christian Theocracy than under the Roman Emperors, or under the English Georges? There are no means, of course, of proving the point either way; but are we prepared in *matter of fact* to hold the affirmative? If not, *cui bono* the mediaeval system?

The conclusion I am disposed to acquiesce in is this:— that certain ages, i.e. the ages of barbarism, are more susceptible of religious impressions than other ages; and call for, need, the visible rule of Religion; that, as every animal knows its own wants, and distinguishes by instinct between food and poison, so a ruder people asks for a strong form of religion, armed with temporal sanctions, and it is good for it; whereas other ages reject it, and it would be bad for

327

them. Mortara's case would have excited as much admiration six centuries ago as it rouses indignation now; and, in matter of fact, it was a good thing for men thus to be compelled to be Christians, and a bad thing for them now. I don't say that it made *more* true Christians, but it was the way by which Christians, were they more or fewer, were to be made. A mediaeval system now would but foster the worst hypocrisy,—not because this age is worse than that, but because imagination acts more powerfully upon barbarians, and reason on traders, *savants,* and newspaper readers.

I have not said a word to deny the abstract duty of using force, etc. etc., any more than I deny the merit of leaving lands to the Church and founding monasteries;—but Prudence looks to the expedient.

Dec. 4, 1860.

I am very anxious not to be defending a paradox, and you will do me a great service if you keep me from such an absurdity. I will try to make my meaning clearer; and, if I succeed in this, I shall *ipso facto,* as I hope, be recommending it.

My *assumption* is, that the revealed object of the institution of the Church is to save souls.

My *position* is, that there is no *probability in facts* (i.e. no *evidence*), that one organisation of society saves more souls than another.

And further, that there *is* an *antecedent probability* the other way (viz. that one organisation of society is *not* in fact better suited for this great object than another, except accidentally), from the circumstance that the world—that is, human society, *in maligno positus est;* from which it is natural to suspect that organisations, abstractedly good (whether in themselves or in portions of themselves), are so intimately bound up *ab initio* with their own corruptions, that they are likely not to be good in fact, and that they need not work well in the concrete.

From which I would draw the *conclusion,* that the mediaeval political system, whatever good principles it might contain, and whatever good provisions it might enforce, still, as being only accidentally better fitted than another system for saving souls, is not, in the Divine Purpose, included in that object.

On the other hand, that one system (i.e. the mediaeval and others besides it) accidentally, i.e. at a given time and place, is better suited than another for the object, I not only grant, but would maintain. And I fully concede, that this or that method of State action (humanly speaking) is absolutely necessary at a certain crisis, in order to extricate the Church from existing difficulties, and set her on her course again;—though this remark applies to Victor Emmanuel quite as well as to Charlemagne (without of course denying the sin of the one and the merit of the other), and, moreover, allows me to consider that a system, e.g. the mediaeval, enforced out of season may save fewer souls than some other system.

My meaning will be further illustrated by the objections you propose, as I should view them.

(1) "Take marriage as the basis of natural society. . . . Surely Christian marriage is an immense gain to Catholic nations as distinguished from Protestant."

Certainly, if you could have it, and not other things with it, which can never be *in mundo maligno.* That recognition

329

of a Christian doctrine must be taken as a *part of a whole,* and the question is not, whether the particular provision is or is not a good, but whether the whole state of legislation, mediaeval organisation, the system did not necessarily *de facto,* and, in virtue of its containing much that is Christian, also contain much that is unchristian.

(2) "Surely Christian monarchy is an immense gain to Christians who possess it, as contrasted with 'the kings of the Gentiles.'"

That is, an immense gain *towards the saving of souls?* I grant that State protection, patronage, sanction, is such, i.e. in its abstract idea, but is State patronage always so in fact, and in the concrete? I say, no, because in fact patronage always has been, always will be, something besides patronage, *in mundo maligno;* it will be interference. When the State gives, it will always take. The *Quid pro quo* in Christian Legislation is Imperial Prerogative. Constantine built churches, and delivered his opinion about orthodoxy and heresy. He honoured bishops, but he introduced himself, and preached to them, in their Ecumenical Assembly, and called himself a "bishop for external matters." We must consider, then, what State Patronage in the concrete *connotes;* viz. State influence in holy things. It is a beneficial thing for bishops to be princes, as we learn from the history of the Middle Ages. I am not speaking against ecclesiastical establishments; I am but asking whether there is proof that the Church saves *more* souls when established, than when persecuted, or than when tolerated.

(3) You say, "It is no reflection on the *bonitas* of the *optimum,* that *corruptio optimi est pessima.*" Well, I consider that that *corruptio* is coincident, synchronous, with the introduction of the *optimum;* so that in fact the *opti-*

330

mum and *pessimum* always go together. Is it clear, then, that the mediocre, neutral, i.e. toleration, may not in certain states of society save as many souls, nay more souls, than an *optimo-pessimum*. May not I prefer, at this day, for the saving of souls, a Gallio for my ruler to a Philip II., a Gamaliel to a St. Louis?

(4) You say, "Strange and startling as the facts are" (of Rome in the fifteenth century, etc.), "these dangers were inherent in the spiritual authority itself." I should read this sentence, "These evils were inherent (considering *mundus in maligno positus est*) in the spiritual authority in *fact* and in concrete, if exalted to a temporal throne."

(5) "What would the mediaeval times have been *without* the mediaeval system?" Much worse than they were; because, as I have said in my former letter, the system was suited to the times; but that does not prove that it was suited to all times, to these times; and, if not suited to all times, how can it be included in that object which *is* for all times? How can you speak of the Gospel converting first the individual, then the State, as if the two were in the same order? The mediaeval system was a great triumph for the Gospel, and I am puzzled to say what it was in the way of benefit for the souls of men, considered as a whole.

(6) "Will you stop short of a Church of the Catacombs?" This implies that I think some other organisation of society *better fitted* for saving souls than the mediaeval. I meant to say no such thing, I meant to say that, *in its day*, the mediaeval system was best fitted, but not in another day, that it had great advantages, but greater counterbalancing disadvantages; that it could not be called a divine object, assuming (1) that the Gospel aims at saving souls, and (2) *mundus in maligno positus est;* that, while it was suitable

331

to the times in which it was found, it was not suitable to such times as these. I certainly think that (humanly speaking) it would lessen, not increase, the number of the elect in the nineteenth century, and that it would be as great a mistake to apply Ferdinand's or Philip II.'s system to England, as to have established the Bill of Rights, etc etc., in the Jesuit missions of Paraguay.

I have one difficulty of my own. A blessing comes on a State adopting Christianity. What is meant by this? and 1, is it a *temporal* blessing on the body politic? or 2, a blessing on the *individual* rulers? or 3, a spiritual blessing on the population?

As to my own objection, which you draw out, I am inclined, as far as I see, to answer *distinguendo:—Beatus populus*—this either means—(1) people, or (2) State polity. If the former, surely *beatus,* and no mistake, and the people will develop its faith in a corresponding State polity. This is the high sense of the word *nation,* including both the *matter* and the *form* of a people; of which the instance is Spain for many centuries down to this day. But if the latter, *subdistinguo,* the *populus* is not blest directly, but, if blest, blest indirectly *through* the State or Ruler. And he is blest or not, according as he acts (1) with the people passive or neutral, or (2) against the people. (1) Thus St. Stephen of Hungary, and St. Oswald of the Northumbrians, were blessed (and their people through them) because they carried their people with them; but (2) I cannot see that prince or people would gain any blessing by any such forcible attempts as those of James II to make the English Catholic.

I have expressed this view incidentally in my second lecture on "Catholicism in England."

Now you may say that Catholicism has often been established also; true, but Catholicism does not depend on its establishment for its existence; but it can do without it, and often dispenses with it to an advantage. A Catholic nation, *as a matter of course*, establishes Catholicism, because it is a Catholic nation; but in such a case *Catholicism comes first and establishment comes second;* the establishment is the spontaneous act of the people; it is a national movement, the Catholic people do it, and not the Catholic Church. It is *but an accident* of a particular state of things, the result of the fervour of the people; it is the will of the masses; but I repeat, it is not necessary for Catholicism— not necessary, I maintain, and Ireland is my proof of it.

333

CHAPTER XXX

RELIGION AND MODERN SOCIETY[1]

IN A LONG course of years I have made many mistakes. I have nothing of that high perfection which belongs to the writings of saints, viz., that error cannot be found in them; but what I trust that I may claim all through what I have written, is this,—an honest intention, an absence of private ends, a temper of obedience, a willingness to be corrected, a dread of error, a desire to serve Holy Church, and, through Divine mercy, a fair measure of success. And, I rejoice to say, to one great mischief I have from the first opposed myself. For thirty, forty, fifty years I have resisted to the best of my powers the spirit of Liberalism in religion. Never did Holy Church need champions against it more sorely than now, when, alas! it is an error overspreading, as a snare, the whole earth; and on this great occasion, when it is natural for one who is in my place to look out upon the world, and upon Holy Church as in it, and upon her future, it will not, I hope, be considered out of place, if I renew the protest against it which I have made so often.

Liberalism in religion is the doctrine that there is no positive truth in religion, but that one creed is as good as another, and this is the teaching which is gaining substance and force daily. It is inconsistent with any recognition of any religion, as *true*. It teaches that all are to be tolerated, for all are matters of opinion. Revealed religion is not a truth, but a sentiment and a taste; not an objective fact, not miraculous; and it is the right of each individual to make it say just what strikes his fancy. Devotion is not necessarily founded on faith. Men may go to Protestant Churches and to Catholic, may get good from both and belong to neither. They may fraternise together in spiritual thoughts and feelings, without having any views at all of doctrines in common, or seeing the need of them. Since, then, religion is so personal a peculiarity and so private a possession, we must of necessity ignore it in the intercourse of man with man. If a man puts on a new religion every morning, what is that to you? It is as impertinent to think about a man's religion as about his sources of income or his management of his family. Religion is in no sense the bond of society.

Hitherto the civil power has been Christian. Even in countries separated from the Church, as in my own, the *dictum* was in force, when I was young, that: "Christianity was the law of the land." Now, everywhere that goodly framework of society, which is the creation of Christianity, is throwing off Christianity. The *dictum* to which I have referred, with a hundred others which followed upon it, is gone, or is going everywhere; and, by the end of the century, unless the Almighty interferes, it will be *forgotten*. Hitherto, it has been considered that religion alone, with its supernatural sanctions, was strong enough to secure submission of the masses of our population to law and order; now the Philosophers and Politicians are bent on satisfying this problem without the aid of Christianity. Instead of the Church's authority and teaching, they would

substitute first of all a universal and thoroughly secular education, calculated to bring home to every individual that to
be orderly, industrious, and sober is his personal interest.
Then, for great working principles to take the place of
religion, for the use of the masses thus carefully educated,
it provides—the broad fundamental ethical truths, of justice, benevolence, veracity, and the like; proved experience;
and those natural laws which exist and act spontaneously
in society, and in social matters, whether physical or psychological; for instance, in government, trade, finance, sanitary
experiments, and the intercourse of nations. As to Religion,
it is a private luxury, which a man may have if he will; but
which of course he must pay for, and which he must not
obtrude upon others, or indulge in to their annoyance.

The general [nature] of this great *apostasia* is one and
the same everywhere; but in detail, and in character, it
varies in different countries. For myself, I would rather
speak of it in my own country, which I know. There, I
think it threatens to have a formidable success; though it
is not easy to see what will be its ultimate issue. At first
sight it might be thought that Englishmen are too religious
for a movement which, on the continent, seems to be
founded on infidelity; but the misfortune with us is, that,
though it ends in infidelity as in other places, it does not
necessarily arise out of infidelity. It must be recollected
that the religious sects, which sprang up in England three
centuries ago, and which are so powerful now, have ever
been fiercely opposed to the Union of Church and State,
and would advocate the unChristianising of the monarchy
and all that belongs to it, under the notion that such a catas-
trophe would make Christianity much more pure and much
more powerful.

Next the liberal principle is forced on us from the necessity of the case. Consider what follows from the very fact of these many sects. They constitute the religion, it is supposed, of half the population; and recollect, our mode of government is popular. Every dozen men taken at random whom you meet in the streets have a share in political power,—when you inquire into their forms of belief, perhaps they represent one or other of as many as seven religions; how can they possibly act together in municipal or in national matters, if each insists on the recognition of his own religious denomination? All action would be at a deadlock unless the subject of religion was ignored. We cannot help ourselves.

And, thirdly, it must be borne in mind, that there is much in the liberalistic theory which is good and true; for example, not to say more, the precepts of justice, truthfulness, sobriety, self-command, benevolence, which, as I have already noted, are among its avowed principles, and the natural laws of society. It is not till we find that this array of principles is intended to supersede, to block out, religion, that we pronounce it to be evil. There never was a device of the Enemy so cleverly framed and with such promise of success. And already it has answered to the expectations which have been formed of it. It is sweeping into its own ranks great numbers of able, earnest, virtuous men, elderly men of approved antecedents, young men with a career before them.

Such is the state of things in England, and it is well that it should be realised by all of us; but it must not be supposed for a moment that I am afraid of it. I lament it deeply, because I foresee that it may be the ruin of many souls; but I have no fear at all that it really can do aught of serious

337

harm to the Word of God, to Holy Church, to our Almighty King, the Lion of the tribe of Judah, Faithful and True, or to His Vicar on earth. Christianity has been too often in what seemed deadly peril, that we should fear for it any new trial now. So far is certain; on the other hand, what is uncertain, and in these great contests commonly uncertain, and what is commonly a great surprise, when it is witnessed, is the particular mode by which, in the event, Providence rescues and saves His elect inheritance. Sometimes our enemy is turned into a friend; sometimes he is despoiled of that special virulence of evil which was so threatening; sometimes he falls to pieces of himself; sometimes he does just so much as is beneficial, and then is removed. Commonly the Church has nothing more to do than to go on in her own proper duties, in confidence and peace; to stand still and to see the salvation of God.

> The meek spirited shall possess the earth,
> And shall be refreshed in the multitude of peace.

CHAPTER XXXI

THE CONSTITUTION AS A

POLITICAL PRINCIPLE[1]

THE PROPOSITION I have undertaken to maintain is this:—
That the British Constitution is made for a state of peace,
and not for a state of war; and that war tries it in the same
way, to use a homely illustration, that it tries a spoon to use
it for a knife, or a scythe or hay-fork to make it do the work
of a spade. I express myself thus generally, in order to give
to those who should do me the honour of reading me the
most expeditious insight into the view which I wish to set
before them. But, if I must speak accurately, my meaning
is this,—that, whereas a Nation has two aspects, internal
and external, one as regards its own members, and one as
regards foreigners, and whereas its government has two
duties, one towards its subjects, and one towards its allies
or enemies, the British State is great in its home department,
which is its primary object, foreign affairs being its secondary; while France or Russia, Prussia or Austria, contemplates in the first place foreign affairs, and is great in
their management, and makes the home department only
its second object. And further, that, if England be great
abroad, as she is, it is not so much the State, as the People
or Nation, which is the cause of her greatness, and that not

339

by means but in spite of the Constitution, or, if by means of it in any measure, clumsily so and circuitously; on the other hand, that, if foreign powers are ever great in the management of their own people, and make men of them, this they do in spite of their polity, and rather by the accidental qualifications of the individual ruler; or if by their polity, still with inconvenience and effort. Other explanations I may add to the above as I proceed, but this is sufficient for the present.

1. *States and Constitutions*

Now I hope you will have patience with me, if I begin by setting down what I mean by a State, and by a Constitution.

First of all, it is plain that every one has a power of his own to act this way or that, as he pleases. And, as not one or two, but every one has it, it is equally plain, that, if all exercised it to the full, at least the stronger part of mankind would always be in conflict with each other, and no one would enjoy the benefit of it; so that it is the interest of every one to give up some portion of his birth-freedom in this or that direction, in order to secure more freedom on the whole; exchanging a freedom which is now large and now narrow, according as the accidents of his conflicts with others are more or less favourable to himself, for a certain definite range of freedom prescribed and guaranteed by settled engagements or laws. In other words, Society is necessary for the well-being of human nature. The result, aimed at and effected by these mutual arrangements, is called a State or Standing; that is, in contrast with the appearance presented by a people before and apart from such arrangements, which is not a standing, but a chronic condition of commotion and disorder.

And next, as this State or settlement of a people, is brought about by mutual arrangements, that is, by laws or rules, there is need, from the nature of the case, of some power over and above the People itself to maintain and enforce them. This living guardian of the laws is called the Government, and a governing power is thus involved in the very notion of Society. Let the Government be suspended, and at once the State is threatened with dissolution, which at best is only a matter of time.

Here then is the problem: The social state is necessary for man, but it seems to contain in itself the elements of its own undoing. It requires a power to enforce the laws, and to rule the unruly; but what law is to control that power, and to rule the ruler? According to the common adage, "Quis custodiat ipsos custodes?" Who is to hinder the governor dispensing with the law in his own favour? History shows us that this problem is as ordinary as it is perplexing.

The expedient, by which the State is kept *in statu* and its ruler is ruled, is called its Constitution; and this has next to be explained. Now a Constitution really is not a mere code of laws, as is plain at once; for the very problem is how to confine power within the law, and in order to the maintenance of law. The ruling power can, and may, overturn law and law-makers, as Cromwell did, by the same sword with which he protects them. Acts of Parliament, Magna Charta, the Bill of Rights, the Reform Bill, none of these are the British Constitution. What then is conveyed in that word? I would answer as follows:—

As the individuals have characters of their own, so have races. Most men have their strong and their weak points, and points neither good nor bad, but idiosyncratic. And so of races: one is brave and sensitive of its honour; another romantic; another industrious, or long-headed, or religious. One is barbarous, another civilized. Moreover, growing out of these varieties or idiosyncrasies, and corresponding to them, will be found in these several races, and proper to each, a certain assemblage of beliefs, convictions, rules, usages, traditions, proverbs, and principles; some political, some social, some moral; and these tending to some definite form of government and *modus vivendi,* or polity, as their natural scope. And this being the case, when a given race has that polity which is intended for it by nature, it is in the same state of repose and contentment which an individual enjoys who has the food, or the comforts, the stimulants, sedatives, or restoratives, which are suited to his *diathesis* and his need.

This then is the Constitution of a State: securing, as it does, the national unity by at once strengthening and controlling its governing power. It is something more than law; it is the embodiment of special ideas, ideas perhaps which have been held by a race for ages, which are of immemorial usage, which have fixed themselves in its innermost heart, which are in its eyes sacred to it, and have practically the force of eternal truths, whether they be such or not. These ideas are sometimes trivial, and, at first sight, even absurd: sometimes they are superstitious, sometimes they are great or beautiful; but to those to whom they belong they are first principles, watch-words, common property, natural ties, a cause to fight for, an occasion of self-sacrifice. They are the expressions of some or other sentiment,—of loyalty, of order, of duty, of honour, of faith, of justice, of glory. They are the creative and conservative

342

influences of Society; they erect nations into States, and invest States with Constitutions. They inspire and sway, as well as restrain, the ruler of a people, for he himself is but one of that people to which they belong.

2. Constitutional Principles and Their Varieties

It is a common saying that political power is founded on opinion; this is true, if the word "opinion" be understood in the widest sense of which it is capable. A State depends and rests, not simply on force of arms, not on logic, not on anything short of the sentiment and will of those who are governed. This doctrine does not imply instability and change as inherent characteristics of a body politic. Since no one can put off his opinions in a moment, or by willing it, since those opinions may be instincts, principles, beliefs, convictions, since they may be self-evident, since they may be religious truths, it may be easily understood how a national polity, as being the creation and development of a multitude of men having all the same opinions, may stand of itself, and be most firmly established, and may be practically secure against reverse. And thus it is that countries become settled, with a definite form of social union, and an ascendancy of law and order; not as if that particular settlement, union, form, order, and law were self-sanctioned and self-supported, but because it is founded in the national mind, and maintained by the force of a living tradition. This, then, is what I mean by a State; and, being the production and outcome of a people, it is necessarily for the good of the people, and it has two main elements, power and liberty,—for without power there is no protection, and without liberty there is nothing to protect. The seat of power is the Government; the seat of liberty is the Constitution.

You will say that this implies that every State must have a Constitution; so I think it has, in the sense in which I have explained the word. As the governing power may be feeble and unready, so the check upon its arbitrary exercise may be partial and uncertain; it may be rude, circuitous, abrupt, or violent; it need not be scientifically recognized and defined; but there never has been, there never can be, in any political body, an instance of unmitigated absolutism. Human nature does not allow of it. In pure despotisms, the practical limitation of the ruler's power lies in his personal fears, in the use of the dagger or the bowstring. These expedients have been brought into exercise before now, both by our foes, the Russians, and still more so, by our friends, the Turks. Nay, when the present [Crimean] war began, some of our self-made politicians put forward the pleasant suggestion that the Czar's assassination at the hands of his subjects, maddened by taxes and blockades, was a possible path to the triumph of the allies.

Such is the lawless remedy which nature finds for a lawless tyranny; and no one will deny that such a savage justice is national in certain states of Society, and has a traditional authority, and may in a certain sense be called Constitutional. As society becomes civilized, the checks on arbitrary power assume a form in accordance with a more cultivated morality. We have one curious specimen of a Constitutional principle, preserved to us in the Medo-Persian Empire. It was a wholesome and subtle provision, adopting the semblance of an abject servility suitable to the idea of a despotism, which proclaimed the judgment of the despot infallible, and his word irrevocable. Alexander felt what it was to do

irrevocable acts in the physical order, when, in the pleni-
tude of his sovereignty, he actually killed his friend in the
banquet; and, as to the vulgar multitude, this same natural
result, the remedy or penalty of reckless power, is expressed
in the unpolite proverb, "Give a rogue rope enough, and he
will hang himself." With a parallel significance, then, it was
made a sacred principle among the Medo-Persians, which
awed and sobered the monarch himself, from its surpassing
inconvenience, that what he once had uttered had the force
of fate. It was the punishment of his greatness, that, when
Darius would have saved the prophet Daniel from the
operation of a law, which the king had been flattered into
promulgating, he could not do so.

A similar check upon the tyranny of power, assuming the
character of veneration and homage, is the form and etiquette which is so commonly thrown round a monarch. By
irresistible custom, a ceremonial more or less stringent has
been made almost to enter into his essential idea, for we
know majesty without its externals is a jest; and, while to
lay it aside is to relinquish the discriminating badge which
is his claim upon the homage of his subjects, to observe it
is to surrender himself manacled and fettered into their
hands. It is said a king of Spain was roasted to death because the proper official was not found in time to wheel
away his royal person from the fire. If etiquette hindered
him from saving his own life, etiquette might also interpose
an obstacle to his taking the life of another. If it was so
necessary for Sancho Panza, governor of Barataria, to eat
his dinner with the sanction of the court physician on every
dish, other great functionaries of State might possibly be
conditions of other indulgences on his part which were less
reasonable and less imperative. As for our own most gra-

cious Sovereign [Queen Victoria], she is honoured with the Constitutional prerogative that "the king can do no wrong"; that is, he can do no political act of his own mere will at all.

It is, then, no paradox to say that every State has in some sense a Constitution; that is, a set of traditions, depending, not on formal enactment, but on national acceptance, in one way or other restrictive of the ruler's power; though in one country more scientifically developed than another, or more distinctly recognized, or more skilfully and fully adapted to their end. There is a sort of analogy between the political and the physical sense of the word. A man of good constitution is one who has something more than life,—viz., a bodily soundness, organic and functional, which will bring him safely through hardships, or illnesses, or dissipations. On the other hand, no one is altogether without a constitution: to say he has nothing to fall back upon, when his health is tried, is almost to pronounce that his life is an accident, and that he may at any moment be carried off. And, in like manner, that must be pronounced no State, but a mere fortuitous collection of individuals, which has no unity stronger than despotism, or deeper than law.

I am not sure how far it bears upon the main proposition to which these remarks are meant to conduct us, but at least it will illustrate the general subject, if I ask your leave to specify, as regards the depository of political power, four Constitutional principles, distinct in kind from each other, which, among other parallel ones, have had an historical existence. If they must have names given them, they may be called respectively the principles of co-ordination, subordination, delegation, and participation.

1. As all political power implies unity, the word *co-ordination* may seem inconsistent with its essential idea: and

346

yet there is a state of society, in which the limitation of despotism is by the voice of the people so unequivocally committed to an external authority, that we must speak of it as the Constitution of such a State, in spite of the seeming anomaly. Such is the recognition of the authority of Religion, as existing in its own substantive institutions, external to the strictly political framework, which even in pagan countries has been at times successfully used to curb the extravagances of absolute power. Putting paganism aside, we find in the history both of Israel and of Judah the tyranny of kings brought within due limits by the priests and prophets, as by legitimate and self-dependent authorities. The same has been the case in Christian times. The Church is essentially a popular institution, defending the cause and encouraging the talents of the lower classes, and interposing an external barrier in favour of high or low against the ambition and the rapacity of the temporal power. "If the Christian Church had not existed," says M. Guizot, "the whole world would have been abandoned to unmitigated material force." However, as the corrective principle is in this instance external to the State, though having its root internally in national opinion, it cannot, except improperly, be termed Constitutional.

2. Next I come to the principle of *subordination*, which has been commonly found in young, semi-barbarous states both in Europe and Asia, and has attained its most perfect form in what is called the Feudal System. It has had a military origin; and, after the pattern of an army, is carried out in an hierarchy of chiefs, one under the other, each of whom in consequence had direct jurisdiction only over a few. First came the *suzerain*, or lord paramount, who had the allegiance of a certain number of princes, dukes, counts, or

even kings. These were his feudatories,—that is, they owed him certain military services, and held their respective territories of him. Their vassals, in turn, were the barons, each under his own prince or duke, and owing him a similar service. Under the barons were the soldiers, each settled down on his own portion of land, with the peasants of the soil as his serfs, and with similar feudal duties to his own baron.

A system like this furnished a most perfect expedient against absolutism. Power was distributed among many persons, without confusion or the chance of collision; and, while the paucity of vassals under one and the same rule gave less scope to tyrannical excesses, it created an effective public opinion, which is strongest when the relation between governor and governed is most intimate. Moreover, if any one were disposed to play the tyrant, there were several distinct parties in a condition to unite against him; the barons and lower class against the king, the king and the lower class against the barons. The barbarities of the middle ages have been associated in men's minds with this system; but, whatever they were, they surely took place in spite of it, not through it,—just as the anti-Catholic virulence of the present race of Englishmen is mitigated, not caused, by the British Constitution.

3. By the principle of *delegation,* I mean that according to which power is committed for a certain time to individuals, with a commensurate responsibility, to be met whenever that time has expired. Thus the Roman Dictator, elected on great emergencies, was autocrat during the term of his rule. Thus a commander of an army has unfettered powers to do what he will, while his command continues; or the captain of a ship; but afterwards his acts are open to

inquiry, and, if so be, to animadversion. There are great advantages to a system like this; it is the mode of bringing out great men, and of working great measures. You choose the fittest man for each department; you frankly trust him, you heap powers upon him, you generously support him with your authority, you let him have his own way, you let him do his best. Afterwards you review his proceedings; you reward or censure him. Such again, in fact, is with us the liberty of the press, censorship being simply unconstitutional, and the courts of law, the remedy against seditious, libellous, or demoralizing publications. Here, too, your advantage is great; you form public opinion, and you ascertain the national mind.

4. The very opposite to this is the principle of *participation*. It is that by which a People would leave nothing to its rulers, but has itself, or by its immediate instruments, a concurrent part in everything that is done. Acting on the notion that no one is to be trusted, even for a time, and that every act of its officials is to be jealously watched, it never commits power without embarrassing its exercise. Instead of making a venture for the transcendent, it keeps fast by a safe mediocrity. It rather trusts a dozen persons than one to do its work. This is the great principle of boards and officers, engaged in checking each other, with a second apparatus to check the first apparatus, and other functionaries to keep an eye on both of them,—Tom helping Jack, and Jack waiting for Bill, till the end is lost in the means. Such seems to have been the principle of the military duties performed by the Aulic Council in Germany, which virtually co-operated with Napoleon in his victories in that country. Such is the great principle of committees of taste, which have covered this fair land with architectural mon-

strosities. And as being closely allied to the principle of comprehension and compromise (a principle, necessary indeed, in some shape, but admitting of ruinous excess), it has had an influence on our national action in matters more serious than architecture or sculpture. And it has told directly upon our political efficiency.

3. *Self-Government and Social Initiative*

In saying that a free State will not be strong, I am far indeed from saying that a People with what is called a free Constitution will not be active, powerful, influential, and successful. I am only saying that it will do its great deeds, not through the medium of its government, or *politically,* but through the medium of its individual members, or *nationally.* Self-government, which is another name for political weakness, may really be the means or the token of national greatness. Athens, as a State, was wanting in the elements of integrity, firmness, and consistency; but perhaps that political deficiency was the very condition and a result of her intellectual activity.

I will allow more than this readily. Not only in cases such as that of Athens, is the State's loss the Nation's gain, but further, most of those very functions which in despotisms are undertaken by the State may be performed in free countries by the Nation. For instance, roads, the posts, railways, bridges, aqueducts, and the like, in absolute monarchies, are governmental matters; but they may be left to private energy, where self-government prevails. Letter-carriage indeed involves an extent of system and a punctuality in work, which is too much for any combination of individuals; but the care of Religion, which is a governmental work in Russia, and partly so in England, is left to private competi-

350

tion in the United States. Education, in like manner, is sometimes provided by the State, sometimes left to religious denominations, sometimes to private zeal and charity. The Fine Arts sometimes depend on the patronage of Court or Government; sometimes are given in charge to Academies; sometimes to committees or vestries.

I do not say that a Nation will manage all these departments equally well, or so well as a despotic government; and some departments it will not be able to manage at all. Did I think it could manage all, I should have nothing to write about. I am distinctly maintaining that the war department it cannot manage; that is my very point. It cannot conduct a war; but not from any fault in the nation, or with any resulting disparagement to popular governments and Constitutional States, but merely because we cannot have all things at once in this world, however big we are, and because, in the nature of things, one thing cannot be another. I do not say that a Constitutional State never must risk war, never must engage in war, never will conquer in war; but that its strong point lies in the other direction. If we would see what liberty, independence, self-government, a popular Constitution, can do, we must look to times of tranquillity. In peace a self-governing nation is prosperous in itself, and influential in the wide world. Its special works, the sciences, the useful arts, literature, the interests of knowledge generally, material comfort, the means and appliances of a happy life, thrive especially in peace. And thus such a nation spreads abroad, and subdues the world, and reigns in the admiration and gratitude and deference of man, by the use of weapons which war shivers to pieces. Alas! that mortals do not know themselves, and will not (according to the proverb) cut their coat according to their cloth!

351

REASON AND FAITH

REASON AND FAITH

THE READINGS IN this final Part indicate quite briefly the direction taken by Newman's reflections on religion. They can only point out the path toward the great bulk of his religious writings, which are formally theological. Since one of his leading themes is the analogous relationship between the natural and the supernatural orders, however, his philosophically relevant remarks on natural religion do help to orient the searching mind toward the Christian faith and life.

The succinct criticism of Hume's theory of miracle, Selection (32), seeks to remove an obstacle in the path of the modern man's acceptance of a transcendent and redeeming God. Newman does not think that Paley and Whately have grasped the point of Hume's contention that any criterion for the antecedent probability of miracles must be drawn from our past experience of uniformly occurring causal sequence in nature, i.e., from a region where the probability favors a God who acts according to uniform natural laws. Newman has already criticized Hume in Selection (5) for not distinguishing between a uniform order of sequence and a causal relation, and between general regularity and inexorable necessity in natural laws. His present point is that our conception of the physical order is a matter of interpretation, and cannot be kept in artificial isolation from the moral order in weighing the antecedent probability of miracles. Their likelihood is established by referring to a moral use of divine causal power, when God intends to communicate new truths to men through a visible subordination of the physical set of uniformities. Furthermore, the specific question of Judaeo-Christian miracles concerns a concrete, historical record of personal lives, rather than a purely abstract analysis of terms. Thus Newman argues that miracles are compatible with the course of nature, provided that the latter is viewed with sufficient precision and contextual concreteness.

Newman's own synthesis of the physical and moral viewpoints rests upon his analogical and sacramental view of the material world, sketched in Selection (33). The analogy which holds between the visible and the spiritual orders is that of sign to thing signified, and hence it requires the interpretative activity of the human mind to make the relation explicit and fruitful. Yet this sort of interpretative ordering does not deprive physical events and human history of their intrinsic structure, laws, and worth. From the side of God, the divine purpose does not run roughshod over the things of this visible world and does not abrogate their immanent laws. God works ordinarily in and through the prevailing natural and historical orders, even in achieving the economy of grace. And from the human side, we have to realize that the providence and governance of God are manifested in the visible realm and yet are also concealed by it. There is a fundamental polarity involved here, since our mind can approach human experience both in its fac-

356

tuality and in its symbolic import, both by the method of the physical and historical sciences and by that of teleology and religious significance.

When we do take the visible world in its sign-function, we can discover the religious import of our daily experience. Selection (34) describes how the interpretative mind gives a natural religious response on the basis of the three natural informants about God: material things, historical existence, and the moral acts of conscience. Newman makes his teaching on natural religion continuous with his account of the real assent to God, since the latter provides the stable context within which the religious interpretation and practical attitude reasonably develop. Like the idea of the university and that of the constitution, the idea of religion is a real and powerful molder of human society. Newman does not approach the phenomena of natural religious life in a reductionist spirit, and does not exclude a special providential aid through an original revelation or other social means of deepening our real apprehension of the meaning of religion. He retains the descriptive approach to the acts and values characterizing the religious response to God on the part of man the sinner and hoper. In the concrete, our natural religious outlook does not center around the order in physical events or the satisfaction of certain psychological needs, but around God's personal presence in the hearts of men and in their history. Conscience teaches us about God as our judge, powerful provider, and revealer of Truth. Hence natural religion remains fundamentally open to the Christian message: it is there to be transformed rather than eliminated.

With Selection (35) we are reaching the limits of our philosophical study of Newman, since it deals explicitly

357

with the relations of faith and reason. This theme perennially attracts the attention of philosophers and theologians aware of the claims made for revealed religion. Our text is taken from one of Newman's Oxford sermons delivered in 1839, while he was still serving as Vicar of St. Mary's. Its main theme about the reasonable solidarity between our everyday acts of informal reasoning and the act of supernatural faith remains central to his mature position. When he came to re-edit this sermon during his Catholic days, he kept the integral text with the addition of a few notes to show its basic agreement with his final teaching on how concrete reasoning reaches certitude outside the sphere of formal demonstration. "Faith is properly an assent, and an assent without doubt, or a certitude," concerning truths revealed by the personal God.[1] One of his later refinements is that we do not deliberately begin with an act of trust in our knowing powers, but we must actually use them and bring out their reliability in practice. Newman stresses in this sermon that faith is not an irrational act or sentiment but an exercise of reason itself, working in concrete matters where we must venture something to make any progress. The act of religious faith suits our human condition of moving toward the eternal God through temporal modes of being and acting. Our readings conclude with the invocation in Selection (36) to the Father of lights, a reminder that Newman is essentially a man of prayer throughout all of his philosophical investigations.

CHAPTER XXXII

CRITIQUE OF HUME'S VIEW OF MIRACLES[1]

IN PROOF OF miraculous occurrences, we must have recourse to the same kind of evidence as that by which we determine the truth of historical accounts in general. For though Miracles, in consequence of their extraordinary nature, challenge a fuller and more accurate investigation, still they do not admit an investigation conducted on different principles,—Testimony being the main assignable medium of proof for past events of any kind. And this being indisputable, it is almost equally so that the Christian Miracles are attested by evidence even stronger than can be produced for any of those historical facts which we most firmly believe. This has been felt by unbelievers; who have been, in consequence, led to deny the admissibility of even the strongest testimony, if offered in behalf of miraculous events, and thus to get rid of the only means by which they can be proved to have taken place.

It has accordingly been asserted, that all events inconsistent with the course of nature bear in their very front such strong and decisive marks of falsehood and absurdity, that it is needless to examine the evidence adduced for them.[2] "Where men are heated by zeal and enthusiasm," says Hume, with a distant but evident allusion to the Christian Miracles, "there is no degree of human testimony so strong as may not be procured for the greatest absurdity; and those who will be so silly as to examine the affair by that medium, and seek particular flaws in the testimony, are almost sure to be confounded."[3] Of these antecedent objections, which are supposed to decide the question, the most popular is founded on the frequent occurrence of wonderful tales in every age and country—generally, too, connected with Religion; and since the more we are in a situation to examine these accounts, the more fabulous they are proved to be, there would certainly be hence a fair presumption against the Scripture narrative, did it resemble them in its circumstances and proposed object. A more refined argument is that advanced by Hume, in the first part of his *Essay on Miracles,* in which it is maintained against the credibility of a Miracle, that it is more probable that the testimony should be false than that the Miracle should be true.

This latter objection has been so ably met by various writers, that, though prior in the order of the argument to the former, it need not be considered here. It derives its force from the assumption, that a Miracle is strictly a causeless phenomenon, a self-originating violation of nature; and is solved by referring the event to divine agency, a principle which (it cannot be denied) has originated works indicative of power at least as great as any Miracle requires. An adequate cause being thus found for the production of a Miracle, the objection vanishes, as far as the mere question of power is concerned; and it remains to be considered whether the anomalous fact be of such a character as to admit of being referred to the Supreme Being. For if it can-

360

not with propriety be referred to Him, it remains as improbable as if no such agent were known to exist. At this point, then, I propose taking up the argument; and by examining what Miracles are in their nature and circumstances referable to Divine agency, I shall be providing a reply to the former of the objections just noticed, in which the alleged similarity of all miraculous narratives one to another, is made a reason for a common rejection of all.

In examining what Miracles may properly be ascribed to the Deity, Hume supplies us with an observation so just, when taken in its full extent, that I shall make it the groundwork of the inquiry on which I am entering. As the Deity, he says, discovers Himself to us by His works, we have no rational grounds for ascribing to Him attributes or actions dissimilar from those which His works convey. It follows, then, that in discriminating between those Miracles which can and those which cannot be ascribed to God, we must be guided by the information with which experience furnishes us concerning His wisdom, goodness, and other attributes. Since a Miracle is an act out of the known track of Divine agency, as regards the physical system, it is almost indispensable to show its consistency with the Divine agency, at least, in some other point of view; if, that is, it is recognized as the work of the same power. Now, I contend that this reasonable demand is satisfied in the Jewish and Christian Scriptures, in which we find a narrative of Miracles altogether answering in their character and circumstances to those general ideas which the ordinary course of Divine Providence enables us to form concerning the attributes and actions of God.

While writers expatiate so largely on the laws of nature, they altogether forget the existence of a moral system: a system which, though but partially understood, and but general in its appointments as acting upon free agents, is as intelligible in its laws and provisions as the material world. Connected with this moral government, we find certain instincts of mind; such as conscience, a sense of responsibility, and an approbation of virtue; an innate desire of knowledge, and an almost universal feeling of the necessity of religious observances; while, in fact, Virtue is, on the whole, rewarded, and Vice punished. And though we meet with many and striking anomalies, yet it is evident they are but anomalies, and possibly but in appearance so, and with reference to our partial information.

These two systems, the Physical and the Moral, sometimes act in union, and sometimes in opposition to each other; and as the order of nature certainly does in many cases interfere with the operation of moral laws (as, for instance, when good men die prematurely, or the gifts of nature are lavished on the bad), there is nothing to shock probability in the idea that a great moral object should be effected by an interruption of physical order. But, further than this, however physical laws may embarrass the operation of the moral system, still on the whole they are subservient to it; contributing, as is evident, to the welfare and convenience of man, providing for his mental gratification as well as animal enjoyment, sometimes even supplying correctives to his moral disorders. If, then, the economy of nature has so constant a reference to an ulterior plan, a Miracle is a deviation from the subordinate for the sake of the superior system, and is very far indeed from improbable, when a great moral end cannot be effected except at the expense of physical regularity. Nor can it be fairly said to argue an imperfection in the Divine plans, that this interference should be necessary. For we must view the system of Providence as a whole; which is not more imperfect because of the mutual action of its parts, than a machine, the separate wheels of which effect each other's movements.

Now the Miracles of the Jewish and Christian Religions must be considered as immediate effects of Divine Power beyond the action of nature, for an important moral end; and are in consequence accounted for by producing, not a physical, but a final cause. We are not left to contemplate the bare anomalies, and from the mere necessity of the case to refer them to the supposed agency of the Deity. The power of displaying them is, according to the Scripture narrative, intrusted to certain individuals, who stand forward as their interpreters, giving them a voice and language, and a dignity demanding our regard; who set them forth as evidences of the greatest of moral ends, a Revelation from God,—as instruments in His hand of affecting a direct intercourse between Himself and His creatures, which otherwise could not have been effected,—as vouchers for the truth of a message which they deliver. This is plain and intelligible; there is an easy connection between the miraculous nature of their works and the truth of their words; the fact of their superhuman power is a reasonable ground for belief in their superhuman knowledge. Considering, then, our instinctive sense of duty and moral obligation, yet the weak sanction which reason gives to the practice of virtue, and withal the uncertainty of the mind when advancing beyond the first elements of right and wrong; considering, moreover, the feeling which wise men have entertained of the need of some heavenly guide to instruct and confirm them in goodness, and that unextinguishable desire for a Divine message which has led men in all ages to acquiesce even in pretended revelations, rather than forego the consolation thus afforded them; and again, the possibility (to say the least) of our being destined for a future state of being, the nature and circumstances of which it may concern us much to know, though from nature we know nothing; considering, lastly, our experience of a watchful and merciful Providence, and the impracticability already noticed of a Revelation without a Miracle, it is hardly too much to affirm that the moral system points to an interference with the course of nature, and that Miracles wrought in evidence of a Divine communication, instead of being antecedently improbable, are, when directly attested, entitled to a respectful and impartial consideration.

When the various antecedent objections which ingenious men have urged against Miracles are brought together, they will be found nearly all to arise from forgetfulness of the existence of moral laws. In their zeal to perfect the laws of matter they most unphilosophically overlook a more sublime system, which contains disclosures not only of the Being but of the Will of God. Thus, Hume, in a passage above referred to, observes, "Though the Being to whom the Miracle is ascribed be Almighty, it does not, upon that account, become a whit more probable, since it is impossible for us to know the attributes or actions of such a Being, otherwise than from the experience which we have of His productions in the usual course of nature. This still reduces us to past observation, and obliges us to compare the instances of the violation of truth in the testimony of men with those of the violation of the laws of nature by Miracles, in order to judge which of them is most likely and probable."[4] Here the moral government of God, with the course of which the Miracle entirely accords, is altogether

364

kept out of sight. With a like heedlessness of the moral character of a Miracle, another writer [Voltaire], notorious for his irreligion, objects that it argues mutability in the Deity, and implies that the physical system was not created good, as needing improvement. And a recent author [Bentham] adopts a similarly partial and inconclusive mode of reasoning, when he confuses the Christian Miracles with fables of apparitions and witches, and would examine them on the strict principle of those legal forms which from their secular object go far to exclude all religious discussion of the question.

Such reasoners seem to suppose, that when the agency of the Deity is introduced to account for Miracles, it is the illogical introduction of an unknown cause, a reference to a mere name, the offspring, perhaps, of popular superstition; or, if more than a name, to a cause that can be known only by means of the physical creation; and hence they consider Religion as founded in the mere weakness or eccentricity of the intellect, not in actual intimations of a Divine government as contained in the moral world. From an apparent impatience of investigating a system which is but partially revealed, they esteem the laws of the material system alone worthy the notice of a scientific mind; and rid themselves of the annoyance which the importunity of a claim to miraculous power occasions them, by discarding all the circumstances which fix its antecedent probability, all in which one Miracle differs from another, the professed author, object, design, character, and human instruments.

When this partial procedure is resisted, the *a priori* objections of sceptical writers at once lose their force. Facts are only so far improbable as they fall under no general rule; whereas it is as parts of an existing system that the Miracles

365

of Scripture demand our attention, as resulting from known attributes of God, and corresponding to the ordinary arrangements of His providence. Even as detached events they might excite a rational awe towards the mysterious Author of nature. But they are presented to us, not as unconnected and unmeaning occurrences, but as holding a place in an extensive plan of Divine government, completing the moral system, connecting Man and his Maker, and introducing him to the means of securing his happiness in another and eternal state of being.

A more subtle question remains, respecting the possible existence of causes in nature, to us unknown, by the supposed operation of which the apparent anomalies may be reconciled to the ordinary laws of the system. It has already been admitted that some difficulty will at times attend the discrimination of miraculous from merely uncommon events; and it must be borne in mind that in this, as in all questions from which demonstration is excluded, it is impossible, from the nature of the case, absolutely to disprove any, even the wildest, hypothesis which may be framed. It may freely be granted, moreover, that some of the Scripture Miracles, if they stood alone, might reasonably be referred to natural principles of which we were ignorant, or resolved into some happy combination of accidental circumstances. For our purpose, it is quite sufficient if there be a considerable number which no sober judgment would attempt to deprive of their supernatural character by any supposition of our ignorance of natural laws, or of exaggeration in the narrative. Raising the dead and giving sight to the blind by a word, feeding a multitude with the casual provisions which one individual among them had with him, healing persons at a distance, and walking on the water, are facts, even separately taken, far beyond the conceivable effects of artifice or accident; and much more so when they meet together in one and the same history. And here Hume's argument from general experience is in point, which at least proves that the ordinary powers of nature are unequal to the production of works of this kind.

It becomes, then, a balance of opposite probabilities, whether gratuitously to suppose a multitude of perfectly unknown causes, and these, moreover, meeting in one and the same history, or to have recourse to one, and that a known power, then miraculously exerted for an extraordinary and worthy object. We may safely say no sound reasoner will hesitate on which alternative to decide. While, then, a fair proportion of the Scripture Miracles are indisputably deserving of their name, but a weak objection can be derived from the case of the few which, owing to accidental circumstances, bear at the present day less decisive marks of supernatural agency. For, be it remembered (and it is a strong confirmatory proof that the Jewish and Christian Miracles are really what they profess to be) that though the miraculous character of some of them is more doubtful in one age than in another, yet the progress of Science has made no approximation to a general explication of them on natural principles. While discoveries in Optics and Chemistry have accounted for a host of apparent miracles, they hardly touch upon those of the Jewish and Christian systems. Here is no phantasmagoria to be detected, no analysis or synthesis of substances, ignitions, explosions, and other customary resources of the juggler's art.

367

CHAPTER XXXIII

THE UNIVERSE AS FACT AND SYMBOL[1]

[DURING MY preparation of *The Arians of the Fourth Century,*] the broad philosophy of Clement and Origen carried me away; the philosophy, not the theological doctrine; and I have drawn out some features of it in my volume, with the zeal and freshness, but with the partiality, of a neophyte. Some portions of their teaching, magnificent in themselves, came like music to my inward ear, as if the response to ideas, which, with little external to encourage them, I had cherished so long. These were based on the mystical or sacramental principle, and spoke of the various Economies or Dispensations of the Eternal. I understood these passages to mean that the exterior world, physical and historical, was but the manifestation to our senses of realities greater than itself. Nature was a parable: Scripture was an allegory: pagan literature, philosophy, and mythology, properly understood, were but a preparation for the Gospel. The Greek poets and sages were in a certain sense prophets; for "thoughts beyond their thought to those high bards were given." There had been a directly divine dispensation granted to the Jews; but there had been in some sense a dispensation carried on in favour of the Gentiles. He who had taken the seed of Jacob for His elect people had not therefore cast the rest of mankind out of His sight.

In the fulness of time both Judaism and Paganism had come to nought; the outward framework, which concealed yet suggested the Living Truth, had never been intended to last, and it was dissolving under the beams of the Sun of Justice which shone behind it and through it. The process of change had been slow; it had been done not rashly, but by rule and measure, "at sundry times and in divers manners," first one disclosure and then another, till the whole evangelical doctrine was brought into full manifestation. And thus room was made for the anticipation of further and deeper disclosures, of truths still under the veil of the letter, and in their reason to be revealed. The visible world still remains without its divine interpretation; Holy Church in her sacraments and her hierarchical appointments, will remain, even to the end of the world, after all but a symbol of those heavenly facts which fill eternity. Her mysteries are but the expressions in human language of truths to which the human mind is unequal.

Christianity, nor Christianity only, but all God's dealings with His creatures have two aspects, one external, one internal. What one of the earliest Fathers says of its highest ordinance, is true of it altogether, and of all other divine dispensations: they are two-fold, "having one part heavenly, and one part earthly." This is the law of Providence here below; it works beneath a veil, and what is visible in its course does but shadow out at most, and sometimes obscures and disguises what is invisible. The world in which we are placed has its own system of laws and principles, which, as far as our knowledge of it goes, is, when once set in motion, sufficient to account for itself,—as complete and independent as if there was nothing beyond it. Ordinarily speaking, nothing happens, nothing goes on in the world, but may be satisfactorily traced to some other event or fact in it, or has a sufficient result in other events or facts in it, without the necessity of our following it into a higher system of things in order to explain its existence, or to give it a meaning.

We will not stop to dwell on exceptions to this general statement, or on the narrowness of our knowledge of things: but what is every day said and acted on proves that this is at least the impression made upon most minds by the course of things in which we find ourselves. The sun rises and sets on a law; the tides ebb and flow upon a law; the earth is covered with verdure or buried in the ocean, it grows old and it grows young again, by the operation of fixed laws. Life, whether vegetable or animal, is subjected to a similar external and general rule. Men grow to maturity, then decay, and die. Moreover, they form into society, and society has its principles. Nations move forward by laws which act as a kind of destiny over them, and which are as vigorous now as a thousand years ago. And these laws of the social and political world run into the physical, making all that is seen one and one only system; a horse stumbles, and an oppressed people is rid of their tyrant; a volcano changes populous cities into a dull lake; a gorge has of old time opened, and the river rolls on, bearing on its bosom the destined site of some great mart, which else had never been. We cannot set limits either to the extent or to the minuteness of this wonderful web of causes and effects, in which all we see is involved. It reaches to the skies; it penetrates into our very thoughts, habits, and will.

Such is confessedly the world in which our Almighty

Creator has placed us. If then He is still actively present with His own work, present with nations and with individuals, He must be acting by means of its ordinary system, or by quickening, or as it were, stimulating its powers, or by superseding or interrupting it; in other words, by means of what is called nature, or by miracle; and whereas strictly miraculous interference must be, from the nature of the case, rare, it stands to reason that, unless He has simply retired, and has left the world ordinarily to itself,—content with having originally imposed on it certain general laws, which will for the most part work out the ends which He contemplates,—He is acting through, with, and beneath those physical, social, and moral laws, of which our experience informs us. Now it has ever been a firm article of Christian faith, that His Providence is in fact not general merely, but is, on the contrary, thus particular and personal; and that, as there is a particular Providence, so of necessity that Providence is secretly concurring and co-operating with that system which meets the eye, and which is commonly recognized among men as existing. It is not too much to say that this is the one great rule on which the Divine Dispensations with mankind have been and are conducted, that the visible world is the instrument, yet the veil, of the world invisible,—the veil, yet still partially the symbol and index: so that all that exists or happens visibly, conceals and yet suggests, and above all subserves, a system of persons, facts, and events beyond itself.

Thus the course of things has a natural termination as well as a natural origin: it tends towards final causes while it springs from physical; it is ever issuing from things which we see round about us; it is ever passing on into what is matter of faith, not of sight. What is called and seems to be

371

cause and effect, is rather an order of sequence, and does not preclude, nay, perhaps implies, the presence of unseen spiritual agency as its real author. This is the animating principle both of the Church's ritual and of Scripture interpretation; in the latter it is the basis of the theory of double sense; in the former it makes ceremonies and observances to be signs, seals, means, and pledges of supernatural grace. It is the mystical principle in the one, it is the sacramental in the other. All that is seen,—the world, the Bible, the Church, the civil polity, and man himself,—are types, and, in their degree and place, representatives and organs of an unseen world, truer and higher than themselves. The only difference between them is, that some things bear their supernatural character upon their surface, are historically creations of the supernatural system, or are perceptibly instrumental, or obviously symbolical: while others rather seem to be complete in themselves, or run counter to the unseen system which they really subserve, and thereby make demands upon our faith.

This may be illustrated from the creation of man, The Creator "formed man of the dust of the ground, *and* breathed into his nostrils the breath of life, and man became a living soul." He first formed a material tabernacle, and then endued it with an unseen life. Now some philosophers, somewhat after the manner of the ancient Gnostics, have speculated on the probability of man's being originally of some brute nature, some vast misshapen lizard of the primeval period, which at length by the force of nature, from whatever secret causes, was exalted into a rational being, and gradually shaped its proportions and refined its properties by the influence of the rational principle which got possession of it.[2] Such a theory is of course irreconcilable with the letter of the sacred text, to say no more; but it

372

bears an analogy, and at least supplies an illustration, to many facts and events which take place in this world.

When Providence would make a Revelation, He does not begin anew, but uses the existing system; He does not visibly send an Angel, but He commissions or inspires one of our own fellows. When He would bless us, He makes a man His priest. When He would consecrate or quicken us, He takes the elements of this world as the means of real but unseen spiritual influences. When He would set up a divine polity, He takes a polity which already is, or one in course of forming. Nor does He interfere with its natural growth, development, or dependence on things visible. He does not shut it up in a desert, and there supply it with institutions unlike those which might naturally come to it from the contact and intercourse of the external world. He does but modify, quicken, or direct the powers of nature or the laws of society. Or if He works miracles, still it is without superseding the ordinary course of things. He multiplies the flocks or the descendants of Jacob, or in due season He may work signal or public miracles for their deliverance from Egypt; but still the operation of ordinary causes, the influence of political arrangements, and what is called the march of events, are seen in such providences as truly, and can be pointed out as convincingly, as if an Angel and a pillar of a cloud were not with them.

Thus the great characteristic of Revelation is addition, substitution. Things look the same as before, though now an invisible power has taken hold upon them. This power does not unclothe the creature, but clothes it. Men dream everywhere; it gives visions. Men journey everywhere; it sends "the Angels of God to meet them." Men may elsewhere be hospitable to their brethren: now they entertain Angels. Men carry on a work; but it is a blessing from some

373

ancestor that is breathing on and through it unseen. A nation migrates and seizes on a country; but all along its proceedings are hallowed by prophecy, and promise, and providence beforehand, and used for religious ends afterwards. Israel was as much a political power, as man is an animal. The rites and ceremonies enjoined upon the people might be found elsewhere, but were not less divine notwithstanding. Circumcision was also practised in Egypt, frequent ablutions may be the custom of the East, the veil of Moses may have been the symbol of other rulers (if so be) before him—though the fact has to be proved; a Holy of Holies, an altar, a sacrifice, a sacerdotal caste, *in* these points the Mosaic law resembled, yet *as to* these it differed from, the nations round about. The Israelitish polity had a beginning, a middle, and an end, like other things of time and place; its captivities were the natural consequences, its monarchy was the natural expedient, of a state of political weakness. Its territory was a battle-ground, and its power was the alternate ally, of the rival empires of Egypt and Assyria. Heathen travellers may have surveyed the Holy Land, and have thought it but a narrow slip of Syria. So it was; what then? till the comparative anatomist can be said by his science to disprove the rationality and responsibility of man, the politician or geographer of this world does nothing, by dissertations in his own particular line of thought, towards quenching the secret light of Israel, or dispossessing its angelic guardians of the height of Sion or of the sepulchres of the prophets. Its history is twofold, worldly to the world, and heavenly to the heirs of heaven.

What is true of Judaism is true of Christianity. The kingdom of Christ, though not of this world, yet is in the world, and has a visible, material, social shape. It consists of men, and it has developed according to the laws under which combinations of men develop. It has an external aspect similar to all other kingdoms. We may generalize and include it as one among the various kinds of polity, as one among the empires, which have been upon the earth. It is called the fifth kingdom; and as being numbered with the previous four which were earthly, it is thereby, in fact, compared with them. We may write its history, and make it look as like those which were before or contemporary with it, as a man is like a monkey.

Now we come at length to Mr. Milman: this is what he has been doing [in his *History of Christianity Under the Empire*]. He has been viewing the history of the Church on the side of the world. Its rise from nothing, the gradual aggrandizement of its bishops, the consolidation of its polity and government, its relation to powers of the earth, its intercourse with foreign philosophies and religions, its conflict with external and internal enemies, the mutual action for good or for evil which has been carried on between it and foreign systems, political and intellectual, its large extension, its growth and resolution into a monarchy, its temporal greatness, its gradual divisions and decay, and the natural causes which operated throughout,—these are the subjects in which he delights, to which he has dedicated himself,—that is, as far as they can be detached from their directly religious bearing; and unless readers understand this, they will think that what is but *a contemplation of what is outside,* is intended by him for *a denial of what is inside.* It is to be feared that too many persons will unfairly run away from his book with the notion that to ignore the Almighty in ecclesiastical history is really to deny Him.

CHAPTER XXXIV

NATURAL RELIGION[1]

THE WHOLE TENOR of Scripture from beginning to end is to this effect: the matter of revelation is not a mere collection of truths, not a philosophical view, not a religious sentiment or spirit, not a special morality, poured out upon mankind as a stream might pour itself into the sea, mixing with the world's thought, modifying, purifying, invigorating it;—but an authoritative teaching, which bears witness to itself, and keeps itself together as one, in contrast to the assemblage of opinions on all sides of it, and speaks to all men, as being ever and every where one and the same, and claiming to be received intelligently, by all whom it addresses, as one doctrine, discipline, and devotion directly given from above. In consequence, the exhibition of credentials, that is, of evidence, that it is what it professes to be, is essential to Christianity, as it comes to us; for we are not left at liberty to pick and choose out of its contents according to our judgment, but must receive it all, as we find it, if we accept it at all. It is a religion in addition to the religion of nature; and as nature has an intrinsic claim upon us to be obeyed and used, so what is over and above nature, or supernatural, must also bring with it valid testimonials of its right to demand our homage.

Next, as to its relation to nature. As I have said, Christianity is simply an addition to it; it does not supersede or contradict it; it recognizes and depends on it, and that of necessity: for how possibly can it prove its claims except by an appeal to what men have already? be it ever so miraculous, it cannot dispense with nature; this would be to cut the ground from under it; for what would be the worth of evidences in favour of a revelation which denied the authority of that system of thought, and those courses of reasoning, out of which those evidences necessarily grew?

And in agreement with this obvious conclusion we find in Scripture our Lord and His Apostles always treating Christianity as the completion and supplement of Natural Religion, and of previous revelations; as when He says that the Father testified of Him; that not to know Him was not to know the Father; and as St. Paul at Athens appeals to the "Unknown God," and says that "He that made the world now declareth to all men to do penance, because He hath appointed a day to judge the world by the man whom He hath appointed." As then our Lord and His Apostles appeal to the God of Nature, we must follow them in that appeal; and, to do this with the better effect, we must first inquire into the chief doctrines and the grounds of Natural Religion.

By Religion I mean the Knowledge of God, of His Will, and of our duties towards Him; and there are three main channels which Nature furnishes for our acquiring this knowledge, viz. our own minds, the voice of mankind, and the course of the world, that is, of human life and human affairs. The informations which these three convey to us teach us the Being and Attributes of God, our responsibility to Him, our dependence on Him, our prospect of reward or punishment, to be somehow brought about, according as

377

we obey or disobey Him. And the most authoritative of these three means of knowledge, as being specially our own, is our own mind, whose informations give us the rule by which we test, interpret, and correct what is presented to us for belief, whether by the universal testimony of mankind, or by the history of society and of the world.

Our great internal teacher of religion is, as I have said in an earlier part of this Essay, our Conscience.[2] Conscience is a personal guide, and I use it because I must use myself; I am as little able to think by any mind but my own as to breathe with another's lungs. Conscience is nearer to me than any other means of knowledge. And as it is given to me, so also is it given to others; and being carried about by every individual in his own breast, and requiring nothing besides itself, it is thus adapted for the communication to each separately of that knowledge which is most momentous to him individually,—adapted for the use of all classes and conditions of men, for high and low, young and old, men and women, independently of books, educated reasoning, of physical knowledge, or of philosophy. Conscience, too, teaches us, not only that God is, but what He is; it provides for the mind a real image of Him, as a medium of worship; it gives us a rule of right and wrong, as being His rule, and a code of moral duties. Moreover, it is so constituted that, if obeyed, it becomes clearer in its injunctions, and wider in their range, and corrects and completes the accidental feebleness of its initial teachings. Conscience, then, considered as our guide, is fully furnished for its office. I say all this without entering into the question how far external assistances are in all cases necessary to the action of the mind, because in fact man does not live in

378

isolation, but is every where found as a member of society. I am not concerned here with abstract questions.

Now conscience suggests to us many things about that Master, whom by means of it we perceive, but its most prominent teaching, and its cardinal and distinguishing truth, is that He is our Judge. In consequence, the special Attribute under which it brings Him before us, to which it subordinates all other Attributes, is that of justice— retributive justice. We learn from its informations to conceive of the Almighty, primarily, not as a God of Wisdom, of Knowledge, of Power, of Benevolence, but as a God of Judgment and Justice; as One who, not simply for the good of the offender, but as an end good in itself, and as a principle of government, ordains that the offender should suffer for his offence. If it tells us any thing at all of the characteristics of the Divine Mind, it certainly tells us this; and, considering that our shortcomings are far more frequent and important than our fulfillment of the duties enjoined upon us, and that of this point we are fully aware ourselves, it follows that the aspect under which Almighty God is presented to us by Nature, is (to use a figure) of One who is angry with us, and threatens evil. Hence its effect is to burden and sadden the religious mind, and is in contrast with the enjoyment derivable from the exercise of the affections, and from the perception of beauty, whether in the material universe or in the creations of the intellect. This is that fearful antagonism brought out with such soul-piercing reality by Lucretius, when he speaks so dishonourably of what he considers the heavy yoke of religion, and the "aeternas poenas in morte timendum"; and, on the other hand, rejoices in his "Alma Venus," "quae rerum naturam sola gubernas." And we may appeal to him for the fact, while we repudiate his view of it.

Such being the *prima facie* aspect of religion which the teachings of Conscience bring before us individually, in the next place let us consider what are the doctrines, and what the influences, as we find it embodied in those various rites and devotions which have taken root in the many races of mankind, since the beginning of history, and before history, all over the earth. Of these also Lucretius gives us a specimen; and they accord in form and complexion with that doctrine about duty and responsibility, which he so bitterly hates and loathes. It is scarcely necessary to insist, that wherever religion exists in a popular shape, it has almost invariably worn its dark side outwards. It is founded in one way or other on the sense of sin; and without that vivid sense it would hardly have any precepts or any observances. Its many varieties all proclaim or imply that man is in a degraded, servile condition, and requires expiation, reconciliation, and some great change of nature. This is suggested to us in the many ways in which we are told of a realm of light and a realm of darkness, of an elect fold and a regenerate state. It is suggested in the almost ubiquitous and ever-recurring institution of a Priesthood; for wherever there is a priest, there is the notion of sin, pollution, and retribution, as, on the other hand, of intercession and mediation. Also, still more directly, is the notion of our guilt impressed upon us by the doctrine of future punishment, and that eternal, which is found in mythologies and creeds of such various parentage.

Of these distinct rites and doctrines embodying the severe side of Natural Religion, the most remarkable is that of atonement, that is, "a substitution of something offered, or some personal suffering, for a penalty which would other-wise be exacted"; most remarkable, I say, both from its close connexion with the notion of vicarious satisfaction, and, on the other hand, from its universality. "The practice of atonement," says the author, whose definition of the word I have just given, "is remarkable for its antiquity and universality, proved by the earliest records that have come down to us of all nations, and by the testimony of ancient and modern travellers. In the oldest books of the Hebrew Scriptures, we have numerous instances of expiatory rites, where atonement is the prominent feature. At the earliest date, to which we can carry our inquiries by means of the heathen records, we meet with the same notion of atone-ment. If we pursue our inquiries through the accounts left us by the Greek and Roman writers of the barbarous na-tions with which they were acquainted, from India to Britain, we shall find the same notions and similar practices of atonement. From the most popular portion of our own literature, our narratives of voyages and travels, every one, probably, who reads at all will be able to find for himself abundant proof that the notion has been as permanent as it is universal. It shows itself among the various tribes of Africa, the islanders of the South Seas, and even that most peculiar race, the natives of Australia, either in the shape of some offering, or some mutilation of the person."[3]

These ceremonial acknowledgments, in so many distinct forms of worship, of the existing degradation of the human race, of course imply a brighter, as well as a threatening aspect of Natural Religion; for why should men adopt any rites of deprecation or of purification at all, unless they had some hope of attaining to a better condition than their present? Of this happier side of religion I will speak presently; here, however, a question of another kind occurs, viz. whether the notion of atonement can be admitted among the doctrines of Natural Religion,—I mean, on the ground that it is inconsistent with those teachings of Conscience, which I have recognized above, as the rule and corrective of every other information on the subject. If there is any truth brought home to us by conscience, it is this, that we are personally responsible for what we do, that we have no means of shifting our responsibility, and that dereliction of duty involves punishment; how, it may be asked, can acts of ours of any kind—how can even amendment of life—undo the past? And if even our own subsequent acts of obedience bring with them no promise of reversing what has once been committed, how can external rites, or the actions of another (as of a priest), be substitutes for that punishment which is the connatural fruit and intrinsic development of violation of the sense of duty?

I think this objection avails as far as this, that amendment is no reparation, and that no ceremonies or penances can in themselves exercise any vicarious virtue in our behalf, and that, if they avail, they only avail in the intermediate season of probation, that in some way we must make them our own, and that, when the time comes, which conscience forebodes, of our being called to judgment, then, at least, we shall have to stand in and by ourselves, whatever we shall have by that time become, and must bear our own burden. But it is plain that in this final account, as it lies between us and our Master, He alone can decide how the past and the present will stand together who is our Creator and our Judge.

In thus making it a necessary point to adjust the religions

of the world with the intimations of our conscience, I am suggesting the reason why I confine myself to such religions as have had their rise in barbarous times, and do not recognize the religion of what is called civilization, as having legitimately a part in the delineation of Natural Religion. It may at first sight seem strange, that, considering I have laid such stress upon the progressive nature of man, I should take my ideas of his religion from his initial, and not his final testimony about its doctrines; and it may be urged that the religion of civilized times is quite opposite in character to the rites and traditions of barbarians, and has nothing of that gloom and sternness, on which I have insisted as their characteristic. Thus the Greek Mythology was for the most part cheerful and graceful, and its new gods certainly more genial and indulgent than the old ones. And, in like manner, the religion of philosophy is more noble and more humane than those primitive conceptions which were sufficient for early kings and warriors.

But my answer to this objection is obvious: the progress of which man's nature is capable is a development, not a destruction of its original state; it must subserve the elements from which it proceeds, in order to be a true development and not a perversion. And those popular rituals do in fact subserve and complete that nature with which man is born. It is otherwise with the religion of so-called civilization; such religion does but contradict the religion of barbarism; and since this civilization itself is not a development of man's whole nature, but mainly of the intellect, recognizing indeed the moral sense, but ignoring the conscience, no wonder that the religion in which it issues has no sympathy either with the hopes and fears of the awakened soul, or with those frightful presentiments which are

383

expressed in the worship and traditions of the heathen. This artificial religion, then, has no place in the inquiry; first, because it comes of a one-sided progress of mind, and next, for the very reason that it contradicts informants which speak with greater authority than itself.

Now we come to the third natural informant on the subject of Religion; I mean the system and the course of the world. This established order of things, in which we find ourselves, if it has a Creator, must surely speak of His will in its broad outlines and its main issues. This principle being laid down as certain, when we come to apply it to things as they are, our first feeling is one of surprise and (I may say) of dismay, that His control of this living world is so indirect, and His action so obscure. This is the first lesson that we gain from the course of human affairs.

What strikes the mind so forcibly and so painfully is, His absence (if I may so speak) from His own world.[4] It is a silence that speaks. It is as if others had got possession of His work. Why does not He, our Maker and Ruler, give us some immediate knowledge of Himself? Why does He not write His Moral Nature in large letters upon the face of history, and bring the blind, tumultuous rush of its events into a celestial, hierarchical order? Why does he not grant us in the structure of society at least so much of a revelation of Himself as the religions of the heathen attempt to supply? Why from the beginning of time has no one uniform steady light guided all families of the earth, and all individual men, how to please Him? Why is it possible without absurdity to deny His will, His attributes, His existence? Why does He not walk with us one by one, as He is said to have walked with his chosen men of old time? We both see and know each other; why, if we cannot have the sight of Him, have we not at least the knowledge?

384

On the contrary, He is specially "a Hidden God"; and with our best efforts we can only glean from the surface of the world some faint and fragmentary views of Him. I see only a choice of alternatives in explanation of so critical a fact:—either there is no Creator, or He has disowned His creatures. Are then the dim shadows of His Presence in the affairs of men but a fancy of our own, or, on the other hand, has He hid His face and the light of His countenance, because we have in some special way dishonoured Him? My true informant, my burdened conscience, gives me at once the true answer to each of these antagonist questions:—it pronounces without any misgiving that God exists:—and it pronounces too quite as surely that I am alienated from Him; that "His Hand is not shortened, but that our iniquities have divided between us and our God." Thus it solves the world's mystery, and sees in that mystery only a confirmation of its own original teaching.

Let us pass on to another great fact of experience, bearing on Religion, which confirms this testimony both of conscience and of the forms of worship which prevail among mankind;—I mean, the amount of suffering, bodily and mental, which is our portion in this life. Not only is the Creator far off, but some being of malignant nature seems, as I have said, to have got hold of us, and to be making us his sport. Let us say there are a thousand millions of men on the earth at this time; who can weigh and measure the aggregate of pain which this one generation has endured and will endure from birth to death? Then add to this all the pain which has fallen and will fall upon our race through centuries past and to come. Is there not then some great gulf fixed between us and the good God? Here again the testimony of the system of nature is more than corroborated by those popular traditions about the unseen state, which are found in mythologies and superstitions, ancient and modern; for those traditions speak, not only of present misery, but of pain and evil hereafter, and even without end. But this dreadful addition is not necessary for the conclusion which I am here wishing to draw. The real mystery is, not that evil should never have an end, but that it should ever have had a beginning. Even a universal restitution could not undo what had been, or account for evil being the necessary condition of good. How are we to explain it, the existence of God being taken for granted, except by saying that another will, besides His, has had a part in the disposition of His work, that there is a quarrel without remedy, a chronic alienation, between God and man?

I have implied that the laws on which this world is governed do not go so far as to prove that evil will never die out of the creation; nevertheless, they look in that direction. No experience indeed of life can assure us about the future, but it can and does give us means of conjecturing what is likely to be; and those conjectures coincide with our natural forebodings. Experience enables us to ascertain the moral constitution of man, and thereby to presage his future from his present. It teaches us, first, that he is not sufficient for his own happiness, but is dependent upon the sensible objects which surround him, and that these he cannot take with him when he leaves the world; secondly, that disobedience to his sense of right is even by itself misery, and that he carries that misery about him, wherever he is, though no divine retribution followed upon it; and thirdly, that he cannot change his nature and his habits by wishing, but is simply himself, and will ever be himself and what he now is, wherever he is, as long as he continues to be,—or at least that pain has no natural tendency to make him other

386

than he is, and that the longer he lives, the more difficult he is to change. How can we meet these not irrational anticipations, except by shutting our eyes, turning away from them, and saying that we have no call, no right, to think of them at present, or to make ourselves miserable about what is not certain, and may be not true?

Such is the severe aspect of Natural Religion: also it is the most prominent aspect, because the multitude of men follow their own likings and wills, and not the decisions of their sense of right and wrong. To them Religion is a mere yoke, as Lucretius describes it; not a satisfaction or refuge, but a terror and a superstition. However, I must not for an instant be supposed to mean, that this is its only, its chief, or its legitimate aspect. All Religion, so far as it is genuine, is a blessing, Natural as well as Revealed. I have insisted on its severe aspect in the first place, because, from the circumstances of human nature, though not by the fault of Religion, such is the shape in which we first encounter it. Its large and deep foundation is the sense of sin and guilt, and without this sense there is for man, as he is, no genuine religion. Otherwise, it is but counterfeit and hollow; and that is the reason why this so-called religion of civilization and philosophy is so great a mockery. However, true as this judgment is which I pass on philosophical religion, and troubled as are the existing relations between God and man, as both the voice of mankind and the facts of Divine Government testify, equally true are other general laws which govern those relations, and they speak another language, and compensate for what is stern in the teaching of nature, without tending to deny that sternness.

The first of these laws, relieving the aspect of Natural Religion, is the very fact that religious beliefs and institutions, of some kind or other, are of such general acceptance in all times and places. Why should men subject themselves to the tyranny which Lucretius denounces, unless they had either experience or hope of benefits to themselves by so doing? Though it be mere hope of benefits, that alone is a great alleviation of the gloom and misery which their religious rites presuppose or occasion; for thereby they have a prospect, more or less clear, of some happier state in reserve for them, or at least the chances of it. If they simply despaired of their fortunes, they would not care about religion. And hope of future good, as we know, sweetens all suffering.

Moreover, they have an earnest of that future in the real and recurring blessings of life, the enjoyment of the gifts of the earth, and of domestic affection and social intercourse, which is sufficient to affect and subdue even the most guilty of men in his better moments, reminding him that he is not utterly cast off by Him whom nevertheless he is not given to know. Or, in the Apostle's words, though the Creator once "suffered all nations to walk in their own ways," still, "He left not Himself without testimony, doing good from heaven, giving rains and fruitful seasons, filling our hearts with food and gladness."

Nor are these blessings of physical nature the only tokens in the Divine System, which in that heathen time, and indeed in every age, bring home to our experience the fact of a Good God, in spite of the tumult and confusion of the world. It is possible to give an interpretation to the course of things, by which every event or occurrence in its order becomes providential: and though that interpretation does not hold good unless the world is contemplated from a particular point of view, in one given aspect, and with certain

388

inward experiences, and personal first principles and judgments, yet these may be fairly pronounced to be common conditions of human thought, that is, till they are wilfully or accidentally lost; and they issue in fact, in leading the great majority of men to recognize the Hand of unseen power, directing in mercy or in judgment the physical and moral system. In the prominent events of the world, past and contemporary, the fate, evil or happy, of great men, the rise and fall of states, popular revolutions, decisive battles, the migration of races, the replenishing of the earth, earthquakes and pestilences, critical discoveries and inventions, the history of philosophy, the advancement of knowledge, in these the spontaneous piety of the human mind discerns a Divine Supervision.

Nay, there is a general feeling, originating directly in the workings of conscience, that a similar governance is extended over the persons of individuals, who thereby both fulfil the purposes and receive the just recompenses of an Omnipotent Providence. Good to the good, and evil to the evil, is instinctively felt to be, even from what we see, amid whatever obscurity and confusion, the universal rule of God's dealings with us. Hence come the great proverbs, indigenous in both Christian and heathen nations, that punishment is sure, though slow, that murder will out, that treason never prospers, that pride will have a fall, that honesty is the best policy, and that curses fall on the heads of those who utter them. To the unsophisticated apprehension of the many, the successive passages of life, social, or political, are so many miracles, if that is to be accounted miraculous which brings before them the immediate Divine Presence; and should it be objected that this is an illogical exercise of reason, I answer, that since it actually brings them to a right conclusion, and was intended to bring them to it, if logic finds fault with it, so much the worse for logic.

Again, prayer is essential to religion, and, where prayer is, there is a natural relief and solace in all trouble, great or ordinary: nor prayer is not less general in mankind at large than is faith in Providence. It has ever been in use, both as a personal and as a social practice. Here again, if, in order to determine what the Religion of Nature is, we may justly have recourse to the spontaneous acts and proceedings of our race, as viewed on a large field, we may safely say that prayer, as well as hope, is a constituent of man's religion. Nor is it a fair objection to this argument, to say that such prayers and rites as have obtained in various places and times, are in their character, object, and scope inconsistent with each other; because their contrarieties do not come into the idea of religion, as such, at all, and the very fact of their discordance destroys their right to be taken into account, so far as they are discordant; for what is not universal has no claim to be considered natural, right, or of divine origin. Thus we may determine prayer to be part of Natural Religion, from such instances of the usage as are supplied by the priests of Baal and by dancing Dervishes, without therefore including in our notions of prayer the frantic excesses of the one, or the artistic spinning of the other, or sanctioning their respective objects of belief, Baal or Mahomet.

As prayer is the voice of man to God, so Revelation is the voice of God to man. Accordingly, it is another alleviation of the darkness and distress which weigh upon the religions of the world, that in one way or other such religions are founded on some idea of express revelation, coming from the unseen agents whose anger they deprecate; nay, that the very rites and observances, by which they hope to gain the favour of these beings, are by these beings themselves communicated and appointed. The Religion of Nature has not been a deduction of reason, or the joint, voluntary manifesto of a multitude meeting together and pledging themselves to each other, as men move resolutions now for some political or social purpose, but it has been a tradition or an interposition vouchsafed to a people from above. To such an interposition men even ascribed their civil polity or citizenship, which did not originate in any plebiscite, but in *dii minores* or heroes, and was inaugurated with portents or palladia, and protected and prospered by oracles and auguries. Here is an evidence, too, how congenial the notion of a revelation is to the human mind, so that the expectation of it may truly be considered an integral part of Natural Religion.

Among the observances imposed by these professed revelations, none is more remarkable, or more general, than the rite of sacrifice, in which guilt was removed or blessing gained by an offering, which availed instead of the merits of the offerer. This too, as well as the notion of divine interpositions, may be considered almost an integral part of the Religion of Nature and an alleviation of its gloom. But it does not stand by itself; I have already spoken of the doctrine of atonement, under which it falls, and which, if what is universal is natural, enters into the idea of religious service. And what the nature of man suggests, the providential system of the world sanctions by enforcing. It is the law, or the permission, given to our whole race, to use the Apostle's words, to "bear one another's burdens"; and this, as I said when on the subject of Atonement, is quite consistent with his antithesis that "every one must bear his own burden."

391

The final burden of responsibility when we are called to judgment is our own; but among the media by which we are prepared for that judgment are the exertions and pains taken in our behalf by others.

On this vicarious principle, by which we appropriate to ourselves what others do for us, the whole structure of society is raised. Parents work and endure pain, that their children may prosper; children suffer for the sin of their parents, who have died before it bore fruit. "Delirant reges, plectuntur Achivi." Sometimes it is a compulsory, sometimes a willing mediation. The punishment which is earned by the husband falls upon the wife; the benefits in which all classes partake are wrought out by the unhealthy or dangerous toil of the few. Soldiers endure wounds and death for those who sit at home; and ministers of state fall victims to their zeal for their countrymen, who do little else than criticize their actions. And so in some measure or way this law embraces all of us. We all suffer for each other, and gain by each other's sufferings; for man never stands alone here, though he will stand by himself one day hereafter; but here he is a social being, and goes forward to his long home as one of a large company.

Butler, it need scarcely be said, is the great master of this doctrine, as it is brought out in the system of nature. In answer to the objection to the Christian doctrine of satisfaction, that it "represents God as indifferent whether He punishes the innocent or the guilty," he observes that "the world is a constitution or system, whose parts have a mutual reference to each other; and that there is a scheme of things gradually carrying on, called the course of nature, to the carrying on of which God has appointed us, in various ways, to contribute. And in the daily course of natural providence, it is appointed that innocent people should suffer for the faults of the guilty. Finally, indeed and upon the whole, every one shall receive according to his personal deserts; but during the progress, and, for aught we know, even in order to the completion of this moral scheme, vicarious punishments may be fit, and absolutely necessary. We see in what variety of ways one person's sufferings contribute to the relief of another; and being familiarized to it, men are not shocked with it. So the reason of their insisting on objections against the [doctrine of] satisfaction is, either that they do not consider God's settled and uniform appointments as His appointments at all; or else they forget that vicarious punishment is a providential appointment of every day's experience."[5] I will but add, that, since all human suffering is in its last resolution the punishment of sin, and punishment implies a Judge and a rule of justice, he who undergoes the punishment of another in his stead may be said in a certain sense to satisfy the claims of justice towards that other in his own person.

One concluding remark has to be made here. In all sacrifices it was especially required that the thing offered should be something rare, and unblemished; and in like manner in all atonements and all satisfactions, not only was the innocent taken for the guilty, but it was a point of special importance that the victim should be spotless, and the more manifest that spotlessness, the more efficacious was the sacrifice. This leads me to a last principle which I shall notice as proper to Natural Religion, and as lightening the prophecies of evil in which it is founded; I mean the doctrine of meritorious intercession. The man in the Gospel did

393

but speak for the human race every where, when he said, "God heareth not sinners; but if a man be a worshipper of God, and doth His will, him He heareth." Hence every religion has had its eminent devotees, exalted above the body of the people, mortified men, brought nearer to the Source of good by austerities, self-inflictions, and prayer, who have influence with Him, and extend a shelter and gain blessings for those who become their clients. A belief like this has been, of course, attended by numberless superstitions; but those superstitions vary with times and places, and the belief itself in the mediatorial power of the good and holy has been one and the same every where. Nor is this belief an idea of past times only or of heathen countries. It is one of the most natural visions of the young and innocent. And all of us, the more keenly we feel our own distance from holy persons, the more are we drawn near to them, as if forgetting that distance, and proud of them because they are so unlike ourselves, as being specimens of what our nature may be, and with some vague hope that we, their relations by blood, may profit in our own persons by their holiness.

Such, then, in outline is that system of natural beliefs and sentiments, which, though true and divine, is still possible to us independently of Revelation, and is the preparation for it; though in Christians themselves it cannot really be separated from their Christianity, and never is possessed in its higher forms in any people without some portion of those inward aids which Christianity imparts to us, and those endemic traditions which have their first origin in a paradisiacal illumination.

Revelation begins where Natural Religion fails. The Religion of Nature is a mere inchoation, and needs a complement,—it can have but one complement, and that very complement is Christianity. Natural Religion is based upon the sense of sin; it recognizes the disease, but it cannot find, it does but look out for the remedy. That remedy, both for guilt and for moral impotence, is found in the central doctrine of Revelation, the Mediation of Christ.

CHAPTER XXXV

FAITH AS AN EXERCISE OF REASON[1]

I NOW PROCEED to state distinctly what I conceive to be the relation of Faith to Reason. I observe, then, as follows:—

We are surrounded by beings which exist quite independently of us,—exist whether we exist, or cease to exist, whether we have cognizance of them or no. These we commonly separate into two great divisions, material and immaterial. Of the material we have direct knowledge through the senses; we are sensible of the existence of persons and things, of their properties and modes, of their relations toward each other, and the courses of action which they carry on. Of all these we are directly cognizant through the senses; we see and hear what passes, and that immediately. As to immaterial beings, that we have faculties analogous to sense by which we have direct knowledge of their presence, does not appear, except indeed as regards our own soul and its acts. But so far is certain at least, that we are not conscious of possessing them; and we account it, and rightly, to be enthusiasm to profess such consciousness. At times, indeed, that consciousness has been imparted, as in some of the appearances of God to man contained in Scripture: but, in the ordinary course of things, whatever direct intercourse goes on between the soul and immaterial beings, whether we perceive them or not, and are influenced by them or not, certainly we have no consciousness of that perception or influence, such as our senses convey to us in the perception of things material. The senses, then, are the only instruments which we know to be granted to us for direct and immediate acquaintance with things external to us. Moreover, it is obvious that even our senses convey us but a little way out of ourselves, and introduce us to the external world only under circumstances, under conditions of time and place, and of certain media through which they act. We must be near things to touch them; we must be interrupted by no simultaneous sounds to hear them; we must have light to see them; we can neither see, hear, nor touch things past or future.

Now, Reason is that faculty of the mind by which this deficiency is supplied; by which knowledge of things external to us, of beings, facts, and events, is attained beyond the range of sense. It ascertains for us not natural things only, or immaterial only, or present only, or past, or future; but, even if limited in its power, it is unlimited in its range, viewed as a faculty, though, of course, in individuals it varies in range also. It reaches to the ends of the universe, and to the throne of God beyond them; it brings us knowledge, whether clear or uncertain, still knowledge, in whatever degree of perfection, from every side; but, at the same time, with this characteristic, that it obtains it indirectly, not directly.

Reason does not really perceive any thing; but it is a faculty of proceeding from things that are perceived to things which are not; the existence of which it certifies to us on the hypothesis of something else being known to exist, in other words, being assumed to be true.

Such is Reason, simply considered; and hence the fitness of a number of words which are commonly used to denote it and its acts. For instance; its act is usually considered a process, which, of course, a progress of thought from one idea to the other must be; an exercise of mind, which perception through the senses can hardly be called; or, again, an investigation, or an analysis; or it is said to compare, discriminate, judge, and decide: all which words imply, not simply assent to the reality of certain external facts, but a search into grounds, and an assent upon grounds. It is, then, the faculty of gaining knowledge upon grounds given; and its exercise lies in asserting one thing, because of some other thing; and, when its exercise is conducted rightly, it leads to knowledge; when wrongly, to apparent knowledge, to opinion, and error.

Now, if this be Reason, an act or process of Faith, simply considered, is certainly an exercise of Reason; whether a right exercise or not is a farther question; and, whether so to call it, is a sufficient account of it, is a farther question. It is an acceptance of things as real, which the senses do not convey, upon certain previous grounds; it is an instrument of indirect knowledge concerning things external to us,—the process being such as the following: "I assent to this doctrine as true, because I have been taught it"; or, "because superiors tell me so"; or, "because good men think so"; or, "because very different men think so"; or, "because all men"; or, "most men"; or, "because it is established"; or, "because persons whom I trust say that it was once guaranteed by miracles"; or, "because one who is said to have wrought miracles," or "who says he wrought them," "has taught it"; or, "because I have seen one who saw the miracles"; or "because I saw what I took to be a miracle"; or for all or some of these reasons together. Some such exercise of Reason is the act of Faith, considered in its nature.

On the other hand, Faith plainly lies exposed to the popular charge of being a faulty exercise of Reason, as being conducted on insufficient grounds; and, I suppose, so much must be allowed on all hands, either that it is illogical, or that the mind has some grounds which are not fully brought out, when the process is thus exhibited. In other words, that when the mind savingly believes, the reasoning which that belief involves, if it be logical, does not merely proceed from the actual evidence, but from other grounds besides.

I say, there is this alternative in viewing the particular process of Reason which is involved in Faith;—to say either that the process is illogical, or the subject-matter more or less special and recondite; the act of inference faulty, or the premisses undeveloped; that Faith is weak, or that it is unearthly. Scripture says that it is unearthly, and the world says that it is weak.

This, then, being the imputation brought against Faith, that it is the reasoning of a weak mind, whereas it is in truth the reasoning of a divinely enlightened one, let me now, in a few words, attempt to show the analogy of this state of things, with what takes place in regard to other exercises of Reason also; that is, I shall attempt to show that Faith is not the only exercise of Reason, which, when critically examined, would be called unreasonable, and yet is not so.

(1) In truth, nothing is more common among men of a reasoning turn than to consider that no one reasons well but themselves. All men of course think that they them-

selves are right and others wrong, who differ from them; and so far all men must find fault with the reasonings of others, since no one proposes to act without reasons of some kind. Accordingly, so far as men are accustomed to analyze the opinions of others and to contemplate their processes of thought, they are tempted to despise them as illogical. If any one sets about examining why his neighbours are on one side in political questions, not on another; why for or against certain measures, of a social, economical, or civil nature; why they belong to this religious party, not to that; why they hold this or that doctrine; why they have certain tastes in literature; or why they hold certain views in matters of opinion; it is needless to say that, if he measures their grounds merely by the reasons which they produce, he will have no difficulty in holding them up to ridicule, or even to censure.

And so again as to the deductions made from definite facts common to all. From the sight of the same sky one may augur fine weather, another bad; from the signs of the times one the coming in of good, another of evil; from the same actions of individuals one infers moral greatness, another depravity or perversity, one simplicity, another craft; upon the same evidence one justifies, another condemns. The miracles of Christianity were in early times imputed by some to magic, others they converted; the union of its professors was ascribed to seditious and traitorous aims by some, while others it moved to say, "See how these Christians love one another." The phenomena of the physical world have given rise to a variety of theories, that is, of alleged facts, at which they are supposed to point; theories of astronomy, chemistry, and physiology; theories religious and atheistical. The same events are considered to prove a particular providence, and not; to attest the divinity of one religion or of another. The downfall of the Roman Empire was to Pagans a refutation, to Christians an evidence, of Christianity. Such is the diversity with which men reason, showing us that Faith is not the only exercise of Reason, which approves itself to some and not to others, or which is, in the common sense of the word, irrational.

Nor can it fairly be said that such varieties do arise from deficiency in the power of reasoning in the multitude; and that Faith, such as I have described it, is but proved thereby to be a specimen of such deficiency. This is what men of clear intellects are not slow to imagine. Clear, strong, steady intellects, if they are not deep, will look on these differences in deduction chiefly as failures in the reasoning faculty, and will despise them or excuse them accordingly. Such are the men who are commonly latitudinarians in religion on the one hand, or innovators on the other; men of exact or acute but shallow minds, who consider all men wrong but themselves, yet think it no matter though they be; who regard the pursuit of truth only as a syllogistic process, and failure in attaining it as arising merely from a want of mental conformity with the laws on which just reasoning is conducted.

But surely there is no greater mistake than this. For the experience of life contains abundant evidence that in practical matters, when their minds are really roused, men commonly are not bad reasoners. Men do not mistake when their interest is concerned. They have an instinctive sense in which direction their path lies towards it, and how they must act consistently with self-preservation or self-aggrandisement. And so in the case of questions in which party spirit, or political opinion, or ethical principle, or personal feeling, is concerned, men have a surprising sagacity, often

401

unknown to themselves, in finding their own place. However remote the connexion between the point in question and their own creed, or habits, or feelings, the principles which they profess guide them unerringly to their legitimate issues; and thus it often happens that in apparently indifferent practices or usages or sentiments, or in questions of science, or politics, or literature, we can almost prophesy beforehand, from their religious or moral views, where certain persons will stand, and often can defend them far better than they defend themselves. The same thing is proved from the internal consistency of such religious creeds as are allowed time and space to develop freely; such as Primitive Christianity, or the Medieval system, or Calvinism—a consistency which nevertheless is wrought out in and through the rude and inaccurate minds of the multitude. Again, it is proved from the uniformity observable in the course of the same doctrine in different ages and countries, whether it be political, religious, or philosophical; the laws of Reason forcing it on into the same developments, the same successive phases, the same rise, and the same decay, so that its recorded history in one century will almost suit its prospective course in the next.

All this shows, that in spite of the inaccuracy in expression, or (if we will) in thought, which prevails in the world, men on the whole do not reason incorrectly. If their reason itself were in fault, they would reason each in his own way: whereas they form into schools, and that not merely from imitation and sympathy, but certainly from internal compulsion, from the constraining influence of their several principles. They may argue badly, but they reason well; that is, their professed grounds are no sufficient measures of their real ones. And in like manner, though the evidence with which Faith is content is apparently inadequate to its purpose, yet this is no proof of real weakness or imperfection in its reasoning. It seems to be contrary to Reason, yet is not; it is but independent of and distinct from what are called philosophical inquiries, intellectual systems, courses of argument, and the like.

So much on the general phenomena which attend the exercise of this great faculty, one of the characteristics of human over brute natures. Whether we consider processes of Faith or other exercise of Reason, men advance forward on grounds which they do not, or cannot produce, or if they could, yet could not prove to be true, on latent or antecedent grounds which they take for granted.

(2) Next, let it be observed, that however full and however precise our producible grounds may be, however systematic our method, however clear and tangible our evidence, yet when our argument is traced down to its simple elements, there must ever be something assumed ultimately which is incapable of proof, and without which our conclusions will be as illogical as Faith is apt to seem to men of the world.

To take the case of actual evidence, and that of the strongest kind. Now, whatever it be, its cogency must be a thing taken for granted; so far it is its own evidence, and can only be received on instinct or prejudice. For instance, we trust our senses, and that in spite of their often deceiving us.[2] They even contradict each other at times, yet we trust them. But even were they ever consistent, never unfaithful, still their fidelity would not be thereby proved. We consider that there is so strong an antecedent probability that they are faithful, that we dispense with proof. We take the point for granted; or, if we have grounds for it, these either

403

lie in our secret belief in the stability of nature, or in the preserving presence and uniformity of Divine Providence,—which, again, are points assumed. As, then, the senses may and do deceive us, and yet we trust them from a secret instinct, so it need not be weakness or rashness, if upon a certain presentiment of mind we trust to the fidelity of testimony offered for a Revelation.

Again; we rely implicitly on our memory, and that, too, in spite of its being obviously unstable and treacherous. And we trust to memory for the truth of most of our opinions; the grounds on which we hold them not being at a given moment all present to our minds. We trust to memory to inform us what we do hold and what we do not. It may be said, that without such assumption the world could not go on: true; and in the same way the Church could not go on without Faith. Acquiescence in testimony, or in evidence not stronger than testimony, is the only method, as far as we see, by which the next world can be revealed to us.

The same remarks apply to our assumption of the fidelity of our reasoning powers; which in certain instances we implicitly believe, though we know they have deceived us in others.

Were it not for these instincts, it cannot be doubted but our experience of the deceivableness of Senses, Memory, and Reason, would perplex us much as to our practical reliance on them in matters of this world. And so, as regards the matters of another, they who have not that instinctive apprehension of the Omnipresence of God and His unwearied and minute Providence which holiness and love create within us, must not be surprised to find that the evidence of Christianity does not perform an office which was never intended for it,—viz. that of recommending itself

404

as well as the Revelation. Nothing, then, which Scripture says about Faith, however startling it may be at first sight, is inconsistent with the state in which we find ourselves by nature with reference to the acquisition of knowledge generally,—a state in which we must assume something to prove anything, and can gain nothing without a venture.

(3) To proceed. Next let it be considered, that the following law seems to hold in our attainment of knowledge, that according to its desirableness, whether in point of excellence, or range, or intricacy, so is the subtlety of the evidence on which it is received. We are so constituted, that if we insist upon being as sure as is conceivable, in every step of our course, we must be content to creep along the ground, and can never soar. If we are intended for great ends, we are called to great hazards; and, whereas we are given absolute certainty in nothing, we must in all things choose between doubt and inactivity, and the conviction that we are under the eye of One who, for whatever reason, exercises us with the less evidence when He might give us the greater.[3] He has put it into our hands, who loves us; and He bids us examine it, indeed, with our best judgment, reject this and accept that, but still all the while as loving Him in our turn; not coldly and critically, but with the thought of His presence, and the reflection that perchance by the defects of the evidence He is trying our love of its matter; and that perchance it is a law of His Providence to speak less loudly the more He promises.

For instance, the touch is the most certain and cautious, but it is the most circumscribed of our senses, and reaches but an arm's length. The eye, which takes in a far wider range, acts only in the light. Reason, which extends beyond the province of sense or the present time, is circuitous and

405

indirect in its conveyance of knowledge, which, even when distinct, is traced out pale and faint, as distant objects on the horizon. And Faith, again, by which we get to know divine things, rests on the evidence of testimony, weak in proportion to the excellence of the blessing attested. And as Reason, with its great conclusions, is confessedly a higher instrument than Sense with its secure premisses, so Faith rises above Reason, in its subject-matter, more than it falls below it in the obscurity of its process. And it is, I say, but agreeable to analogy, that Divine Truth should be attained by so subtle and indirect a method, a method less tangible than others, less open to analysis, reducible but partially to the forms of Reason, and the ready sport of objection and cavil.

(4) Further, much might be observed concerning the special delicacy and abstruseness of such reasoning processes as attend the acquisition of all higher knowledge. It is not too much to say that there is no one of the greater achievements of the Reason, which would show to advantage, which would be apparently justified and protected from criticism, if thrown into the technical forms which the science of argument requires. The most remarkable victories of genius, remarkable both in their originality and the confidence with which they have been pursued, have been gained, as though by invisible weapons, by ways of thought so recondite and intricate that the mass of men are obliged to take them on trust, till the event or other evidence confirms them.

Such are the methods which penetrating intellects have invented in mathematical science, which look like sophisms till they issue in truths.[4] Here, even in the severest of disciplines, and in absolutely demonstrative processes, the instrument of discovery is so subtle, that technical expressions and formulae are of necessity substituted for it, to thread the labyrinth withal, by way of tempering its difficulties to the grosser reason of the many. Or, let it be considered how rare and immaterial (if I may use the words) is metaphysical proof: how difficult to embrace, even when presented to us by philosophers in whose clearness of mind and good sense we fully confide; and what a vain system of words without ideas such men seem to be piling up, while perhaps we are obliged to confess that it must be we who are dull, not they who are fanciful; and that, whatever be the character of their investigations, we want the vigour or flexibility of mind to judge them. Or let us attempt to ascertain the passage of the mind, when slight indications in things present are made the informants of what is to be. Consider the preternatural sagacity with which a great general knows what his friends and enemies are about, and what will be the final result, and where, of their combined movements,—and then say whether, if he were required to argue the matter in word or on paper, all his most brilliant conjectures might not be refuted, and all his producible reasons exposed as illogical.

And, in an analogous way, Faith is a process of the Reason, in which so much of the grounds of inference cannot be exhibited, so much lies in the character of the mind itself, in its general view of things, its estimate of the probable and the improbable, its impressions concerning God's will, and its anticipations derived from its own inbred wishes, that it will ever seem to the world irrational and despicable;—till, that is, the event confirms it. The act of mind, for instance, by which an unlearned person savingly believes the Gospel, on the word of his teacher, may be analogous to the exercise of sagacity in a great statesman or general, supernatural grace doing for the uncultivated reason what genius does for them.

(5) Now it is a singular confirmation of this view of the subject, that the reasonings of inspired men in Scripture, nay, of God Himself, are of this recondite nature; so much so, that irreverent minds scarcely hesitate to treat them with the same contempt which they manifest towards the faith of ordinary Christians. St. Paul's arguments have been long ago abandoned even by men who professed to be defenders of Christianity. Nor can it be said surely that the line of thought (if I may dare so to speak), on which some of our Ever-blessed Saviour's discourses proceed, is more intelligible to our feeble minds. And here, moreover, let it be noted that, supposing the kind of reasoning which we call Faith to be of the subtle character which I am maintaining, and the instances of professed reasoning found in Scripture to be of a like subtlety, light is thrown upon another remarkable circumstance, which no one can deny, and which some have made an objection,—I mean, the indirectness of the Scripture proof on which the Catholic doctrines rest. It may be, that such a peculiarity in the inspired text is the proper correlative of Faith; such a text the proper matter for Faith to work upon; so that a Scripture such as we have, and not such as the Pentateuch was to the Jews, may be implied in our being under Faith and not under the Law.

(6) Lastly, it should be observed that the analogy which I have been pursuing extends to moral actions, and their properties and objects, as well as to intellectual exercises. According as objects are great, the mode of attaining them is extraordinary; and again, according as it is extraordinary, so is the merit of the action. Here, instead of going to Scrip-

ture, or to a religious standard, let me appeal to the world's judgment in the matter. Military fame, for instance, power, character for greatness of mind, distinction in experimental science, are all sought and attained by risks and adventures. Courage does not consist in calculation, but in fighting against chances. The statesman whose name endures, is he who ventures upon measures which seem perilous, and yet succeed, and can be only justified on looking back upon them. Firmness and greatness of soul are shown, when a ruler stands his ground on his instinctive perception of a truth which the many scoff at, and which seems failing. The religious enthusiast bows the hearts of men to a voluntary obedience, who has the keenness to see, and the boldness to appeal to, principles and feelings deep buried within them, which they know not themselves, which he himself but by glimpses and at times realizes, and which he pursues from the intensity, not the steadiness of his view of them.

And so in all things, great objects exact a venture, and a sacrifice is the condition of honour. And what is true in the world, why should it not be true also in the kingdom of God? We must "launch out into the deep, and let down our nets for a draught"; we must in the morning sow our seed, and in the evening withhold not our hand, for we know not whether shall prosper, either this or that. "He that observeth the wind shall not sow, and he that regardeth the clouds shall not reap." He that fails nine times and succeeds the tenth, is a more honourable man that he who hides his talent in a napkin; and so, even though the feelings which prompt us to see God in all things, and to recognize supernatural works in matters of the world, mislead us at times, though they make us trust in evidence which we ought not to admit, and partially incur with justice the imputation of credulity, yet a Faith which generously apprehends Eternal Truth, though at times it degenerates into superstition, is far better than that cold, sceptical, critical tone of mind, which has no inward sense of an overruling, ever-present Providence, no desire to approach its God, but sits at home waiting for the fearful clearness of His visible coming, whom it might seek and find in due measure amid the twilight of the present world.

CHAPTER XXXVI

PRAYER TO THE FATHER OF LIGHTS[1]

O GRACIOUS AND merciful God, Father of Lights, I humbly pray and beseech Thee, that in all my exercises of Reason, Thy gift, I may use it, as Thou wouldst have me use it, in the obedience of Faith, with a view to Thy Glory, with an aim at Thy Truth, in dutiful submission to Thy Will, for the comfort of Thine elect, for the edification of Holy Jerusalem, Thy Church, and in recollection of Thine own solemn warning: "Every idle word that men shall speak, they shall give an account thereof in the day of judgment; for by thy words, thou shalt be justified, and by thy words, thou shalt be condemned."

NOTES

Full bibliographical information is given here only for those works which are not included in the Bibliographical Note. The few notes by Newman himself are here placed within squared brackets, and the other notes are by the editor.

General Introduction

1. Manuscript, January 5, 1860. Most of the MS quotations in this Reader are taken from "Newman's Philosophical Papers," MS A.46.3, preserved at the Birmingham Oratory and used with the kind permission of C. S. Dessain, C. O. Microfilms are available for study at Yale, Illinois, and Notre Dame universities. The importance of the present text is noted by C. S. Dessain, C. O., "Cardinal Newman on the Theory and Practice of Knowledge: The Purpose of the *Grammar of Assent*," *The Downside Review*, 75 (1957), 1-23.

2. *Apologia*, 10. On the Oriel Noetics and Newman's relation with Whately, see A. D. Culler, *The Imperial Intellect*, 35-45; Maisie Ward, *Young Mr. Newman*, 74-76, 93-95, 115-116.

3. Richard Whately, *Elements of Logic* (ninth ed., Louisville: Morton and Griswold, 1854), 180.

4. *John Henry Newman, Autobiographical Writings*, edited by H. Tristram, C. O., 61.

5. *An Essay on the Development of Christian Doctrine* (first ed., New York: Appleton, n. d.), 88-89. There are many significant remarks and quotations on scientific method found in the first edition (1845) of *Development* and eliminated from the 1878 revision.

6. Sermon on "The Philosophical Temper, First Enjoined by the Gospel," in *Oxford Sermons*, 5-6; the next quotation is *ibid.*, 11. Compare A. N. Whitehead's remark that "the faith in the possibility of science, generated antecedently to development of modern scientific theory, is an unconscious derivative from medieval theology. . . . The faith in the order of nature which has made possible the growth of science is a particular

example of a deeper faith." *Science and the Modern World* (New York: Macmillan, 1925), 19, 27. Newman stresses the habits of mind which permit a study of nature, whereas Whitehead focuses upon the belief that nature is orderly. For a detailed study of the several philosophies influencing Newman's mind, consult G. Rombold, "Das Wesen der Person nach John Henry Newman," *Newman-Studien* IV, 21-78.

7. Joseph Butler, *The Analogy of Religion,* Introduction, in *The Works of Joseph Butler,* edited by W. E. Gladstone (2 vols., Oxford: Clarendon Press, 1896), I, 5, 11. See J. Robinson, "Newman's Use of Butler's Arguments," *The Downside Review,* 76 (1958), 161-180.

8. *The Analogy of Religion,* Introduction (Gladstone, I, 9). Newman's affinity with the Patristic thinkers is brought out by D. Gorce, *Newman et les pères* (second ed., Bruges: Beyaert, 1947).

9. *University,* 97. The Aristotelian element in Newman is examined in two studies by F. M. Willam: "Die philosophischen Grundpositionen Newmans," *Newman-Studien* III, 111-156, and *Aristotelische Erkenntnislehre bei Whately und Newman* (Freiburg i. B.: Herder, 1960).

10. "The Benedictine Schools," in *Historical Sketches,* II, 476. Newman recognized that "Patristic and scholastic theology each involved a creative action of the intellect," (*ibid.,* II, 475) and that a similar creative effort is required by theologians and philosophers today.

11. *Grammar,* 49; the next quotation is *ibid.,* 141. In correcting his own previous talk about trusting our knowing powers, Newman remarks: "It seems to me unphilosophical to speak of trusting ourselves." (*Ibid.,* 47.) Cf. C. B. Keogh, *Introduction to the Philosophy of Cardinal Newman* (unpublished dissertation, Louvain University, 1950), 15-183.

12. Letter to William Froude, April 29, 1879, in *Newman-Froude Correspondence,* 204. A good description of Newman's concrete mode of thinking is given by A. J. Boekraad, *The Personal Conquest of Truth according to J. H. Newman,* especially chapter six.

13. *Grammar,* 133. In the tradition of Descartes, Locke, and the Scottish school, Newman refers to self-knowledge as a type of intuition. Cf. J. Artz, "Newman and Intuition," *Philosophy Today,* 1 (1957), 10-15.

14. *University,* 206.

15. *Apologia,* 177.

16. Letter to T. W. Allies, November 22, 1860, in *Allies,* 111. Newman sometimes distinguishes "investigation" (a study of intellectual difficulties, while still assenting to revelation) from "inquiry," in which the assent of faith is itself revoked. (*Grammar,* 144.)

17. *Grammar,* 56, where Newman argues for the energizing presence of purposive mind in all the phases and regions of the universe. See P. J. McLaughlin, "Newman and Science," in *A Tribute to Newman,* 307-336.

18. This MS text of November 16, 1861, is quoted in J. M. Cameron, "The Night-Battle: Newman and Empiricism," *Victorian Studies,* 4 (1960) 101. Cameron concentrates upon the Hume-Newman relationship and also mentions Newman's relevance for analytic philosophy. In *The Uses of Argument* (Cambridge: the University Press, 1958), S. E. Toul-

min states: "By treating logic as generalised jurisprudence and testing our ideas against our actual practice of argument-assessment, rather than against a philosopher's ideal, we shall eventually build up a picture very different from the traditional one." (10)

19. *Grammar*, 273.

20. *Ibid.*, 265; Sermon on "The Individuality of the Soul," in *Sermons and Discourses*, I, 189. The comparison with existentialism is discussed by D. Gorce, "Newman existentialiste?" *Newman-Studien* III, 203-224.

PART ONE: THE CONCRETE WAY OF KNOWING

Introduction

1. *Grammar*, 121.

2. *Ibid.*, 133. J. Artz gives an excellent introduction: "Newman's Contribution to Theory of Knowledge," *Philosophy Today*, 4 (1960), 12-25. For more detailed analyses, consult J. F. Cronin, S. S., *Cardinal Newman: His Theory of Knowledge* (Washington: Catholic University of America Press, 1935), and F. Wiedmann, "Theorie des realen Denkens nach John Henry Newman," *Newman-Studien* IV, 144-248.

Selection 1.

1. From *Apologia*, 9-10, 16-17.

2. [It is significant that Butler begins his work with a quotation from Origen], given above in our General Introduction. Thus Newman himself underlines the continuity of his thought with the Fathers and Butler on the analogical structuring of the material and spiritual worlds.

Selection 2.

1. This essay first appeared as a double-column letter from "A" in *The Christian Observer*, 20 (1821), 293-295. The text given here follows the original publication, with some slight corrections from *Two Letters Addressed to The "Christian Observer," Published in That Magazine in 1821 and 1822* (privately reprinted [by Sir W. H. Cope], 1871). Its importance is brought out by F. M. Willam, "Die philosophischen Grundpositionen Newmans," *Newman-Studien* III, 135 ff.

2. [Many of these questions in religion, and of those above in mathematics, may perhaps admit of a probable answer: there are *some*, however, which cannot be answered.] This and the next note by Newman are found only in the original published text.

3. [I should add, however, that Christianity does not require us to believe any thing absurd or contradictory: its most incomprehensible doctrines are not opposed to reason, nor are they in reality more calculated to awaken just incredulity than many demonstrable propositions of human science.] The subject of this essay is reworked in Newman's Sermon on "The Mysteriousness of Our Present Being," in *Parochial and Plain Sermons* (new impression, 8 vols., London: Longmans, Green, 1908-1920), IV, 282-294.

415

Selection 3.

1. From *Newman-Froude Correspondence*, 118-123, 180-181. The year 1859 was as crucial for these correspondents as for Darwin. Except for the one case explained in note 2, all references here to "Hurrell" refer to William Froude's older brother, Richard Hurrell Froude, who had been Newman's close friend at Oxford.

2. This reference is to William Froude's son, also named Richard Hurrell Froude, whom Newman had just received into the Catholic Church.

3. Sir Charles Lyell was the leading geologist of the day.

4. Newman's position is that there is a *common* pattern of concrete reasoning which we use both in everyday inferences and in those leading to religious belief. Hence, as the following Selections show, he deliberately takes his inductive materials on assent and illative reasoning from a broad field, so that we will not think that the human mind requires a special esoteric faculty in order to attain truths about God and religion.

Selection 4.

1. From *Grammar*, 7-10, 32.

Selection 5.

1. From *Grammar*, 33-57, with omissions.

2. Newman's behind-the-scenes difficulties in clarifying the terms "instinct" and "intuition," as designating cognitive acts wherein we do not attend to the mediating factors leading us to their respective objects, are set forth in Selection (15).

3. The analogy between inference to the external world from sense reports and inference to God from phenomena of conscience is pursued in more detail in Selection (14).

Selection 6.

1. From *Grammar*, 57-64, with omissions.

Selection 7.

1. From *Grammar*, 68-74.

2. Newman takes the long quotation which concludes this Selection from his essay, "The Tamworth Reading Room," in *Essays and Sketches*, II, 203-207. All internal quotations within the Tamworth paper are taken from the speech by Sir Robert Peel upon which Newman bases his own comments.

3. The question of whether physico-theology and the study of physics give a foundation to our religious belief is further explored in Selections (12) and (13).

Selection 8.

1. From *Grammar*, 205-206, 229-230, 262-287 (with omissions); *Oxford Sermons*, 256-260, 275. Zeno's *John Henry Newman, Our Way to Certitude* is an extended commentary on the doctrine of the illative sense, which is described in chapter two.

2. [Though Aristotle, in his *Nicomachean Ethics,* speaks of *phronesis* as the virtue of the *opinion-forming part of the soul* generally, and as being concerned generally with contingent matter (VI, 4), or what I have called the concrete, and of its function being, as regards that matter, *to possess truth by way of affirmation or denial* (ibid., 3), he does not treat of it in that work in its general relation to truth and the affirmation of truth, but only as it bears upon *the things done.*] The Greek words of Newman's original note have been replaced here by the corresponding and italicized English words from the Oxford translation. See *The Basic Works of Aristotle,* edited by R. McKeon (New York: Random House, 1941), 1024-1027. Newman clearly indicates his stress on true judgment.

3. Newman is using Hume's well known distinction between Cartesian antecedent skepticism or universal methodic doubt and a consequent skepticism or doubt bearing on particular arguments and uses of the mind. Newman accepts the Humean criticism of the former kind of doubt but adds that, concerning matters of history and sacred tradition, Hume himself follows antecedent skepticism in his assumption against religious witnesses. Cf. David Hume, *An Inquiry concerning Human Understanding,* section xii, edited by C. W. Hendel (New York: Liberal Arts Press, 1955), 158-160.

Selection 9.

1. From *Grammar,* 120-141.

2. John Locke, *An Essay concerning Human Understanding,* IV, xv, 2, edited by A. C. Fraser (reprint edition, 2 vols., New York: Dover Publications, 1959), vol. II, p. 364.

3. This quotation and the next one are from Locke, *ibid.,* IV, xvi, 6 (Fraser, II, 375, 376).

4. Locke, *ibid.,* IV, xix, 1 (Fraser, II, 428-429). Newman refers us to his *Development,* 304-313, where he admits Locke's argument against sheer enthusiasm in religious questions and yet criticizes Locke for subordinating the assent of faith to proofs of reason. In this latter passage, Newman presents the views of Aquinas and Suarez on faith and reason, by taking long quotations from the *Essay on the Human Understanding* written by Bishop Huet, a fideistic French Catholic.

5. Newman is applying Mill's canons of agreement, difference, residues, and concomitant variations, to show that there is neither a reductive identity nor an exclusive causal connection between inference and assent. See *John Stuart Mill's Philosophy of Scientific Method,* edited by E. Nagel (New York: Hafner, 1950), 211-233.

6. See Selection (5).

7. J. E. Gambier, *An Introduction to the Study of Moral Evidence; or of That Species of Reasoning Which Relates to Matters of Fact and Practice* (second ed., London: Rivington, 1808), 5-6. Although Newman disagrees with Gambier's position that there are degrees of assent and no certitude in assent, nevertheless this book sheds some light on Newman's own thought. For it emphasizes the need for a distinct logical analysis of

our actual reasoning in factual and practical matters, distinguishes this moral reasoning from the demonstrations obtainable in formal logic and mathematics, and holds that there is some determinate evidence enabling us to reason properly and reach defensible probabilities on concrete issues and human events.

8. The argument here depends upon showing that there are exceptions to Locke's limitation of certainty to intuition, demonstration, and sense perception of present actual existence. Whereas Locke treats assent as a non-certitudinal acceptance of propositions which are probable in varying degrees (*An Essay concerning Human Understanding*, IV, xv, 3, and xvi, 1 [Fraser, II, 365, 369]), Newman suggests that assent can properly be certitudinal and unconditional, and be so in some cases where we do not have Locke's intuitive and demonstrative types of knowledge.

9. Here, Newman uses the analysis of ordinary discourse to further his argument.

Selection 10.

1. From a rough draft in *Newman-Froude Correspondence*, 199-209. Newman quotes from several of Froude's previous letters, as well as from some of his own books.

2. William Froude's brother, Richard Hurrell Froude.

3. B. G. Niebuhr wrote a history of ancient Rome.

Selection 11.

1. From a Letter to John Walker, in Ward's *Life*, II, 43. Newman's notion of converging probabilities lends itself readily to the metaphor of the many-stranded cable of moral demonstration. When one of Newman's critics characterized his concrete kind of reasoning as "practical," however, Newman made the following capital distinction. "We commonly use the word ["practical"] in opposition to speculative when we use it of arguments, that is of what is sufficient, not for belief, or assurance of truth, but for action. But I mean to assert that probable arguments may lead to a conclusion which is not only safe to act upon, but is to be embraced as true." Manuscript note of April 27, 1876. This is quoted by E. Przywara, *Ringen der Gegenwart* (2 vols., Augsburg: Filser, 1929), II, 826, n. 14. Newman scholars owe a longstanding debt to Przywara for publishing and commenting on the significance of many manuscript papers. On the nondeductive, interlocking type of evidential system, cf. N. Rescher, "A Theory of Evidence," *Philosophy of Science*, 25 (1958), 83-94.

PART TWO: KNOWLEDGE AND THE PERSONAL GOD

Introduction

1. *University*, 23-24. Joseph Butler also defends the plural sources of evidence concerning God, in *The Analogy of Religion*, Introduction (Gladstone, I, 12).

2. MS note, November 7, 1859; see the context in Selection (14).

3. Letter to Henry Wilberforce, August 20, 1869, in Ward's *Life*, II,

254, 255. The story about the King of Spain is elucidated in Selection (31).

4. William Wordsworth, *The Excursion*, IV, 225-227.

Selection 12.

1. From *University*, 34-35, 54, 196, 311-313, 326-332 (with omissions); *Oxford Sermons*, 194-195.

2. [I use the word, not in the sense of "Naturalis Theologia," but in the sense in which Paley uses it in the work which he has so entitled.] Newman clearly does not want us to confuse the metaphysical treatises on natural theology with the physico-theological tradition culminating in William Paley's *Natural Theology* (1802).

3. T. B. Macaulay, "Ranke's History of the Popes," in *Critical and Miscellaneous Essays* (4 vols., Philadelphia: Carey and Hart, 1842-1843), III, 321-322. Newman was also a careful reader of Macaulay's essay on "Lord Bacon," *ibid.*, II, 286-402.

4. [*"Physical* phenomena, *taken by themselves"*; that is, apart from psychological phenomena, apart from moral considerations, apart from the moral principles by which they must be interpreted, and apart from that idea of God which wakes up in the mind under the stimulus of intellectual training. The question is, whether physical phenomena logically *teach* us, or on the other hand logically *remind* us of the Being of a God. In either case, if they do not bring to us this cardinal truth, we are, in St. Paul's words, "without excuse."] Newman added this note to the third (1872) edition of his *Oxford Sermons* in order to make it clear that he was not denying the presence of evidence about God in the physical world, but was pointing out the contextual and interpretative conditions required by our minds in order to grasp the theistic significance of such evidence. He was not arguing for a reminiscence-theory of knowledge of God but for the need to avoid separating our study of physical phenomena from all the other intellectual resources of our mind.

Selection 13.

1. Letter to W. R. Brownlow, in Ward's *Life*, II, 269.

2. See Selection (5).

Selection 14.

1. These sections from MS A.46.3, were all written during 1859 (February 24, November 7, and December 3), when Newman's mind was fermenting with ideas for his *Grammar of Assent*, his general defense of Christianity, and his discussion with Froude.

2. H. M. Chalybäus, *Historical Survey of Speculative Philosophy from Kant to Hegel*, English translation from fourth German edition by A. Tulk (London: Longman, 1854), 16-58 (on Kant). Chalybäus gives a subjectivist reading of Kant, especially on sensibility and consciousness, and approves of the psychological developments of Reinhold and Fries. Thus Newman (who did not read Kant directly) views Kant primarily as a subjectivist confined to representations in consciousness.

Selection 15.

1. Most of Newman's Letters to Charles Meynell are printed in Ward's *Life,* II, 256-261; the corrected text of the complete correspondence is given in the Appendix to Zeno, *John Henry Newman, Our Way to Certitude,* 226-270, upon which the present Selection is based.

2. Meynell was worried that, if Newman denied the possibility of two straight lines enclosing a space only because a straight line is a notion, someone might then infer that not only the geometrical axioms but also those of the moral law are purely notional products of our own mind.

3. Meynell called Newman's attention to the view of Maine de Biran that we know causality primarily through our inner experience of ourselves as willing or exerting energy to produce effects, and that we infer other things on the basis of the experience of resistance. But Newman separates the two cases: we infer the existence of material things from the experience of resistance, but since we do not experience any strict act of willing on the part of matter, we cannot attribute causality to it.

4. Meynell warned Newman that his teaching on our inferential knowledge of external things would probably be classified by philosophical authorities as a form of idealism or, at most, of hypothetical realism.

5. In testing Newman's argument that assent is useless if it is only the double of inference, Meynell mentioned the counter-argument that conscious reflection is only an echo of direct knowledge and yet is not therefore deemed to be nothing. But Newman's strong sense of the intentional differentiation of acts and objects led him to challenge whether reflective consciousness is indeed only an echo of direct awareness.

Selection 16.

1. From a Letter to Frederick Rogers, Lord Blachford, in Ward's *Life,* II, 571. Blachford consulted Newman about a paper on brute consciousness which Blachford was preparing for the Metaphysical Society, of which T. H. Huxley was a leading member.

Selection 17.

1. This letter to someone having intellectual difficulties about religion is taken from Ward's *Life,* II, 330-331.

Selection 18.

1. From MS A.46.3; written November 17, 1859, with an addition dated August 31, 1864. Newman himself labels this paper a "Proof of Theism." On his notion of conscience, cf. F. J. Kaiser, *The Concept of Conscience according to John Henry Newman* (Washington: Catholic University of America Press, 1958).

Selection 19.

1. From "Rise and Progress of Universities," in *Essays and Sketches,* II, 316-318; *University,* 169-171, 177-178. Newman restricts himself here to methodological substitutes for conscience. Elsewhere, he recognizes the existence of pathological cases in which the acts of conscience are not present. "For myself, as my writings show, I have never based the belief in a God on any argument from merely external nature, but simply as

implied in the fact and deducible from the existence of conscience, nor do I see any difficulty in the notion of the existence of a being endued with reason (at least in its lower degrees), yet without a conscience. The other day there was an interesting account in the *Times* of the Asylum for the Homicidal Insane, and the writer mentioned that of the worst man there the physicians said that he was not properly mad, but only had no sort of perception of the difference between right and wrong. If such being had in a former age of the world developed human faculties, his existence would be horrible; but, if not so, he might be a sort of semi-idiot or fool, clever, cunning, wayward, selfish, something like the Undines of Frankenstein, who are described as being more than an organism, as having a spirit, yet not a soul. Because he had no conscience, he would have no idea of a God." Letter to Mr. Cox, January 28, 1865; text in J. Seynaeve, *Cardinal Newman's Doctrine on Holy Scripture*, appendix-page 148°.

2. This conception of the gentleman as a replacement for the man of religious conscience furnishes the context for understanding Newman's admiring and yet radically critical portrait of the gentleman or "the *beau-ideal* of the world," in *University*, 185-187.

3. Anthony Ashley Cooper, Earl of Shaftesbury, *Characteristicks of Men, Manners, Opinions, Times* (3 vols., [without place or publisher], 1711-1714), I, 174, 175. Newman recognized in this book one of the major sources for British ethical naturalism.

Selection 20.

1. From *Grammar*, 75-89.

2. Even though we do not include here the discussion of the Trinity, Newman's credal and theological context is worthy of note.

3. Newman himself evokes the personal character of Cicero and St. John Chrysostom in his *Essays and Sketches*, I, 3-53; III, 157-232. Cf. T. S. Bokenkotter, *Cardinal Newman as a Historian* (Louvain: Publications Universitaires, 1960).

4. Here, the method of difference is used to distinguish conscience from practical norms based on beauty, pleasure, utility, social welfare, and social convention. Yet Newman is careful to include the acts of moral sense within the sphere of conscience, so that ethics will not be divorced in its root from religion. Within the integrated personal agent, moral sense is the source of ethics, and conscience the source of personal religion.

PART THREE: RELIGION AND SOCIAL DEVELOPMENT

Introduction.

1. *Development*, 38. The psychological, institutional, and dogmatic aspects of the theory of development are examined in J.-H. Walgrave, O. P., *Newman the Theologian.*

Selection 21.

1. From *Development*, 31-38.

2. In this thematic introductory paragraph, Newman moves swiftly

toward the interpretative judgment as the principal human factor underlying growth in the apprehension, criticism, and social realization of the
meanings embodied in the central human ideas.

Selection 22.

1. From *Development,* 159-191, with omissions.

2. St. Vincent of Lerins, *The Commonitories,* 23; compare the modern
translation by R. E. Morris (New York: Fathers of the Church, Inc.,
1949), 309-310.

3. Edward Gibbon, *The History of the Decline and Fall of the Roman
Empire,* chapter 49 (6 vols., New York: Bigelow, Smith, n.d.). V, 162.

4. Henry Hallam, *The Constitutional History of England* (fifth ed.,
New York: Harper, n.d.), 195, 196.

5. Newman quotes this intensely autobiographical passage from his
"Tracts for the Times," number 85, in *Essays and Sketches,* I, 282-283.
There, he also makes this observation: "I have not said that it is a happy
thing never to *add* to what you have, but that it is not happier to *take
away.*" (*Ibid.,* 282.) There is a similar stress on accumulating fresh certitudes in *Grammar,* 187-193.

6. St. Leo the Great, *Letters,* 162; compare the modern translation by
E. Hunt, C. S. C. (New York: Fathers of the Church, Inc., 1957), 252.

7. St. Vincent of Lerins defends progress in the Church, "but it must
be progress in the proper sense of the word, and not a change in faith.
Progress means that each thing grows within itself, whereas change implies that one thing is transformed into another. Hence, it must be that
understanding, knowledge, and wisdom grow and advance mightily and
strongly in individuals as well as in the community, in a single person as
well as in the Church as a whole, and this gradually according to age and
history. But they must progress within their own limits, that is, in accordance with the same kind of dogma, frame of mind, and intellectual approach." *The Commonitories,* 39 (Morris translation, 309).

Selection 23.

1. From C. S. Dessain, C. O., "An Unpublished Paper by Cardinal
Newman on the Development of Doctrine," *The Journal of Theological
Studies,* n. s. 9 (1958), 331-332. Newman uses this example to show how
the Fathers and later theologians have developed the truths of revelation
and yet remained faithful to the mind of Christ.

Selection 24.

1. Draft of a Letter to Pope Leo XIII, in Ward's *Life,* II, 501-502.
H. F. Davis has a comparative study on "Newman and Thomism,"
Newman-Studien III, 157-169. He maintains that there is "a great contrast between the *methods* of Thomism and Newmanism, complete agreement between their *world-views,* and little common ground in the sphere
of *metaphysics.*" (*Ibid.,* 159). Newman himself said: "I have no suspicion and do not anticipate, that I shall be found in substance to dis-
agree with St. Thomas." MS Letter to Robert Whitty, S. J., December 20,
1878.

Selection 25.

1. From a manuscript of May 24, 1861, entitled "An Essay on the Inspiration of Holy Scripture," printed in J. Seynaeve, *Cardinal Newman's Doctrine on Holy Scripture,* appendix-pages 60-69*, with omissions. Newman adduces the case of Galileo as one of the critical points of growth toward maturity on the part of Catholic Scripture-scholars. Galileo gives his own sound views on science and Scripture in his "Letter to the Grand Duchess Christina," in *Discoveries and Opinions of Galileo,* edited by S. Drake (New York: Doubleday Anchor, 1957), 175-216.

2. The question-marks are Newman's own.

3. For a full description of the religious difficulties associated with geological findings in the period just before Darwin, see C. C. Gillispie, *Genesis and Geology* (Cambridge: Harvard University Press, 1951).

4. See Newman's essay, "On Consulting the Faithful in Matters of Doctrine," *Cross Currents,* 2(1951-52), 69-97.

Selection 26.

1. From *University,* 202-207, 303-305.

2. For another treatment of this difficulty, see the Sermon on the "Contest between Faith and Sight," in *Sermons and Discourses,* I, 124.

Selection 27.

1. From *University,* 40-46, 91, 97-101, 146-148.

2. Aristotle, *Rhetoric,* I, 5, 1361a; cf. *The Basic Works of Aristotle* (McKeon, 1340-1341).

3. Within this educational context, Newman means by "philosophy" that comparative and reflective use of reason which enables us to grasp the relation, order, and methodological limits of the various kinds of knowledges being taught in the university. Cf. the commentary by Wolfgang Renz, O. S. B., *Newmans Idee einer Universität* (Freiburg i. S.: Universitätsverlag, 1958), 134-160, who discusses the unitive form for the knowledges in the university as proposed by Newman ("philosophy") and Pius IX ("religion").

4. Consult John Locke, *Some Thoughts concerning Education,* sections 201-211, in *The Educational Writings of John Locke,* edited by J. W. Adamson (Cambridge: the University Press, 1922), 169-175.

Selection 28.

1. From "Lectures on the History of the Turks," in *Historical Sketches,* I, 161-170, with omissions.

Selection 29.

1. Letters to T. W. Allies, from *Allies,* 111-114, 120-125 (with omissions), 131-132. The internal quotations are taken from Allies' letters to Newman.

Selection 30.

1. This is Newman's *biglietto* speech or response to his official notification in Rome about the cardinalate, reported in Ward's *Life,* II, 460-462, 463.

Selection 31.

1. From "Who's to Blame?" in *Discussions and Arguments*, 311-313, 314-324, 331-333. The particular question of blame concerned the British conduct of the Crimean War.

PART FOUR: REASON AND FAITH

Introduction.

1. *Oxford Sermons*, Preface to the third edition, xvi. Chapter 7 of P. Flanagan's *Newman, Faith and the Believer* analyzes the act of faith as a personal and certitudinal assent. On the influence of Newman's notion of faith, see Roger Aubert, *Le Problème de l'acte de foi* (second ed., Louvain: Publications Universitaires, 1950), 343-356, 468-469, 564-575, 751-752.

Selection 32.

1. From *Miracles*, 13-22, 53-55.

2. [I. e., it is pretended to try *past* events on the principles used in conjecturing *future; viz.,* on the antecedent probability and examples.] A similar shift is noticeable when Hume, in treating of causal inference, substitutes a psychological account of prediction for an analysis of causal inference concerning presently existing things.

3. *An Inquiry concerning Human Understanding*, x (Hendel, 133-134, n. 9). In Selections (5) and (6), Newman had already suggested by his distinctions between causality and physical sequence, uniformity and unconditional necessity of connection, that there are no good grounds for any a priori dismissal of miracles as being incompatible with the course of nature. His theory of concrete reasoning then described the common pattern for finding certitude in historical testimony, a pattern to which our investigation of proposed miracles is no exception. Finally, his comparative approach to natural religion in Selection (34) offers a positive basis for dealing with miraculous stories in various religions, without dismissing them all as groundless.

4. Hume, *ibid.* (Hendel, 139).

Selection 33.

1. From *Apologia*, 24-25; "Milman's View of Christianity," in *Essays and Sketches*, II, 221-226. The latter text is taken from Newman's review-article on H. H. Milman's *History of Christianity Under the Empire* (1840).

2. This was written twenty years before Darwin made the problem of human evolution more specific as a scientific hypothesis. Newman's fearless response to this latter hypothesis is given in a manuscript notation of 1863: "There is as much want of simplicity in the idea of the creation of distinct species as in that of the creation of trees in full growth, or of rocks with fossils [already present] in them. I mean that it is as strange that monkeys should be so like men, with no *historical* connection between them, as that there should be no course of facts by which fossil

bones got into rocks. The one idea stands to the other idea as fluxions to differentials. Differentials are fluxions with the condition of time eliminated. I will either go whole hog with Darwin, or dispensing with time and history altogether, hold, not only the theory of distinct species but that also of the creation of fossil-bearing rocks." This text is quoted in Culler, *The Imperial Intellect*, 267. The distinct-species alternative was repugnant to Newman on several grounds: it violates the canon of simplicity of explanation, it closes the mind to factual similarities, and it evacuates time and history of their developmental significance for both the scientist and the religious thinker. For some present-day Christian evaluations of evolution, consult *Darwin's Vision and Christian Perspectives*, edited by W. J. Ong, S. J. (New York: Macmillan, 1960).

Selection 34.

1. From *Grammar*, 294-310. The delicate question of the relation between natural religion and revelation is well treated by Julius Döpfner, "Das Verhältnis von Natur und Ubernatur bei John Henry Newman," *Newman-Studien* IV, 269-330.

2. See the dictum in Selection (20) that the image which we gradually form of the supreme governor, judge, and provider, from the acts of our conscience, "is the creative principle of religion, as the Moral Sense is the principle of ethics." (*Grammar*, 84) Newman holds that we undergo a process of deepening our apprehension and realization of God from the deliverances of conscience. The immediate basis in the commanding acts of conscience leads us to form an image of God in which His commanding will is most prominent. But as we increase our personal reflection upon the life of conscience, we approach the ultimate religious import of our belief in God, and deepen our image of Him as being morally concerned and providential in His own nature or personal being. "I believe that conscience involves the revelation of a God commanding; this does not oblige me to say that moral obligation depends simply on that command. I believe it to depend not solely on the command but on the nature of God. This is not inconsistent, I am sure, with anything I have meant to say to you [to W. G. Ward], which has all gone to this, viz., that conscience in the sense of moral obligation in my mind is such as distinctly to carry with it the sense of an Obliger; or that the *immediate* shape with which it comes to me is not that of a divine truth but of a divine command as well. The immediate form need not be the ultimate basis. I have only said that my conscience is to me a proof of a God just as a shadow is a proof of a substance. The shadow does not depend on the mere arbitrary *will* of the substance for its shape, but on the *nature* of the substance. No illustration is exactly parallel. As the Word is from the Father's will, yet exists in consequence of the Father's eternal nature, so His word in our hearts [conscience] is from His eternal nature, yet is also an act of His will, and is imposed by His authority. This is what I hold and would express." Letter of Newman, to W. G. Ward, November 26, 1859; quoted in Wilfrid Ward, *William George Ward and the Catholic Revival* (London: Macmillan, 1893), 217.

3. [*Penny Cyclopaedia,* article "Atonement" (abridged).]

4. Newman here refers us to a passage in the *Apologia,* describing the disturbing feeling I have "when I look into this living busy world, and see no reflexion of its Creator." (*Ibid.,* 219.) This text is given in full in the section devoted to Newman's conception of God in J. Collins, *God in Modern Philosophy* (Chicago: Regnery, 1959), 356. Here, Newman's experience can be compared with the hidden God of Pascal and Kierkegaard, the death of God according to Hegel and Nietzsche, and the theme of God's absence developed by Hölderlin and Heidegger.

5. This is an abridgment of Joseph Butler, *The Analogy of Religion,* II, v, 22 (Gladstone, I, 271-273).

Selection 35.

1. From the Sermon on "The Nature of Faith in Relation to Reason," in *Sermons and Discourses,* I, 328-340.

2. In Selection (14), Newman remarks that we must use, not trust, our sense.

3. [Here, by "absolute certainty in nothing," is meant, as I believe, "proofs such as absolutely to make doubt impossible"; and by "between doubt and inactivity," is meant, not formal doubt, but a state of mind which recognizes the possibility of doubting.] This note and the next one were added by Newman as clarifications in the third (1872) edition of his *Oxford Sermons.* He treats the abstract possibility of doubting in much the same way that Newton and Roger Cotes treat the entertainment of nonempirical hypotheses as alternatives to the Newtonian natural philosophy.

4. ["The principle of concrete reasoning," which leads to Faith, "is parallel to the method of proof, which is the foundation of modern mathematical science, as contained in the celebrated Lemma, with which Newton opens his *Principia.*"] (*Grammar,* 243-244.) Thus from first to last, Newman retains the comparison between reasoning in Newtonian natural philosophy and reasoning in matters of religion.

Selection 36.

1. From Ward's *Life,* II, 364-365.

BIBLIOGRAPHICAL NOTE

The following abbreviations are used in the Notes to indicate the particular editions of the Newman sources used in these Selections.

1. *Allies*. Mary H. Allies, *Thomas William Allies*. London: Burns and Oates, 1907.

2. *Apologia*. J. H. Newman, *Apologia Pro Vita Sua*. Edited by C. F. Harrold. New York: Longmans, Green, 1947.

3. *Development*. J. H. Newman, *An Essay on the Development of Christian Doctrine*. Edited by C. F. Harrold. New York: Longmans, Green, 1949.

4. *Discussions and Arguments*. J. H. Newman, *Discussions and Arguments on Various Subjects*. New impression, New York: Longmans, Green, 1924.

5. *Essays and Sketches*. J. H. Newman, *Essays and Sketches*. 3 vols. Edited by C. F. Harrold. New York: Longmans, Green, 1948.

6. *Grammar*. J. H. Newman, *An Essay in Aid of a Grammar of Assent*. Edited by C. F. Harrold. New York: Longmans, Green, 1947.

7. *Historical Sketches*. J. H. Newman, *Historical Sketches*. 2 vols. London: Pickering, 1872.

8. *Miracles*. J. H. Newman, *Two Essays on Biblical and on Ecclesiastical Miracles*. New impression, New York: Longmans, Green, 1924.

9. *Newman-Froude Correspondence*. *Cardinal Newman and William Froude, F. R. S., A Correspondence*. Edited by G. H. Harper. Baltimore: Johns Hopkins Press, 1933.

10. *Oxford Sermons*. J. H. Newman, *Fifteen Sermons Preached Before the University of Oxford*. New impression, New York: Longmans, Green, 1918.

11. *Sermons and Discourses*. J. H. Newman, *Sermons and Discourses*. 2 vols. Edited by C. F. Harrold. New York: Longmans, Green, 1949.

12. *University*. J. H. Newman, *The Idea of a University*. Edited by C. F. Harrold. New York: Longmans, Green, 1947.

13. Ward's *Life*. Wilfrid Ward, *The Life of John Henry Cardinal Newman*. 2 vols. New York: Longmans, Green, 1912.

The vast and important task of preparing a complete edition of the twenty thousand extant letters written by Cardinal Newman is well under way. Under the general editorship of Fr. Dessain, Newman's correspondence is being published by Thomas Nelson and Sons, of Edinburgh, 1961 ff. See C. S. Dessain, "Cardinal Newman's Papers: A Complete Edition of His Letters," *The Dublin Review*, 234 (1960-61), 291-296.

The reader who is building his own Newman library will find four of the major works newly edited with helpful introductions in the Doubleday Image Books series: *Apologia Pro Vita Sua*, edited by Philip Hughes; *An Essay in Aid of a Grammar of Assent*, edited by Etienne Gilson; *An Essay on the Development of Christian Doctrine*, edited by Gustave Weigel, S. J.; and *The Idea of a University*, edited by George Shuster. There are two outstanding anthologies which present Newman's basic theological and philosophical ideas in an orderly way: *A Newman Synthesis*, edited by Erich Przywara (New York: Longmans, Green, 1931), which is arranged around the three themes of man's awareness of sin, his acceptance of Christ, and his path in the Christian life; and *The Living Thoughts of Cardinal Newman*, presented by Henry Tristram, C. O. (New York: Mc-Kay, 1946), the introduction to which is itself an important contribution to Newman studies. Father Tristram is also the editor of *John Henry Newman: Autobiographical Writings* (New York: Sheed and Ward, 1957), which gathers into one well annotated volume Newman's many scattered autobiographical sketches, memoirs, and journals. This collection, along with the new edition being prepared of Newman's correspondence, gives us access to the personal life out of which the whole literary production developed.

Wilfrid Ward's *The Life of John Henry Cardinal Newman* is still the standard biography, valuable both for its presentation of Newman in relation to his contemporaries and for its many letters and manscript notes. The results of subsequent research, especially literary studies, are incorporated into C. F. Harrold, *John Henry Newman, An Expository and Critical Study of His Mind, Thought and Art* (New York: Longmans, Green, 1945). The most perceptive recent study of his spiritual growth and holiness is made by Louis Bouyer, C. O., *Newman: His Life and Spirituality* (New York: Kenedy, 1958). We are fortunate in having two excellent specialized accounts of Newman's early years of spiritual and intellectual ferment. Maisie Ward's *Young Mr. Newman* (New York: Sheed and Ward, 1948) is a lively portrait enriched by numerous extracts from the Newman papers and contemporary sources, whereas R. D. Middleton's *Newman at Oxford: His Religious Development* (New York: Oxford University Press, 1950), gives a circumstantial and scrupulously fair description of the Anglican years.

Much of the present interest in Newman's thought has been sparked by some exciting work done on his theological views. A sensibly balanced introductory study is provided by E. D. Benard: *A Preface to Newman's Theology* (St. Louis: Herder, 1945). The theme of development, based upon Newman's personal experience and his developmental approach to concrete knowledge, belief and the Christian doctrinal tradition, is central in *Newman the Theologian*, by J.-H. Walgrave, O. P. (New York: Sheed and Ward, 1960), with a critical evaluation of the recent literature. For a comprehensive report on how the advances in Biblical studies have quickened our appreciation of Newman in this field, we can consult Jaak Seynaeve, W. F., *Cardinal Newman's Doctrine on Holy Scripture* (Louvain: Publications Universitaires, 1953), which also presents 150 pages of Newman manuscripts on Holy Scripture. The central question of the act of faith is carefully treated in Philip Flanagan's *Newman, Faith and the Believer* (Westminster: Newman Press, 1946), with a stress upon the personal conscience of the believer.

There are two reliable introductions to Newman's philosophical position which make intelligent use of the manuscripts and scholarly findings. A. J. Boekraad, *The Personal Conquest of Truth according to J. H. Newman* (Louvain: Editions Nauwelaerts, 1955), shows how Newman's theory of knowledge responded to the problems raised by the Enlightenment and religious liberalism; Dr. Zeno, O. F. M. Cap., *John Henry Newman, Our Way to Certitude* (Leiden: Brill, 1957), comments on the illative sense and the question of nominalism and certitude. Since Newman always bears in mind the practical influence of modern educational institutions upon the formation of the mind, his conception of education is integral with his philosophy. The whole story of his involvement with the Catholic University of Ireland is told in illuminating detail by Fergal McGrath, S. J., *Newman's University: Idea and Reality* (New York: Longmans, Green, 1951). In *The Imperial Intellect: A Study of Newman's Educational Ideal* (New Haven: Yale University Press, 1955), A. D. Culler not only places the Irish project within the wider setting of Newman's earlier educational experiences and reflections but also raises the question of a possible tension between the humanistic and the religious aspects of Newman's mind. (See the criticism of Culler's thesis by H. F. Davis, "Newman, Christian or Humanist?" *Blackfriars*, 37 [1956], 516-526.) An entirely new dimension of Newman's outlook is described in Terence Kenny's *The Political Thought of John Henry Newman* (New York: Longmans, Green, 1957), including his nuanced position in respect to the liberal-conservative debate. A sampling of other Newman research is found in two commemorative volumes of essays: *John Henry Newman: Centenary Essays* (London: Burns, Oates, and Washbourne, 1945), and *A Tribute to Newman*, edited by Michael Tierney (Dublin: Browne and Nolan, 1945).

There is a rich harvest of foreign-language studies on Newman, a few of which we can mention. The article on "John Henry Newman," in *Dictionnaire de Théologie Catholique*, volume XI, columns 327-398, is written by two English Oratorians and authorities on Newman: Henry Tristram and Francis Bacchus. Jean Guitton's *La philosophie de Newman* (Paris: Boivin, 1933) gives prominence to the idea of development and compares Newman with Spencer, Hegel, and the Modernists. S. Jankélévitch's French translation of selections, *Oeuvres philosophiques de Newman*

429

(Paris: Aubier, 1945), is specially valuable for the 200-page introduction by Maurice Nédoncelle. Two German studies concentrate upon Newman's philosophy of religion, with its attractive synthesis of the responsible human person and the social conditions in the Church for belief and action: Erich Przywara, *Einführung in Newmans Wesen und Werk* (Freiburg i. B.: Herder, 1922), and Heinrich Fries, *Die Religionsphilosophie Newmans* (Stuttgart: Schwabenverlag, 1948).

A place apart must be reserved for a new venture in international co-operation among Newman scholars. *Newman-Studien* is now edited by Heinrich Fries and Werner Becker, and published at Nurenburg by Glock and Lutz. Four volumes of essays on various aspects of Newman's life and thought have been published to date (I: 1948, II: 1954, III: 1957, IV: 1960). The contributions are in several languages, report the latest findings, include some long monographs, and have a continuing bibliography of writings by and about Newman. This series is an essential tool for doing any advanced work in the Newman area.

INDEX

INDEX

INDEX

INDEX

Metaphysics, 15, 18 f., 169 f., 171, 198, 204

Moral Law, 82 f., 197, 209 ff., 214 f., 223 ff., 341 ff., 361 ff., 370 ff., 420
    moral judgment, 116 f., 209

Mystery, 25, 38, 50 ff., 72 f., 206 f., 369 ff., 384 f., 409 f.

Naturalism, 8 f., 11, 14, 28 f., 87 ff., 173, 181 ff., 248, 292 ff., 320, 335 f., 365 ff., 370 ff., 421. See Nature.

Natural philosophy ("mathematics") See Scientific reasoning.

Nature, 9, 13 f., 28, 37, 51, 85 ff., 168 f., 212, 233, 287, 293 ff., 354 ff., 361 f., 368 ff., 377, 413 f. See Laws of Nature.

Newton, Isaac, 4, 7, 8, 17, 38, 42, 50, 53, 158, 161, 186, 207, 220, 264, 305 f., 426. See Scientific reasoning.

Newman, John Henry, Cardinal
    and analytic philosophy, 29 f., 414 f., 418. See Language.
    and existentialism, 31 f., 415. See Personal self, Concrete reasoning.
    experiential method, 10 f., 17, 31, 45, 81, 105 ff., 127, 130 f., 141, 151 ff., 157, 190 ff., 201
    "human respect," 291
    man of prayer, 358, 411
    manuscripts, 169 f., 172, 190-96, 209-11, 413, 428
    Oxford Movement, 1, 39
    Patristic influence on, 4, 7, 13 f., 26, 368 ff., 414, 415
    philosophical formation, 3-16, 27
    philosophical themes, 16-27
    psychological viewpoint, 18 ff., 31, 131
    religious humanism, 14, 26 f., 241, 429
    sacramental principle, 14, 37, 47 f., 356 f., 361 ff., 368-75. See Analogy.
    theism (personal and realistic), 13, 31, 171, 200, 420

Noetic or Evidential school, 4-7, 21, 56, 166, 413

Opinion, 76 ff., 140
Origen, 13, 368

Paley, W., 167, 355, 419
Pantheism, 169, 181
Passions, 97 ff., 149. See Will.
Peirce, C. S., 39, 46
Perception, 200 f., 228 f.
Personal Self, 23 f., 31 f., 37 f., 49, 79, 106, 141 f., 170, 172, 191, 193 ff., 205, 214 ff., 220 f., 228 f.

Personal or concrete thinking, 18 f., 24, 31, 43 f., 96, 121 ff., 191 ff., 208, 399 ff., 414. See Illative sense, Imagination, Inference, Reasoning informal.

Phenomena, 171 f., 185 f., 204, 221. See Matter.

Philosophy, 14 ff., 18 ff., 130, 170 f., 217, 240, 244, 259, 267, 281 f., 283, 308 ff., 423

Plato and Platonic, 14, 310

Prayer, 48, 390, 411

Principles, 42, 78 ff., 197, 207 f., 262, 266

Probability, 12 f., 25, 37, 39, 44 ff., 47 ff., 57 ff., 77, 126 ff., 140 f., 155, 164, 243, 365 ff., 407, 418
    and scientific fallibilism, 39, 57 ff.

Progress, 32, 107 f., 160, 245, 318 f., 409, 422. See Development.

Providence, 14, 215, 364, 369 ff., 388 f., 410

Przywara, E., 416

Rationalism, 10 ff., 19, 31, 126 f., 238, 271 f.

Reasoning, formal or logical (formalization), 5, 13, 19, 21 f., 29 f., 43 f., 46, 102, 110 ff., 143 ff., 270 ff., 406 f.

Reasoning, informal or implicit (concrete,) 6 ff., 13, 21 f., 29 f., 43 f., 46, 105-25, 270 ff., 397 ff., 401 ff., 424. See Illative sense, Inference, Personal or concrete thinking.

Religion, 54, 76, 100 f., 180, 189, 206 f., 209, 218 f., 228, 355 ff., 376-95, 427 f.
    philosophy of, 26, 48
    religious reasoning, 8, 38
    and social world, 324-38

Scholasticism, 3 f., 16, 20, 44, 170, 267

Scientific reasoning (mathematics, Newtonian natural philosophy), 4, 7 ff., 13, 28 f., 38 ff., 50 ff., 56 ff., 72, 85 ff., 120 f., 135 f., 151 ff., 158 f., 164, 167 ff., 177 ff., 184 ff., 197, 207 f., 241 f., 262 ff., 284-91, 292 ff., 302 ff., 406 f., 413 f. See Newton.

Scripture, 1, 9, 52 f., 284-91, 297 f., 372, 423

Senses, 190 ff., 199 f., 207 f., 211, 221 f., 396 f.

Shaftesbury, Lord, 10, 173, 216 f., 421

Skepticism, 14, 37, 47, 124 f., 157, 169, 195, 275, 417. See Doubt.

435

INDEX

Social love, 245, 251, 316 ff., 339 ff.
Socrates, 178, 275
State, 212 f., 249 f., 316-24, 325 ff., 335 f., 339-51.
State of Nature, 245, 317 ff.
Symbol, 113, 159, 368-75

Testimony or evidence of witness, 155 f., 359 ff.
Theology, 56, 59, 61, 76 f., 150, 158 ff., 180, 183, 187 f., 218, 233 f., 242, 262, 414, 422
  natural theology and physico-theology, 167 ff., 177 ff., 419
Thomas Aquinas, St., 16, 159, 283, 323, 417, 422
Toulmin, S., 30
Tradition and originality, 17, 25, 238 f., 260-80, 281 ff. See Progress.

Trinity, 52, 218, 421
Trust or belief in one's powers, 78 f., 105 ff., 193 ff., 358, 404, 426
Truth, 19, 22, 41, 43 ff., 51, 61, 109, 123 ff., 129, 137, 139 f., 154 ff., 203, 287, 292, 300, 303 f., 335, 418

Universals, 64 f., 82 f.
University, 24 f., 241 ff., 292-315

Vincent of Lerins, St., 261, 277, 421
Voltaire, 38, 365

Ward, W. G., 209
Warfare of ideas, 239, 257
Whately, Richard, 5 f., 355
Whitehead, A. N., 9, 413 f.
Will, 42, 46, 58, 83 ff., 89, 137, 161 ff., 200, 420, 425. See Causality.